ADOPTED,
THE CHINESE WAY

ADOPTED,
THE CHINESE WAY

A Memoir

By

Marguerite Chien Church

ISBN 0-7414-1224-1

Published by:

PUBLISHING.COM

519 West Lancaster Avenue
Haverford, PA 19041-1413
Info@buybooksontheweb.com
www.buybooksontheweb.com
Toll-free (877) BUY BOOK
Local Phone (610) 520-2500
Fax (610) 519-0261

Printed in the United States of America

Printed on Recycled Paper

Published November, 2002

For Eric, Kathy, and Bean

In memory of my mother

Acknowledgments

My special thanks to my friend Marion Ciaccio for her diligent and perceptive editing of my manuscript, done always with grace and tact. I am grateful too to my childhood schoolmate, Tom Constant, for the loan of his many books on China that brought back memories of Peking and of things Chinese that I would otherwise have forgotten. Other former schoolmates have also been generous in answering my many questions, and I thank them for helping me to fill in the blank spaces in my recollections of our Peking years. I wish also to thank my family and the many friends who took the time to read my work, to make helpful suggestions, and to encourage me along the way. Finally, for guiding me through the intricacies of computer formatting and for other technical assistance, I am grateful to my son Eric Eng and his wife, Carolyn, without whom this book could not have been completed.

CONTENTS

Sketches by author.

Foreword

FOR MOST OF MY ADULT LIFE I have been a Chinese-American, an American citizen of Chinese origin. But that was not always the case. For twenty-nine years of my life I was Chinese, not just racially; I was a Chinese national as well. I was happy, and proud, to be Chinese. I had no wish to become anything else. I loved America and its people, but I had no desire to *be* an American. As a child, America had been for me the land of dreams, of fantasy, the Disneyland of today that every child yearns to see. America was the land of the Baby Ruths and Butterfingers we received in packages at Christmastime from friends in America. It was the land of the shiny red apples that arrived each winter packed in wooden crates, each wrapped in its own crinkly tissue. It was Dick Powell and Ruby Keeler dancing their way through Forty-Second Street; and big bands, and broadway shows, hamburgers, and ice cream sodas, the images that Hollywood had brought us. More important, it was the place I would one day go for an advanced education. Then I would return to China to be a part of that elite class called "returned students." I would probably marry another "returned student," and with him be a member of the privileged class to which I was accustomed. I never thought that America would one day be *my* country.

But at the age of twenty-nine I became an American citizen. I am ashamed to say it was not for some lofty ideological reason, not to escape religious or political persecution, not to find a way out of poverty, but simply because it was expedient. By then I was married and living in America. My Chinese-American husband, born in America while his father was a student at Harvard, was being posted overseas by the U.S. State Department. The assignment required that his wife be an American citizen. And so, I became an American, a Chinese-American, but for years I couldn't escape a sense of guilt. It was as if I had turned my back on my heritage. I had forsaken the country of my birth. That guilt stayed with me for years, albeit in a far corner of my mind. It was not until the excesses of Chinese communist government became apparent that my guilt was finally dispelled. Then my choice of nationality became untrivialized. Then I could tell myself I had turned my back on a repressive regime; I was justified in having changed my allegiance, in having chosen to be a part of the land of the free.

Today, America *is* my country. It is also the country of my children. They are American. Racially Chinese, they are as American as any white Anglo-Saxon American descended from the early settlers of this country. But China too is our country. It is the country of my birth, of my heritage, and of theirs. I wanted them to know something of that country, of the family from which they came, and a lifestyle once lived that was far removed from the one they know. In recording my story I have tried to provide a glimpse of the world I knew in the years before World War II. It was a world of rare privilege, an idyllic lifestyle of ease and luxury that even then was seen by few and certainly will not be seen again.

Unfortunately, in my family, none of the generation beyond mine are still alive to help me piece together our family history. I regret daily that I was too busy with my own life to question my parents about their lives before me. I have queried friends and family members who remain, and find that memories of people, places, and experiences we shared differ sharply from person to person. I remember dancing parties at a gazebo in the Winter Palace; a friend insists it was at the Summer Palace that we danced, on the marble boat. I remember hours spent at our concubine's house; my brother says we were seldom there.

So, in recording my memories of family and my early years in Peking, I have relied mostly on my own recollections. Some of those recollections are vivid in my mind, the conversations as clear as if they had been spoken yesterday. Others are dim, and I have had to reconstruct scenes and words as I imagined they *might* have been.

Throughout this memoir I have used the true names of my family members and close friends. However, in cases where I believed the persons would prefer not to be identified, I have changed the names accordingly. I have consistently used the Wade-Giles system in the Romanization of Chinese words because that was the system in use throughout my years in China. However, I have often eliminated the apostrophe from the Wade-Giles spelling of *T'ai T'ai* simply as a matter of convenience. Also, in the name *Yi Tai Tai,* which according to Wade-Giles should be *I T'ai T'ai,* I have used "yi" (pronounced "ee") rather than the correct "I" to avoid having the word mispronounced as "eye." The name "Peking" I have retained for purely sentimental reasons. For lovers of the old city, it remained Peking even after the government moved to Nanking and its name was officially changed to Peiping. Today, once again China's capital, its official name is Beijing, but it was, and always will be, Peking to me.

Chapter 1
Beginnings: *"Kuo Chi"*

DRESSED IN A RED SATIN JACKET, and wrapped in a red brocade quilt, a small bundle of red, the color of happiness, I was delivered into the arms of my American mother. I was one month old. Around my neck was a jade pendant on a thin gold chain, and on each wrist a gold bracelet. The jade pendant, a brilliant lustrous green, was carved with two peaches, the Chinese symbol for long life, an appropriate symbol for an infant starting a new life. I don't recall ever seeing the red clothing, or the quilt, but I remember the bracelets well. They were of twenty-four karat gold, by western standards far too pure for jewelry, too yellow and much too soft. They were made in a wraparound style, each one a thick gold band with a little ball at each end, the soft metal wrapped almost twice around to encircle my tiny infant wrists. I no longer have the bracelets. They were lost sometime during the war together with the Chinese silver dollars we children had saved through the years from the red envelopes we received from our elders at Chinese New Year. The jade pendant, however, rests in my jewel box, a treasured reminder of my origins. In later years I had it set on a double strand of seed pearls. It will one day go to my daughter.

The American woman who was my mother was not the one in whose womb my life began. She was not the one who brought me into the world. She endured none of the discomforts of pregnancy, no nausea in the early months, or backaches as the weeks wore on. She suffered no pains of childbirth. She was not the one to hear my first cries through the dim haze of post-birth exhaustion. Nonetheless, to me she was Mother, the only one whom I called Mother, the only one whom I thought of as my mother.

My father played no part in my conception. He was not the one from whose seed I had grown. His union with my mother produced neither me nor my brothers and sisters. But he was my father, the only one I ever called Daddy, the only one I thought of as my father. My birth parents I thought of not at all. I knew they existed, somewhere in another city. I knew they were related to my father. But not until I was eighteen, when I knew I would soon be meeting them for the first time, did they even enter my thoughts. That another mother had carried me within her womb for nine long months, had felt my first stirrings within her body, had endured the pain of pushing me through that narrow birth canal into the brilliant light of the open world; all that meant little to me. *That* mother had been no more than a receptacle, a vessel to hold the seed whose sprouts would send forth arms and legs, fingers and toes, for the infant me.

It was not her first pregnancy. This would be her eighth.. She had known almost from the start that I might not be hers to keep. If I were born a girl, I was promised to the family of her husband's older brother. She did not question the commitment. Her brother-in-law and his American wife had no children of their own; she had many. It was a good arrangement. It was the Chinese way.

My mother--and throughout this memoir, all references to "my mother" or "my father" are *always* to my adoptive parents--had been bitterly disappointed at her failure to conceive. I cannot believe, however, that any disappointment my father felt was not tempered with relief. He was certainly aware that any offspring of his marriage to my mother would be stigmatized throughout their lifetimes because of their mixed blood. Possibly it was because of this that he did not consult a doctor. Nor did my mother, for her own unspoken reasons, reasons that I did not learn of until many years later. *But that story later.* Each parent felt the fault lay with the other. Both parents wanted children, my mother because of her great love of children and the natural desire to have her own, and my father for the added reason that he needed a son and heir to carry on his line of the Ch'ien family.

After three years of marriage and no signs of pregnancy, my mother began to think of adoption. With so many poor families in China, surely it would be a simple matter to find a couple who would be willing, even happy, to find a good home for a child they could not afford to raise. But when she broached the subject to my father she was surprised at his instant rejection of the idea. "No, that's out of the question. We can't possibly adopt an unknown. We wouldn't know anything about the child's background, whether there were medical problems in the family, either physical or mental. No, I'll ask my brother for one of his."

"What do you mean, 'ask for'? You surely can't just *ask for* a child. How can you expect any of your brothers just to hand over a child to us?" The mere suggestion seemed unthinkable to my mother.

My father explained patiently, "Helen, you don't understand. In China this is the way it's done. Without a son, my line of the Ch'ien family will die with me. My oldest brother has only one child so he has none to give me, but my second brother has two, both boys. Don't you remember? You were the one who gave the first one his English name, Winston. Now I'll ask my brother to give the second one to us."

My mother couldn't believe it could possibly be that easy. "That sounds much too simple," she said. "I can't believe your brother would be willing, and even if he's willing, what about your sister-in-law? Surely she won't want to give up a child."

"I'm sure she'll do whatever is expected of her. Of course I'll have to discuss it with my brother, but I know he'll have no objections." My father was confident. "With no children of my own, I have the right to claim the child of a relative. My brother is the closest to me, so he's the logical one to give up one of his sons. I'm quite sure he won't deny me."

"But how can you say it's your 'right'? No one has the 'right' to someone else's child." My mother was not so easily convinced.

"No, of course I don't have what *you* think of as a legal right, but in China tradition carries as much weight as a written law, and sometimes more. After all, it's in the interests of the whole Ch'ien family; it's not just for my sake alone. You must understand, Helen, that in China the family is far more important than any single individual. Each member of the family must be expected to make some sacrifices for the others.   By taking a child from a brother, all the property owned by our family will be kept within our Ch'ien family, and nothing will pass to a stranger who is no relation. I'm quite sure this is something my brother will do for me, and for the family."

My mother was still skeptical. "I can't help thinking how hard it will be on your sister-in-law. How can she bear to give up a child?" It all seemed too easy. "How old is the boy now?"

"Well, it seems it was just a few months ago that he was born. I don't remember exactly when, but he must be about five or six months old now. His Chinese name is Chao Sen, Ch'ien Chao Sen, but if he comes to us you can give him his English name. You were supposed to choose an English name for him anyway."

My mother was still pondering the whole concept. "Will it be a legal adoption?" she asked. "I mean, will he really be all ours? I mean, they won't be able to change their minds and ask for him back will they?"

"Well, it's not an adoption in the way you think of it. There won't be any legal documents to sign, any adoption papers to register. The transfer will be recorded in the Ch'ien family records, our *chia p'u*, in our family temple, and that will make him our son. It's as simple as that. It's not adoption in the western sense of the word; it's *kuo chi*, simply a transfer of lineage from one branch of the family to another. The boy will still be a part of the larger Ch'ien family."

Richard with my parents

And so, the six-month-old boy became the oldest son in my parents' family. My mother gave him the English name Richard. My father now had a son to carry on his line, and the larger family was assured of the succession of my father's branch. Richard would have all the privileges and rights of inheritance that a natural-born son would have had. Furthermore, all concerns of bloodlines were satisfied. No checking into Richard's background was necessary. His biological father was after all a blood brother of my father and carried the same family genes. Nor was the background of Richard's birth-mother to be questioned, for that would have been thoroughly checked before her marriage into the family.

What a sane and sensible solution to childlessness! A solution I often wish were practiced today in the western world in which I live. Today one of my three children is childless. His wife is reluctant to adopt a stranger, concerned that she might be unable to cope with any congenital problems that might exist. I have spoken often to my other two children, rather pointedly, of the old Chinese custom, but they laugh, and each in his own way has said the same thing. From my daughter Kathy who has three children, "No way, Mom!" And from my son Eric who has two, "Mom, you must be kidding!" I know that even the thought has been ridiculous. I put my Chinese hopes to rest.

My father was the third son in his family. My natural/birth father was the fourth. Like Richard, I was merely transferred from one branch of the family to another, from *Ssu Fang*, the Fourth House to *San Fang*, the Third House, of the Ch'ien family. By the time I came into my parents' family they already had Richard, age ten, and two others: Lois, age six; and Luther, thirteen months. Luther was my natural brother. Like me, he was also the son of my father's younger brother, or that was what he and much of the world were given to understand

Back row, left to right: **Lois, Richard, Mabel.** *Front row:* **Luther, Cousin Amy. me.**

throughout most of his lifetime. *But that story later too.* None of us *kuo chi* children ever considered ourselves "adopted" in the western sense of the word. I use the word simply because there is no English-language equivalent for the Chinese term of transfer of child from relative to relative. We were after all still members of the same family; we were not born to strangers. Lois, however, was adopted from outside the family. She had been a waif, deserted and unwanted by her natural parents and taken in by my mother without the prior approval of my father.

In those days, in China, there was often a stigma attached to a child adopted from outside the family. If the child were a boy, the child's origins must be questionable, as no family of good standing would give up a boy. If a girl, she was obviously an "unwanted" child. In any case, the child was somehow tainted, a lesser person. In most cases, the fact that he was adopted was kept from the child, only to have the knowledge later thrust upon him by other children who either whispered loudly and audibly of the fact, or in some cases taunted him with cries of "you're adopted, you're adopted!" In my case, and in the case of Chinese children *kuo chi* from brother to brother, that stigma never existed. I was always secure in the knowledge that my origins were above reproach. Neither did I have the identity problem that seems to plague so many adopted children of today. I never had to go through the long and arduous task of locating my birth parents to establish my identity. *I know, and have always known, exactly who I am.*

I am the natural daughter of my father's younger brother. I thought of my birth parents as my uncle and aunt, and of my biological siblings as cousins. When called upon to explain my background in greater detail to American friends, I make painstaking efforts to lead them through the complicated maze of my family relationships. At first they seem to understand. *"It's really not that complicated. You were adopted by your aunt and uncle."* But within minutes, *"But your mother was American. That makes you half American." "No"* I try to clarify. *"It's my aunt, my adoptive mother, who's American. My real mother is Chinese, so I'm all Chinese."* And as I speak further of the American aunt who became my mother, the uncle who became my father, the birth parents who were then relegated to the position of aunt and uncle, and the many sisters, brothers, and cousins, all of whose positions were interchanged, I can see their eyes glaze over and I know they are entangled in a web of confusion.

I was twenty-seven when I met Eva for the first time. By then we were both in America. The year was 1952. I had completed college and was working at the Chinese Embassy in Washington as personal and social secretary to the wife of the Chinese Ambassador. Eva had just emigrated from Taiwan with her husband and children. In China her husband had once been a prominent banker and she a renowned hostess both in Shanghai and later in the wartime capital of Chungking. Chungking had become the center for the Allied Forces China Theatre Command and the city was brimming with American officers. Eva had moved among them, a beautiful, popular young Chinese matron, basking in the admiration of generals and colonels. Now, as immigrants, her husband was fortunate, through the intercession of friends, to have obtained a job teaching beginning Chinese at the University of Maryland. The friends must truly have been "friends indeed" to have interceded on his behalf, for his Chinese was heavily laced with his native Shanghai accent, and both his accent and pronunciation of Mandarin Chinese left much to be desired. He and Eva had bought a small two-bedroom house near the campus, and even though they were living in considerably reduced circumstances, Eva continued to entertain, modestly but still with style. I had been told that she was a wonderful cook, and on this occasion, our first meeting, she was creating a special lunch for me alone.

Eva was the oldest child in my birth family and twenty years older than I. My mother had spoken of her many times and of the part she had played in my adoption. At the time, Eva's own family was living in Soochow, but Eva had come to Peking to study at Yenching University, which was only seven miles west of the city. Even though she boarded at the school, she spent almost all her weekends with my parents in Peking. Mother had always spoken of what a beautiful girl she was, of her slender willowy figure, and of her grace and charm. I was eager to meet this paragon of Chinese womanhood who was my blood sister.

As I parked my car in front of the small cottage in College Park, Eva was at the door to greet me. I had a photograph of her as a young girl of sixteen, and another of her in a group picture after her marriage. She was still easily recognizable, but now at forty-seven she was no longer a young girl. Her figure was not as willowy as it had once been and her face was a little fuller, but still she was an attractive woman. I wished, however, that she wasn't wearing quite so much makeup, for hers was truly a case of "gilding the lily." She had a beautiful complexion totally free of blemishes or wrinkles but it was covered with layers of heavy white powder. I learned years later that until the day she died she used nothing but this special powder that she ordered from Shanghai even through the worst years of the Communist takeover. Her eyebrows must have been plucked clean in her younger days when thin eyebrows were in vogue, for now they were drawn in completely with eyebrow pencil, two sharply defined thin black crescents. These, together with the white powder, gave her a kind of painted doll look, albeit it a pretty painted doll. Through the layers of powder, however, she was still a lovely-looking woman and one who retained her good looks into old age.

In later years Eva and I became very close. After her husband's death she moved to an apartment in Mclean, Virginia, to be near me even though she had a son living in nearby Rockville, Maryland. It was during those years that I watched her change from the radiant hostess she had once been to a lonely woman who lived almost entirely in the past. Her only pleasure in life was in remembering her past days of glory. Apart from the frequent times we had her over for lunch or dinner, she telephoned me several times a week. Each time she gave me long and protracted accounts of the glamorous social life she had once had, the parties she had given, the important people who had been her friends, the elegant clothing she had worn, and the people who had clamored for her attention. These remembrances were accompanied by a litany of her current complaints: her loneliness, her boredom, her lack of social life, her sons' inattention, her physical ailments, her incompetent doctors, and her limited financial condition. I encouraged her to get involved in some community activities, to join a senior citizens group, to do some volunteer work, in effect to "get a life," all to no avail. My sympathy soon turned to impatience and I must admit that while she went on and on in the same vein in one conversation after another, I would tuck the phone in the crook of my neck and thumb through a magazine, or work on some knitting, or even watch a TV show. An occasional "hmm" from me was enough to assure her that I was still listening, and after an hour or sometimes more, she would hang up, only to call again a day or two later with the identical replay of past glories and present complaints. It was sad to see her so incapable of coping with life.

At this our first meeting we spoke of Eva's resettlement in the U.S., but inevitably we came to discussing the role she had played in my life. Eva could hardly wait to tell the tale. We conversed in Chinese, albeit a somewhat polyglot version, Chinese with English words mixed in. Eva's English was excellent, but she was still more comfortable in our native Chinese. She asked, "Did you know that I was the one who first suggested to your mother that she ask for you?"

Of course the story had been related to me by my parents, but it had been years since I had heard it. Besides, I wanted to hear her version and to know if she had anything to add to what I already knew. "Well, the main thing was that I knew how much your mother loved children," she continued. "Your house was always full of children. Not only your sister and brothers, but the children of friends too. In fact sometimes she even brought home the children of the servants to play with you."

Mother's brood. *Left to right:* **Richard, Mabel, Lois, friend, Cousin Amy, Luther, me, friend.**

I knew this couldn't have been so. My mother would never have been so insensitive as to have thrust the servant's children into such an awkward position. They would have been miserable. I couldn't help saying something. "Eva, are you sure you're not remembering incorrectly? I can't imagine my mother doing anything like that."

"Well, maybe it wasn't the servants' children, but they seemed to me to be of a lower class," Eva conceded. "I only know they weren't dressed very well and their noses were often running. I do know that your mother treated your servants differently from most Chinese women. She actually went to the servants' homes if they had a sick child. That's something most Chinese women wouldn't do, at least none that I know. Maybe I have it mixed up. Anyway, she always seemed to be surrounded with children and I knew she wanted another girl. She actually told me so. She said that two boys and two girls would be the perfect family. I used to be so envious of your family because your mother gave you children so much attention. She was always helping Richard with his schoolwork or reading to Lois, or holding Luther in her lap and singing to him. I often wished I had a mother like that."

Eva paused for a moment, reflecting on what she had just said, but then continued. "Anyway, that summer, just before I was to go home for summer vacation, I got a letter from *my* mother saying she was pregnant again. Right away I had this brilliant idea. I rushed to your mother to give her the news and said, 'Aunt Helen, my mother is pregnant again. There are so many children already in my family, if this one is born a girl, why don't you ask for her?"

"And my mother thought it was a great idea?" I asked.

"I don't think anything like that had even occurred to her. It took her completely by surprise," Eva continued. "She just laughed and said I was a crazy young girl to think my mother would want to give up another child; that after all, my mother had already given Luther to her. I was persistent, though, and insisted that it was a good idea and that I was going to follow up on it when I was back in Soochow with my own family. Then I think your mother put the whole idea aside. After all, Luther was only four months old at the time and she was all wrapped up in being a mother to him."

"So she didn't follow up on your suggestion?"

"Well, there really wasn't anything for her to follow up on," Eva said. "I was the one who followed up. During the three months I was home I could tell that my mother didn't really care about having any more children so I broached my idea to her. I was really not surprised when she agreed that it was a good idea."

"What if I had been born a boy?" I asked. "Do you think she would she have agreed so readily if I had been a boy?"

"Oh, I don't think that would have had anything to do with it." Eva was quite convinced of this. "My parents already had four boys after all. Besides, your mother wanted another girl, not a boy. For my part, I couldn't help thinking of the wonderful life you would have with Aunt Helen as your mother. I wasn't giving any thought at all to your father's position or the fact that he was wealthy and we were not. I was thinking only of all the love and attention you would receive that you wouldn't get from my family. *My* mother wasn't really a very good mother." Here she paused again, hesitant about her own words. "I shouldn't say that. I'm sure she loved us in her way, but she left us with the servants a great deal. I was brought up pretty much by my grandmother who was a very strong woman. She not only gave me love and attention, but she made sure that I learned all the rules of behavior that a young girl of good family should have. Unfortunately, after she died, the other children suffered from lack of proper guidance, especially Lily, who was brought up almost entirely by the amahs."

This was all fascinating information for me because by then I had met Lily (the youngest of my biological siblings) and could relate what Eva was saying to the impression I had had of her. Pretty as she was, she had not come across well. She had Eva's lovely complexion, the lovelier because it was natural and not yet hidden under makeup. But in her demeanor, her comportment, there had been something lacking. The refinement, the dignity, the modest air, the well-modulated speech of a girl of good Chinese family were not there.

In later years, Lily developed into a woman whose strength and character more than overrode her less than ideal upbringing. During the Communist years, when her husband's business was faltering, she alone sustained her family of six (they had four children). In their basement apartment in Hongkong, using a single hand-operated machine, she began a small business, printing designs on handkerchiefs and dish towels. The business mushroomed into a three-building factory, exporting to countries around the world. But I digress.

Eva went on with her account. "Of course, even though the whole idea was started by me, it was *your* father who did the actual negotiating with *my* father. When you were born a girl, we notified your family right away. Of course your mother was thrilled and would have liked to have you right away but my mother needed a little time to regain her strength before making the trip to Peking."

I interrupted. "Why didn't my mother to go to Soochow to pick me up? It would have been easier on your mother."

Eva was not sure. "Maybe my parents didn't feel it right to have a foreign woman travelling alone. Or maybe my parents were reluctant to play host if she had come. Languagewise it would have been rather awkward for my mother, her not speaking English. Anyway, my mother didn't mind making the trip. Everyone was so happy with the outcome. Your mother was going to have the second girl that she wanted, and my parents knew that their child was going to have even better care than they themselves could provide. As for me, I was probably the most excited of all because I knew I was the one who had brought about the whole thing."

"And my mother said you took part in delivering me to Peking too." I added.

"Yes, my mother and I together took the train--two full days. And just before the train arrived in Peking, we dressed you in the special red clothing we had prepared for you, and my mother hung the jade pendant around your neck and put on the pair of gold bracelets. You really looked very special, like a Chinese New Year's present, all in red. I think my mother was rather proud to be presenting such a perfect gift."

"I still have the jade pendant, you know," I told her.

"Oh I remember the pendant. It was a beautiful color and I was quite envious that you were going to have it." She rambled on. "Your mother met us at the station with the car and driver. When my mother put you in her arms, your mother kept on saying "*hsieh hsieh*," and didn't know how to say any more than thank you. Her Chinese wasn't good enough for her to express herself fully, and my mother could speak no English, so I was in the middle. Your mother kept on saying again and again, "Tell her how grateful I am," and even though I told her I'd already done so, she kept saying, "I am so grateful. Tell her I am so grateful."

"Well, of course she was grateful." I said. "After all, your mother didn't have to give me up. My parents already had three children, so I was a bonus gift."

My mother had given me the bare bones of my adoption, but there were so many unanswered questions. "Eva, even though you said your mother was not enthusiastic about having another child, surely it must have been painful for her giving me away after she had carried me for nine months?"

Eva dismissed this thought summarily. "Oh, I don't think so, but then, I really don't know. I never even thought about it and she never acted as if it bothered her."

I had no children of my own at the time, though I had been married for two years. Still, I found it hard to imagine giving up a child of mine. "I don't think I would be willing to give up a child. Would you?" I asked.

Eva hardly gave a thought to that. "Yes, of course. That is, if one of my brothers needed a child to carry on his family line. One of us would have to give him a child. Though he would probably expect to get one from one of our brothers before he would ask for one of mine. A brother's child would also be a Ch'ien, whereas a child of mine would not be of the Ch'ien family but of my husband's family."

"Well, I'm glad I'm not in a position of having to make a decision like that. Maybe if I had been brought up more Chinese I could go along completely with Chinese customs, but giving up a child for the sake of the family? I'm not sure I could do it."

"Oh you would if you had to." Eva was sure that the Chinese in me would prevail over the western.

But I had more questions. I was curious about the transition. "Did your mother nurse me when I was born?"

"Yes, if she hadn't been nursing, travelling would have been difficult." Eva explained. "Actually, it was the prospect of the train trip to Peking that made it necessary for her to breast feed you. Otherwise, she probably would have had a wet nurse for you as she did for the rest of us. She had to keep her figure you know."

"But what about after you left me with *my* mother? She must have had to get a wet nurse for me?"

Eva did not have an answer to that. "I really don't know what she did. If she had been Chinese, she probably would have, but being a foreigner, she probably fed you from a bottle. I really don't know because my mother and I left Peking almost immediately after we had delivered you."

Eva passed out of my life at that time. It was twenty-seven years later that she came into my life again. My mother saw her again only once when she came to visit me in the Washington area after Eva and her family had already resettled here.

Eva died at age eighty-five, a victim of a massive stroke. The last time I saw her was in a nursing home in Bethesda, Maryland. Without her white Shanghai face powder, without her carefully drawn eyebrows, she was no longer the beauty she had once been. But her once fair complexion remained unwrinkled, and her hands, without a trace of disfiguring arthritis, were as smooth and white as those of a young girl. She lay there, immobile. Her head did not move. There was no trace of recognition in her face. The only movement was in her eyes. They darted about, seeming to follow us with each move we made; yet they looked vacant, not registering. Lily and I stood by her bedside together with a third sister, Kao Kao. Lily held Eva's hands tightly between her own, pleading, begging, for a sign of recognition. "This is your sister, Lily. Do you know me? Look at me, please. Please, *Ta Chieh* (oldest sister), look at me. You *must* know me. It's your sister, Lily." In her anguish she reverted to her native Shanghai dialect. "Please, please, *Ta Chieh*, tell me you know me." She swore that Eva was looking at her, that Eva's hands were pressing hers, responding. She turned to Kao Kao and me in desperation, seeking confirmation. "She sees me. She knows me. I can tell that she knows me."

Kao Kao and I looked at each other, shook our heads. We knew it was not so. With each movement, Eva's eyes darted again, from far right to far left and back again. The four of us had been born sisters, biologically bound by blood. For me, the other three had become cousins when I was *kuo chi* into my parents' family branch. But now, for only the third time in our lives, we were together, sisters once again.

Eva died quietly in her bed shortly after that last meeting.

I never found out if I was bottle-fed or breast-fed by a wet nurse. There were so many unanswered questions. It didn't matter. However I was fed, I was a healthy child with few visible flaws. Though my ears protruded markedly and only a light fuzz covered my head, my mother declared that I was a beautiful baby. Even the blue birthmark, almost standard in newborn Chinese infants, was small--about the size of a U.S. quarter--and conveniently located on my right buttock, invisible to the world. Mother named me Kathleen.

That summer, when I was only four months old, her sister, my Aunt Margaret, came to visit from America. The two were sitting on the patio with me in Aunt Margaret's lap when she observed somewhat hesitantly, "Helen, I don't know if I should even mention this, but have you ever noticed what the servants call Kathleen?"

Mother was a bit perplexed. "What do you mean, what they call her? They call her Kathleen just like we all do. Of course as she gets older they won't call her by her name; they'll call her *Erh Hsiao Chieh*-- for Second Young Mistress--but while she's small it's perfectly all right for them to call her by her name."

Aunt Margaret laughed. "No, no, that's not what I mean at all. It's just that every time they say Kathleen it sounds to me as if they are saying 'gasoline.' Now I'm even beginning to *think* of her as Gasoline."

Mother was quite taken aback. She had become so accustomed to English spoken with Chinese accents that she had never noticed. But now she realized, that with no "th" sound in the Chinese language, the "th" had become an "s," and the Chinese difficulty in pronouncing two consonant sounds together required the addition of an extra syllable between the two syllables of Kathleen.

Just then the baby amah appeared on the patio to say it was time to put me to bed. This time Mother clearly heard the amah say "Gasoline." She could not bear to think of her perfect child so labeled. Without the slightest hesitation she said, "We'll just have to rename her." She was quite emphatic. "We'll name her Margaret, after you."

"No, no, Helen. We don't want two Margarets in the family. We'll have to come up with something else." Looking up, Aunt Margaret saw the glorious patch of white marguerites that were massed in the garden's center flower bed. "Why don't you name her Marguerite? That *is* French for Margaret, and yet wouldn't be the same."

So, that very afternoon Mother renamed me Marguerite, after her sister and the small white daisy-like flowers of our summer garden.

Chapter 2
Birth Family

I WAS EIGHTEEN when I first met my birth family. My first cousin Mary, daughter of my father's second older sister, had volunteered to take me around to introduce me to them and to the rest of my father's family. From the moment we met I liked her. She was ten years older than I, an only daughter, and I think she welcomed me as a kind of younger sister. We sat side by side in the pedicab. It was hot. The temperature must have been over one hundred degrees and the humidity was oppressive, but with the canvas hood of the pedicab up to protect us from the hot summer sun, we were reasonably comfortable. However, I could see the dark patch of sweat that had worked its way through the shirt of the pedicab coolie. His was not an easy lot, hauling two people through the streets of Shanghai in rain or shine, heat or cold. Still, it was much easier than for the rickshaw coolies in Peking who were still running on foot. Though I had been in Shanghai for several weeks and had grown accustomed to the sight of the pedicabs on the streets, I was still marveling at what seemed to me a wonderful invention. The progression from foot-drawn rickshaw to bicycle-drawn pedicab seemed such a simple step. It amazed me that the same practice had not been adopted long ago in Peking.

The streets of the French Concession were tree-lined and quiet. We passed by some lovely old European-style houses. They could have been transplanted from another continent. In fact, except for the pedi-cabs, the occasional street vendor, and a few pedestrians, all Chinese, one would not have known this was China. Soon the coolie pulled up at a narrow three-storied house. It was beside a school and we could hear children's voices in the neighboring compound. Mary paid the coolie and then rang the doorbell. As we stood there by the door I had a mo-ment of sudden panic.

"Mary, do you think they'll like me? What if they don't like me?" We spoke in Chinese, in Mandarin.

She sounded amused. "Of course they'll like you."

"What if I don't like *them*? Are they nice? Do *you* like them?" A flood of questions poured out of me. "Do you think I should have worn a Chinese dress?"

"No, you look just fine. I like your dress. And yes, they are very nice," Mary assured me. "Why are you so worried? You seemed so calm before and suddenly you are nothing but nerves."

I didn't have a chance to answer or to examine my feelings. We heard footsteps behind the door and a voice calling out loudly, "*t'a men lai la, t'a men lai la.*" The amah was telling them we had arrived. An-other voice, "Ho Ho, come down quickly; your sister is here."

The door opened and we were in a rather dark hall. The amah pointed the way up a long flight of stairs where the family had gathered to greet us. Without being told I knew that the older couple must be Fourth Uncle and Aunt. Mary greeted them by speaking their titles, "Fourth Uncle, Fourth Aunt." In proper Chinese fashion I did the same. *No real equivalent of "how do you do" among Chinese; only a speaking of a name or title.* Two young men quickly joined us. A young girl came rushing down the stairs from the floor above. Fourth Aunt em-braced me; then held me at arm's length and said, "No, no, you mustn't call me aunt. We are after all your parents. You are *our* child. You must call us *Niang* and *Tieh.*"

I have no recollection at all of what I answered to that. I must have mumbled something. Though *Niang* and *Tieh* were less commonly used than *Ma Ma,* and *Pa Pa,* they still meant the same thing, and there was no way I was going to call them Mother and Father. I already had a mother, and a father. As far as I was concerned they were to remain Aunt and Uncle. I never addressed them as anything else during the eighteen months I stayed in Shanghai. Was I wrong? to deny them? to reject them as parents? I only knew that I did not want them to reclaim me as theirs. The introductions began.

"This is Ling Ling, your second brother." I spoke his name. We did not shake hands but nodded at each other in acknowledgment.

"And this is Ch'iang Ch'iang, your fourth brother." More nods.

"And this is Ho Ho, your younger sister." She giggled.

Later I came to know Ho Ho as Lily. She seemed to like the use of her English name, which was a literal translation from the Chinese. Eva was not there. She was married and had long since left home. Nor was Kwan Kwan, the third son. The first son I never knew. Perhaps he had died early in life. I was introduced as "your sister, Huan Huan." I was surprised. No one had told me of this name. I already had a fine Chinese name, Jung Huan, chosen for me by my father (the "huan" not the same character or pronounced with the same tone as in Huan Huan). I had always been pleased with that name. Both characters were regarded as male characters, normally assigned to boys. They were strong words, meaning nobility, glory, honor. I felt that my father, in choosing those characters, had thought, or perhaps hoped, that I was destined for more than the average Chinese girl of that day. Now, another name had been added, one that I did not care for. The "huan" was a good character, signifying joy and happiness. It had probably been selected for me at birth and I should have been pleased with the choice, but the name did not make me happy. First, I felt the character was too feminine, lacking in strength and boldness. Then I disliked its double use, which made the name sound like a diminutive. And for totally irrational reasons I somehow regarded the name as frivolous and lacking in dignity. To me it was as if I had been given a foolish name like Gigi, or Dodo, or Lulu. *How seriously I took myself at age eighteen!* In any event, throughout my lifetime, like most Chinese, I kept both names, the "milkname" Huan Huan among the members of my birth family, and Jung Huan, my official and legal Chinese name, used in all other circumstances. My new-found siblings also had formal names that were used outside the family but I was to call them Ling Ko, older brother Ling, and Ch'iang Ko, older brother Ch'iang. They called me Huan Mei, younger sister Huan.

Though in my mind I was adamant that these siblings were to remain cousins, the "Ko" designation for older brother and the "Mei" for younger sister were also used among cousins and their use did not bother me.

The initial moments of that meeting were unsettling for me. First, I had acquired a second set of parents; second, new siblings; and third, a new name. Then, Fourth Aunt, who had just insisted that I call her Mother, exclaimed, "What a pretty girl you are! You look exactly like your pictures! Your father sends us pictures of you and news of your progress frequently you know."

She then proceeded to describe the various pictures they had of me through every stage of my eighteen-year-old life: as a child, riding my tricycle; in my grade school play; at my dance recital; at my grade school graduation; my high school graduation. I suddenly became aware that this family whose existence had meant nothing at all to me, whom I had not thought of once for eighteen years of my life, had not put me out of their lives as I had them. Physically they had relinquished me, but emotionally they still claimed a part of me.

"I have always known exactly who I am." Did I ever say that? I had always *thought* that I knew who I was, had never felt the need to establish my identity. At this moment I was not so sure. Two sets of parents? One set to bring me up, to support me, to guide me; the other, to monitor my progress. Two sets of siblings? Two worlds? One, half-American; the other totally Chinese. Two languages? English in one world, Chinese the other. On that day I was not sure who I was. *I was a hybrid; west grafted onto east; American branches grafted onto Chinese roots..*

During lunch that followed I was at first the center of attention. I found it embarrassing. Fourth Aunt and Fourth Uncle, seated on either side of me, kept filling my plate with choice morsels picked from the generous spread of food before us, but I hardly had time to eat. I was peppered with a barrage of questions from all sides.

From Fourth Uncle, "How was your flight from Peking?"

From Ling Ling: "How did you like riding in an airplane?"

From Fourth Aunt: "How do you like Shanghai?"

Ling Ling again: "Was it rough on the airplane? Were you nervous?"

Ch'iang Ch'iang: "When do you start school? What are you going to major in?"

From Fourth Uncle: "Which of the relatives have you met?"

And from Lily: "Do you have a boyfriend?"

Ling Ling repeated his question. "Was it rough on the airplane? Did you get sick during the flight?"

I looked at Mary desperately, seeking some kind of help, but she only smiled and made me fend for myself.

I did my best to answer all the questions. "Yes, it was exciting being on an airplane. Yes, I think I will like Shanghai. Yes, it was rough sometimes and it made me feel sick. No, I didn't throw up. No, I wasn't scared, but my ears ached terribly."

From Ling Ling: "They say you should yawn or swallow."

"I did. I yawned, and swallowed, and blew my nose again and again but nothing helped. I thought my ears would burst."

I stopped for breath and continued. "So far I've met Erh Ku Ku (second paternal aunt), and Mary of course, and her husband. And yesterday we went to see Erh Po Fu (second paternal uncle, whom I refer to in this memoir as Second Uncle) and Erh Po Mu (Second Aunt, his wife) and cousin Helen."

It was a relief when Mary finally came to my rescue and continued running through the list of relatives I'd yet to meet. Ch'iang Ch'iang asked again when I would be starting at St. John's.

"In two more weeks. I'll be majoring in English."

Lily said proudly, "I'm enrolled in St. Mary's. We start in two weeks too, at the same time as you. Our campus is right next to yours so maybe I'll see you there." St. Mary's was the girls high school that preceded St. John's University, and many of its students went on to St. John's after graduation.

Lily asked again, "Do you have a boyfriend?"

I said that I did not.

She persisted, "Did you have a boyfriend in Peking?"

Again I answered no, whereupon she declared, "I am only fifteen and *I* have a boyfriend." She was obviously quite pleased with herself. She seemed to think I was in need of help. She volunteered, "I know lots of boys. I'll help you find a boyfriend." She seemed obsessed with the idea of boyfriends.

I didn't quite know how I was supposed to feel. Chagrined at my inadequacy, I suspect. After all, I was eighteen and it seemed had been unable to snare an admirer. I wanted to dismiss her by saying that I didn't need her help, but before I could come up with an answer, Fourth Aunt rebuked her, "Stop those foolish questions, Ho Ho," and went on to inquire after my mother. She wanted to know how we were faring in Peking under Japanese occupation in the absence of my father. Fourth Uncle had many questions about our financial state. I assured them that we were managing all right, that we occasionally received funds from my father and that we had income from the rents of the extra rooms in the house.

Lily wanted to know what kind of food we ate at home, Chinese or foreign. She wanted to know if I always wore western clothes. *Oh, why, why hadn't I worn a Chinese dress?*

Blessedly the family's focus eventually turned away from just me. Mary was finally included in the conversation. At last I was able to turn my attention to observing the others at the table. Except for Mary, we all had many features in common. I couldn't help noticing that both Ling Ling and Ch'iang Ch'iang had high nose bridges, almost hawk-like, not the flat noses common to many Chinese. From childhood I had always been teased about *my* big nose. I would look at my profile in the triple mirror in Lois's bedroom, pressing a finger of one hand down hard on the slight bump, and pushing the tip of my nose upward with a finger of the other. It was a decided improvement. I wondered if my nose could be corrected. I tried to convince myself that my nose was not big; it was aquiline. I chose to think of it as aristocratic. Friends said I must be descended from the lost tribe of Jews.

Fourth Uncle had curly hair, almost kinky, again different from the typical Chinese. I don't think he liked it, for I noted that he had it well plastered down. Ling Ling's hair had a curl in it too, as did Ch'iang Ch'iang's. Mine had a slight wave; Lily's was straight. Fourth Aunt had straight hair too, which she wore pulled back from her face into a bun. She had a very high forehead. She must have been about sixty, possibly older. I searched her face for any features that I might have inherited. Possibly the shape of the face, melon-seed, oval, the shape most desired by Chinese women; or the small mouth. Her eyes were almond-shaped, but she did not have the fold in her upper eyelids that are so much prized in China. Those I must have gotten from Fourth Uncle. Lily was an extremely pretty girl and I did not wonder that she had a boyfriend. In fact I would not have been surprised if many young boys were not hanging about hoping to get her attention. She had a beautiful complexion, obviously inherited from Fourth Aunt. She looked more like her mother than

**My birth parents,
Fourth Aunt and Uncle**

her father. I looked more like Fourth Uncle and like Ling Ling and Ch'iang Ch'iang. I wondered if they were assessing me as I was them. I knew that Lily was, and feeling sorry for me that I was without a boyfriend.

After lunch we returned to the living room and I had a chance to look around me. The room itself was nice enough. It was bright and airy with front windows that looked out onto the street and windows on the side that looked down on the neighboring school. The furnishings were rather nondescript, but comfortable and functional. Except for the Chinese paintings on the wall and the crocheted antimacassars that covered the arms and backs of the upholstered chairs, there were few decorative touches. The layout of the house seemed strange to me. There was only the living room and one other room on that floor, Fourth Uncle and Aunt's bedroom. I supposed the other bedrooms were on the floor above. The dining room was downstairs, together with the kitchen and probably the servants' room. I wondered if the same amah who had opened the door for us and served us at lunch had also done the cooking. Probably not. *Surely there must be another servant.*

Before we left, Fourth Aunt and Uncle made it clear that they would like me to stay with them during my time in Shanghai. I knew that this had been a source of discord between my parents, my father feeling it was appropriate, my mother adamantly opposed. Again I don't remember how I responded. There are so many things I can't remember. I must have stumbled my way through something noncommittal. I knew that I did not want this to be my home. They were all nice enough and obviously eager to please me, but they were so different. They were so very Chinese, and I was so very westernized.

Mary and I did not stay long after lunch. When we were ready to leave, Fourth Uncle and Aunt said goodbye on the second floor landing where they had first greeted us. They insisted that I must come again next week. The others came downstairs to the front door. Ling Ling hailed a passing pedicab. As Mary and I boarded, Lily reminded me once again, "I'm going to find you a boyfriend."

The pedicab pulled away and I turned to take a final look at the house. It was such a dreary building, sitting directly on the street, its gray concrete walls almost abutting those of the house next door. The neighboring school was now quiet; the children had gone home for the afternoon. Suddenly I was overwhelmed by a wave of homesickness. I did not want Lily *or* her boyfriends. I didn't want this family into which I had been born. I wanted to be in Peking with *my* family. I longed for the familiar things of home. I missed my room. I missed the quiet of our Peking courtyards. I even missed our houseboy Hsueh and the coolie Pai. Most of all I missed my mother. Why had I been so eager to leave her, to come to Shanghai? I wondered if I could be happy here.

Chapter 3
Home: The Courtyards

SEVERAL YEARS AGO, at our home in Virginia, we were sitting at the dinner table with some newfound friends who had just returned from China. Norman was telling us of the enormous changes that had occurred since he was last there in the early forties. He spoke of how primitive things had been in those days. "The worst thing was the toilets," he said. "In public places they were just holes in the ground, and even in private homes I was surprised that they didn't have flush toilets." *What on earth was he talking about? Everyone I knew had flush toilets.*

I couldn't let that comment pass. "Norman, I can't imagine what kind of homes you were in, but I can assure you that not *all* toilet facilities were primitive. Ours certainly were not. In fact, I always had my own private bathroom, *with* flush toilet, and so did my brothers and sisters."

Our friend made appreciative noises but I knew he was thinking that I was exaggerating. I confess to stretching the truth somewhat, for I did not actually have a bathroom of my own until I was ten or eleven. Before that, I shared both bedroom and bath, first with my brother Luther when we were very small, and later with my sister Lois. As far back as I can remember my oldest brother Richard always had his own bathroom.

Actually, Norman's early impressions of the living conditions in China were closer to the truth than my own, for mine were those of a highly privileged class, a tiny percentage of China's then four hundred million people. In my childhood I was totally unaware of the privileged life we led. I knew only that I had a happy childhood surrounded by a loving family and many friends. It was only much later in life, from the vantage point of the middle-class American citizen that I later became, that I could fully appreciate the luxurious lifestyle of my early years.

Property ownership signified wealth, and by that or any other standard my family had been wealthy. My father owned several properties in Peking. In the city proper, bounded by the massive city walls, we owned two large houses with multiple courtyards, one in the northern part of the city and one in the East City. We also had a small single-courtyard house near the southwest corner of the Forbidden City and a country home in the Western Hills some fifteen miles west of the city. In addition, the Ch'ien family, my father's family, owned a general store in the West city. Though we lived at different times in all of the residential houses, the one in the North City is the one I always think of as my childhood home.

Like all houses in Peking it was completely enclosed by high walls, all of which were topped off with gray roofing tiles. It was located on a quiet *hu'tung* off the main avenue just inside the rear gate (*Hou Men*) of the Inner City, the Imperial City. The word *hut'ung*, most often described as an alley or lane, actually applied to any street that was not a main thoroughfare. Some were indeed only narrow alleys, often unpaved and dirty, but most of the *hut'ungs* that I knew were paved, and many were wide enough for two cars to pass. In affluent areas such as ours

they had sidewalks on both sides. All were bordered by high walls that screened the courtyards of the private homes from public view. The long stretches of gray walls were broken only by an occasional large recessed double gate with its own tiled roof, or by the smaller gates of more modest homes. These were flush with the walls and opened directly onto the *hut'ungs*.

I loved our North City house, the thought of which brings back many happy memories. Though I call it a house, it was not just *a* house

Sketch of North City House

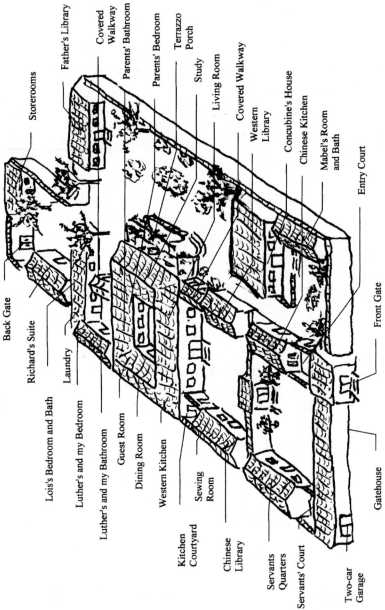

Storerooms

Father's Library

Covered Walkway

Parents' Bathroom

Parents' Bedroom

Study

Terrazzo Porch

Living Room

Covered Walkway

Western Library

Concubine's House

Chinese Kitchen

Mabel's Room and Bath

Entry Court

Front Gate

Back Gate

Richard's Suite

Laundry

Lois's Bedroom and Bath

Luther's and my Bedroom

Luther's and my Bathroom

Guest Room

Dining Room

Western Kitchen

Sewing Room

Kitchen Courtyard

Chinese Library

Servants' Quarters

Servants' Court

Two-car Garage

Gatehouse

Diagram of North City House

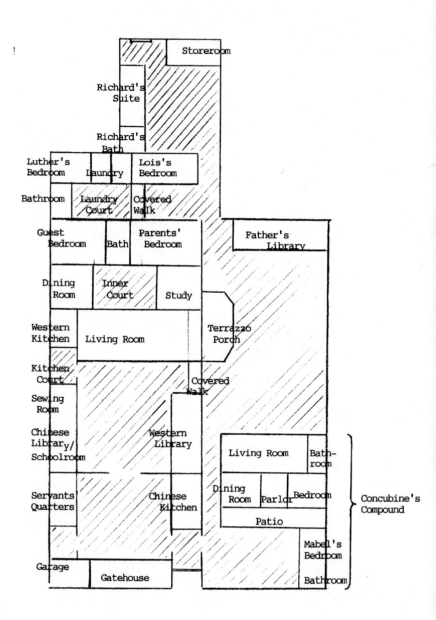

as we think of a house in the west, a single structure divided into separate rooms. On one side of the property was a series of courtyards, each surrounded by rooms that served different purposes. On the other side was the garden, fully planted with trees, shrubs, and flowers. When I think of that house, of how long ago it was that we stopped living in it—sixty-five years--what surprises me is how much I remember of it. Most of the rooms are as vivid in my mind as if I were in them again today. I can see the exact location of a chair, a couch, a wardrobe. I can see the bronze storks on the mantelpiece in the living room, the hexagonal shape of the lamp bases in my parents' bedroom, the procession of small ebony elephants that marched across the mantel in the study,. Yet other rooms are as if they never were. The servants' quarters, for instance. What were they like? Where was their bathroom? Where did they wash? For me, those rooms never were because I was never in them.

The parts that I walked through daily, and lived in and played in, are etched sharply in my memory. The large red double-entry gates opened onto a small entry courtyard with side gates on left and right. On the wall directly facing the front gate hung two vertical red plaques adorned with Chinese characters bearing some auspicious message for house and family. The house was laid out along the traditional style of large multi-courtyard homes, a succession of courtyards on one side, and gardens on the other. Each courtyard was fully paved and surrounded by rooms facing the courtyard. With the Chinese penchant for symmetry, entrance to the rooms was always centered in the court. Off to the side of the principal courtyards were additional, less visible smaller courts for the more mundane functions of the household.

In most multi-courtyard homes, the first courts toward the front of the house were of lesser significance, and the courts progressed in importance to the main courtyard, which was usually toward the rear. Often there were some smaller courts at the very back that were used by poor relations, by family retainers, or used for storage. Such was the case in our house. The first courtyard contained only the servants' quarters and the Chinese kitchen. The gatehouse, which also served as living quarters for our old family retainer Liu Yeh, and the garage backed onto the *hut'ung*. Additional servants' quarters bordered the left side of the courtyard, with a small side-court between their rooms and the two-car garage. On the right, immediately behind the wall of the entry court that held the two Chinese plaques, was the Chinese kitchen.

The Chinese kitchen, that is, the kitchen for the preparation of Chinese food, served the house of my grandfather's concubine on a daily basis and ours only for Chinese banquets or special occasions when the entertaining was to be Chinese style. As was the case with most Chinese kitchens, it was totally detached from the other rooms of the house. Were it not, with so much cooking done on top of the stove and such large amounts of oil used, the grease and cooking odors would surely have permeated the rest of the house. The kitchen was a greasy place and the only way to keep it *looking* clean, if not actually clean, was to apply a fresh coat of whitewash at least once a year. The whitewashed walls could not be scrubbed and the fresh wash simply covered the old, grease and all.

In the winter months this court was a barren place. The windows and doors facing the court were tightly closed against the cold winter air, and except for people passing through it to reach the courtyards beyond, there was no visible activity. However, in the summer months it came alive. Potted oleanders appeared on either side of the court's entrance, and potted pomegranates on either side of the gate leading to the next court. Windows and doors were open and the sounds of life once more emerged. Through it all Chu Shih Fu held court. It was his domain. Chu Shih Fu was our Chinese cook, that is, the cook who prepared our Chinese food, and he held a very special status in the household far beyond that of a mere servant. We addressed him as Chu Shih Fu, or Master Chef Chu, and not by his last name only as we did with most of the other male servants. When I saw him, I always spoke his name and title, just as I did for my aunts and uncles or the friends of my parents. For Chu Shih Fu was no ordinary cook. He was truly a master chef and was much in demand among my father's friends who "borrowed" him frequently when they had important entertaining to do. I am sure they tipped him handsomely for his services and I'm sure it gave my father considerable cachet to have in his employ a gem such as Chu Shih Fu.

He was enormously fat. He looked something like a Japanese sumo wrestler, only several sizes smaller, but instead of a topknot of hair, his head was clean-shaven. I must have seen him frequently as he was in winter, and surely in spring and fall, but in memory it is always summer that I see him. I picture him, bare-chested, clad only in loose cotton trousers, a roll of fat oozing over the wide cloth band that wraps his trousers at the waist. He is resting on a stool outside the kitchen door, fanning himself in a leisurely fashion with a palm-leaf fan, apparently without a care in the world. Inside the hot Chinese kitchen his young coolie assistant is washing and chopping the vegetables, slicing the meat, kneading the dough, scrubbing the pots, stoking the fire. Such menial chores were not for Chu Shih Fu.

But half an hour before mealtime, he finally graces the kitchen with his presence. I see him deftly swishing fresh vegetables around in a large wok, or submerging an entire fish or fowl in sizzling oil. The young coolie is scurrying to have all the ingredients he will need arranged before him. Chu Shih Fu is impatient. "Where is the ginger? Scallions! More garlic!" I am reminded of scenes so often seen on T.V. of operating rooms with surgeon dictating authoritatively to attending nurse, "Scalpel! Forceps! Sutures!" When he lifts the wok, red and orange flames from the hole in the concrete fireplace flare out at the sides. Steam is rising from other pots around him and in the intense heat Chu Shih Fu's bare torso and bald head are glistening with sweat. The coolie hands him a wet towel to mop himself. Miraculously, in minutes it seems, there appear on our table the most succulent meats, the crispest greens, the lightest of steamed breads, and the richest soup, food to satisfy the demanding palate of my gourmet father.

The second courtyard of our house was separated from the first by a wall perhaps ten feet high with a raised, covered double gate at its center. About four feet behind the gate was the customary *ying pi*, the flat panel that has come to be known in the West as a spirit screen. A tiled roof covered both the double gate and the *ying pi*. Though the purpose of the *ying pi* was to stop the passage of evil spirits that supposedly could only travel in a straight line and could not turn corners, for us children it served as a tidy alcove in which to hide when playing hide-and-seek. In any case, in our house this particular spirit screen certainly was a redundant precaution, as any evil spirits intent on entering the second courtyard would already have been stopped on entering the front gate. In the small entry court inside the main gate they would have run headlong into the wall holding the two wall plaques and would not have been able to turn left into the courtyard side of the house or right, into the garden side. However, whoever planned the layout of the house must have felt it better to err on the side of caution, rather than run the risk of having any malignant spirits running amok.

Through the years I've often tried to envision the Chinese concept of evil spirits. Surely they did not resemble the genies who emerge from a bottle in a waft of smoke. Those spirits I think of as floating above the human fray, spiraling, drifting, ethereal. They are light, airy, a cloud of smoke, a breath of air. But not so a Chinese spirit. Him I see as an awkward creature, a Frankenstein monster, unable to lift his legs to step above the raised thresholds of Chinese gateways. He staggers into walls, bumps into concrete objects; he is a bumbling, brainless creature. He cannot rise skyward; he cannot turn. But how does he retreat? Can he move backward? And how is it that these evil spirits, so physically inept, are so feared for the influence they might have on our destinies?

In any case, our courtyards were well protected. Assured that our household would not be plagued by evil spirits, we could pursue our daily activities happily in the second court. It was in this court that my education began: in the Chinese library on the left, reading and writing in two languages, Chinese and English; in the sewing room beside it, sewing and knitting; and in the Western library on the right, sex education. Both libraries played an important part in my young life.

The Chinese library, so-called because it contained my father's collection of Chinese books, doubled as a schoolroom during my early years. Its walls were lined with bookcases, but the room also held five desks and a standing blackboard. Luther and I were taught at home until he reached the fifth grade level and I the fourth. Until that time a private tutor came to the house each morning for our Chinese lessons, and my mother conducted classes for us in English in the afternoons. Luther and I were expected to be seated at our desks well before our tutor, Chao Lao Shih (teacher Chao), arrived at nine o'clock. I remember little about our Chinese lessons but know that we used the same texts that were used in the local schools and in general followed the same program.

Of the three hours Chao Lao Shih spent with us each morning I looked forward most to the last hour, which was always devoted to Chinese writing. I have clear recollections of our lessons in calligraphy. It was what I enjoyed most as it was almost like having a drawing or painting class. And getting out all the attendant paraphernalia was a welcome diversion from sitting before a book reading the Chinese equivalent of "See Jane; see Jane run." Before starting our writing we had to make our own ink in our individual inkstands. Though ink stands come in many

 shapes and sizes--and there are many that are beautifully carved which through the years have become much coveted antiques--the ones used by students were generally four or five

inches square with a flat round well in the center about half an inch deep. In this well we placed a few drops of water, and then with our ink sticks held upright and pressed very firmly against the base of the well, proceeded to grind away, rotating the ink stick until enough of it had dissolved in the water to make a thickened liquid of the right consistency for our writing. To a child this seemed like an interminable task, but it was supposed to steady the hand in preparation for holding the brush. If the ink was too thin, it soaked too quickly through the porous rice paper that was used for calligraphy and created unintended wet blobs. If too thick, the brush strokes had un-inked streaks. Even as a child I had a great deal of patience and never had any trouble getting my ink to the right consistency, but my brother Luther would often tire of the rotating and grinding and stop too soon. His pages of characters would then be punctuated with many blobs of too-wet ink over which the tutor would mark red crosses of disapproval. My calligraphy was considered very good, and the tutor always drew a red circle around each character that was well done. I was proud that I usually had a great many red circles and often double red circles on each page of my work.

Chao Lao Shih placed great emphasis on our holding our brushes correctly--they had to be held firmly and absolutely vertically at all times--and we children dutifully followed instructions, making every effort to hold our brushes erect. It was only by holding the brush in this fashion that one's strokes could show *pi li*, the brush power that was considered essential to good calligraphy and also to good brush-painting. As an adult I had an American friend who became quite competent at Chinese painting. She was vocal in her scorn for the Chinese stress on correct vertical holding of the brush and swore that a good painter could hold the brush with his toes and still show brush power. It annoyed me to have a non-Chinese dismiss so cavalierly a teaching that we Chinese had accepted and followed for years without question. Somehow I felt her words were almost a personal affront. The arrogance in her manner that I had noticed but overlooked in the past now loomed large. She was diminished in my eyes.

When we were introduced to writing with a brush we were provided with writing books, whose pages were marked off in squares with the Chinese characters already printed in red. We then simply painted  our strokes over the red and tried to cover every speck of red with our brushes of black ink. It was like painting in a coloring book except that no retouching was allowed after the stroke was made. Each stroke with black ink was to cover all parts of the red, the fat and the thin, the rounded and the tapered. At first I tried to fill in the red parts I had been unable to cover, but soon realized that my efforts could not escape the teacher's watchful eye. He could always tell. Later we graduated to copying characters from a book into blank squares. This was much more difficult as the contrast between the model characters and our freehand copies became painfully evident.

Chinese notebooks and books open from left to right, the opposite direction from western books. Characters, though written vertically from top to bottom, move from right to left across the page, and at the end of each calligraphy lesson our right wrists were always smudged where they had rested on the freshly written damp black characters. Those who had not thought to roll up their right sleeves had dirty cuffs for the rest of the day.

In the afternoons it was English lessons with my mother. In these we were joined by three others, the children of my parents' friends. Mother was an excellent teacher. She was a firm believer in the phonetic system and drilled us relentlessly from charts she ordered from the Beacon Press in Boston. A large chart was propped up on the blackboard at the head of the class and each child had his own separate small one. I can still see my mother pointing with her stick at the letters. Buh--a--ba; ba--tuh--bat. Cuh--a--ca; ca--tuh--cat. Muh--a--ma; ma--tuh--mat. All her students became good readers and to this day attribute much of their academic success in later life to the good grounding in reading that they received from my mother. She was also a firm believer in the Palmer method of penmanship, and at the end of each day's lesson we practiced row upon row of slanted circles and slanted lines, taking care not to go beyond the horizontal lines in our copy books. All those lessons in penmanship, however, were thrown aside, when in my teenage years my zeal for independence enticed me toward a backhand script.

On the far end of the schoolroom was the sewing room. There, I spent many happy hours with Yu Ku Niang, our sewing amah. Yu Ku Niang was a spinster, as the words "*ku niang*" indicated. Physically, she had not a single attribute to recommend her. She was short and of nondescript shape; not fat, but squat. Her face was round and flat. Small eyes with puffy lids were covered with thick glasses. Her nose was broad; her nostrils wide. And in the crevice where nose meets cheek was a large mole with a single hair growing from it. Throughout my childhood years I was mesmerized by that lone hair. I would note that sometimes it was not there; other days it reappeared. I supposed she cut it from time to time. Try as I would to look elsewhere, I found my eyes drifting to it again and again. I often wondered if she noticed.

It was from Yu Ku Niang that I learned to sew and to knit. My mother started me off in both sewing and knitting, but lacked the patience to see me through my early inept efforts. Yu Ku Niang was the one who kept me company and gave me a love for both. She was wonderfully patient with me. She would pick apart painstakingly the embroidery that I had done badly, or re-cut doll's clothes that otherwise could not possibly have gone over any doll's head. Patiently she would show me where I had gone wrong and guide me through a successful repeat. If a knitted scarf, begun with forty stitches on the needle, had shrunk to thirty, she would rip down to each point where I had dropped a stitch and watch me closely while I repeated the stitches to ensure that no more dropped stitches occurred. With her help, every project started became a project completed. I reveled in the sense of accomplishment. Blanket stitch, feather stitch, satin stitch, buttonholes, French knots--all these things and more I learned from her at an early age and have been grateful to her throughout my life.

But best of all, Yu Ku Niang taught me patience. She taught me not to yank futilely at a knotted thread, and showed me how to pick it apart with care. When the thread repeatedly fell out of the needle's eye, and I was ready to throw the work aside in frustration, she taught me how to pierce the short end of the thread with the needle, and to draw the needle through the pierced thread to hold it securely. When my hands perspired and the sticky needle refused to go through the fabric, she showed me how to run the needle through my hair to make it slide again. She also told me that the surest cure for sweaty fingers was to rub them with a lizard's tail. The thought was not appealing. Lying in bed, I would occasionally see a small lizard running across the ceiling but was never able to catch one, or perhaps I did not try hard enough. Several times I made half-hearted attempts to dislodge one by flicking a towel at it, but the lizard simply dropped to the floor and darted away before I could snare it. Though I was never able to apply that particular remedy, to this day I often find myself running a sticky needle through my hair to ease it through a difficult fabric just as Yu Ku Niang taught me years ago.

Yu Ku Niang had yet another talent. She could draw. I doubt that she could have drawn a table or chair in proper perspective, but entirely freehand she created intricate designs of flowers and leaves, grape vines, peonies, or the tiniest daisies. With a soft lead pencil she drew directly onto the fabric; no practice on paper beforehand. And I would watch in fascination as her designs took shape, the leaves and stems winding in and out across the border of a pillow case, a linen collar, or a large tablecloth. Though I learned many things from Yu Ku Niang, I was never able to create my own designs, satisfying myself with embroidering on hers. Neither did I ever learn to use a Chinese thimble which, unlike the western cup-shaped thimble, was a wide ring worn on the tip of the middle finger. Throughout my adult life I have never forgotten Yu Ku Niang and the lessons learned from her.

Across the courtyard, in the western library, I learned other things. The western library, so-called because the books there were all in English, extended the full length of the courtyard. Bookcases lined the entire back wall. On one end of the room was a round blackwood table with a gray marble top, heavily carved; around the table four matching stools. Here I often sat to do my homework. On the other end of the room was a long couch that backed onto the windows opening onto the courtyard. It was a pleasant room and my friends and I often sat there, sometimes discussing our homework, sometimes just talking.

I must have been about eleven, or possibly twelve years old, when I accidentally came across *the* book. I cannot remember what I was looking for, but at the far end of the highest bookshelf, half obscured by a larger volume, there it was.

"Softly he stroked the silky slope of her loins, down, down between her soft warm buttocks, coming nearer and nearer to the very quick of her. She felt him like a flame of desire, yet tender, and she felt herself melting in the flame. She let herself go. She felt his penis rise against her with silent amazing force and assertion, and she let herself go to him. ----------She quivered again at the potent inexorable entry inside her, so strange and terrible."

Edie and I, our heads close together, eyes glued to the pages before us, were engrossed in the pages of *Lady Chatterley's Lover*. Earlier, as soon as I was sure that no one was within earshot of the telephone, I had called my friend Edie to come over to share my discovery. She could not come until the weekend, but meanwhile I had gone painstakingly through its pages searching for "the good parts." I knew nothing, and cared nothing for the story, only that it was supposed to be full of shocking sexual details. Now I was reading aloud to Edie.

I paused. "What's a 'penis?'" I asked.

"Oh, that's got to be his *thing,*" she decided.

"What do you mean, his *thing?*"

"*You* know, his *thing.*"

I giggled, "We call it a *googoo.*"

"Who's *we?*"

"Our amah. She calls Luther's his *googoo*."

"Well, who cares what we call it. Now we know it's called a penis." She pronounced it penn-iss. "What do you suppose 'the quick' is?" she asked.

"What do you mean, the quick?"

"You just read something about coming nearer to 'the quick'," Edie repeated.

We got out the dictionary again. None of the definitions made sense. "Taking only a short time to do something." That wasn't right. "The sensitive flesh below the nails." That wasn't right either. The closest possible was, "easily aroused."

"Oh what does it matter," Edie said impatiently. "What other stuff did you find?"

I turned to other pages that I had noted.

"What if your mother comes in?" Edie was suddenly concerned.

"If she does, I'll just cover the book up with a pillow. Anyway, I think she's going out to a meeting or something in a little while." I read on.

"The sun through the low window sent in a beam that lit up his thighs and slim belly, and the erect phallus rising darkish and hot-looking from the little cloud of vivid gold-red hair."

"What do you suppose a phallus is." I wondered.

"That's got to be his '*thing*' too," Edie said.

"No, that's his penis." I couldn't help giggling as I said the word aloud. I pronounced it "penn-iss" too.

We looked it up. Edie was right.

"It sounds like men have hair down there," she said.

"No they don't. Luther doesn't."

"Well maybe they get it when they get older. Women do, you know."

From the book's pages we found other passages containing much caressing of loins and breasts, of exquisite rippling, rippling thrills, of soft moans and wild cries, of flaming ecstasy, and of phalluses turgid and quivering. On rereading the book in my adult years I realize that most of it was completely over our heads. There were so many words we couldn't understand. Of course we knew of breasts and thighs, but even words like loins, haunches, flanks were animal parts and not associated with people. The four-letter words that are now common even in a child's world were unknown to us. Some we looked up in the dictionary but didn't understand the definitions. At twelve, we were innocents, and innocents of the most thorough kind. Apart from never having heard the word "penis," all I knew of that piece of anatomy was the limp little thing that I had seen hanging between Luther's legs when we bathed together as children. It was something that boys had, and girls did not. We had had no parental explanations of the birds and bees. We were a step beyond believing that babies were delivered by the stork, but we knew only that sex had to do with our private parts, the parts "down there."

"Do you suppose adults really behave like that?" Edie asked. "I mean, do you think *our* parents do?"

"Who knows? They must do something. It has something to do with how babies get born. It's supposed to be a big thrill but in some parts of the book it sounds as if the woman is going to faint or something. And there's another part in here that sounds as if the whole thing is actually kind of funny. Listen to this." I flipped through the pages until I found the part I remembered. I read aloud, "The butting of his haunches seemed ridiculous to her, and the butting of his penis to come to its little evacuating crisis seemed farcical. Yes, this was love, this ridiculous bouncing of the buttocks, and the wilting of the poor insignificant, moist little penis. This was the divine love!"

Edie and I were in turn enthralled, disgusted, titillated, shocked, and revolted by what we read. We discovered behavior that we could hardly imagine and speech that we could not believe that "nice" people uttered.

I read from another page. "An' if tha shits an' pisses, I'm glad. I don't want a woman as couldna shit nor piss." In the polite society in which we lived, references to these bodily functions were confined to the euphemisms, "Number One" and "Number Two."

Edie said, "My mother would die if she heard me use words like that."

I agreed. "They'd die if they knew we'd found this book."

Well, death was not imminent for either Edie's parents or mine, but while we were still engrossed in the book, the side door opened and Mother appeared in the doorway. We were startled, taken completely by surprise. I caught my breath. I had a pillow on hand, ready precisely for the possibility that someone might enter. I slapped it hastily, perhaps too hastily, onto the offending book. Mother looked a little questioning but did not remark on it.

She greeted Edie and asked what we were up to.

Both of us answered almost in unison. "Oh, we're just talking."

She had her coat and hat on and was clearly ready to leave the house. "Well, I'm off to my meeting. I just wanted to tell you that the cook's making your favorite dessert tonight--strawberry shortcake." And as an afterthought. "Edie, would you like to stay for dinner with us? I know that's one of your favorites too."

Edie moaned. "Oh I can't. My cousin's coming over this afternoon and I have to get home by four."

When Mother had gone, we both breathed more easily. "Boy, that was close," Edie said.

I reassured her. "I don't think she noticed a thing." And I didn't think she *had* noticed. But our guilt must have shown in our faces. Perhaps my face flushed. Or perhaps mothers can read us better than we think. We put the book back very carefully where I had found it, obscured by the large volume beside it as it had originally been. A few days later I looked for it again. It was gone. Our journey in discovery had been short-lived. *So endeth the first lesson.*

Across the back of the second courtyard the main house began. It was much more imposing than the rooms on either side of the courtyard. Whereas the two libraries were only a single step above the level of the courtyard, the main house was raised by four wide steps. Its roof extended well beyond the rooms below, and large pillars supported the projecting eaves creating a sort of loggia that extended along the entire front.

The main house was something of a departure from the usual courtyard style of Chinese homes and was instead much like a detached western house, complete with living room, dining room, kitchen, study, two bedrooms and bath. Whoever was responsible for its design, however, could not escape completely the courtyard concept. All the rooms surrounded a small, purely decorative courtyard whose walls were lined with glazed ceramic planters, mostly green but interspersed with an occasional blue or gold. In the spring and summer the gardener kept the pots filled with a succession of colorful blooms. In the autumn the ivy that covered the walls turned a brilliant glowing red. A solitary stone sundial on a pedestal stood in the center.

The living room extended across the breadth of the house, with the dining room bordering the left side of the small court, and the study bordering the right. The kitchen, that is, the western kitchen, the one used for the cooking of western food, was in the corner between living room and dining room. The two bedrooms and bath extended across the back of the house. No self-respecting western architect would have admitted to planning the layout of the rooms. Since they were arranged around the inner court, each one adjoining the other, access to each room required passing through another to reach it. Our rooms, the children's rooms, were in a separate courtyard behind the main house, and to reach them we had to pass through either the guestroom or my parents' bedroom. The only other way would have been to exit from the front of the main house and go around it through the garden.

The living room was large and somewhat formal. I never chose to sit in it, and we children seldom used it except as a passageway to the rest of the house. Generally, it was reserved for more formal occasions. It was used for dinner parties and for the dances my parents occasionally hosted, and also for my mother's weekly bridge sessions and for her monthly "at homes," which were always attended by twenty or more women friends and some occasional men. On those "at home" days, I hung about the kitchen at the cook's elbow, no better than a puppy waiting for morsels of food to be dropped at its feet. The cook always tolerated my presence and let me eat the crusts from the tea sandwiches. He spread the fillings generously so that there was plenty left on the crusts for me. He also let me scrape the whipped cream bowl after the cream puffs had been filled, and the custard bowl from the custard tarts. Children were not a part of these "at home" afternoons, but occasionally I would be dressed up and invited into the living room to say how-do-you-do to the guests. I can still picture my mother pouring tea. She sat in a rattan "peacock chair," her silhouette framed by the chair's round high back, her silver tea service in front of her on a serving cart. Through the years, that picture of my mother has remained with me. Today I have my own peacock chair. It is worn and threatening to fall apart, but I replace its broken strands of rattan with strips of vinyl and think that with luck it may hold up through my lifetime. It sits by the window in our bedroom, and though it is not quite the right piece of furniture for that room, it brings back memories I am loath to lose.

Despite its stiffness and formality, the living room had some lovely features. Double French doors on the right end of the room opened onto a corridor with two moongates leading from it to the terrazzo porch. Thus, from the French doors, the view of the porch and the garden beyond was always seen through the double round frames of the two moongates. The porch was covered entirely by a wisteria vine, which when in bloom provided a beautiful canopy of purple shade. The wide terrazzo railing was a choice place for us children to sit in the summer heat, its surface cooled by the wisteria vines above. However, we had to vie for space with the many potted flowers with which the gardener seemed determined to envelop the porch. The family spent many an hour on that porch in good weather.

The dining room also had its own French doors, but these opened onto the small inner courtyard, so that this room too had its own view. Unfortunately, my place at the table was always with my back to the French doors, and my view was of the buffet that stood against the back wall. On the buffet was my mother's silver service with silver candelabra on each side. The silver service, complete with samovar, was one of my mother's prize possessions. It was one of a kind, made to order for her by Chinese silversmiths. Dragons, raised in relief, wound around the separate pieces and the handles were carefully executed to resemble bamboo. At that time I had no appreciation of their beauty and would rather have been looking onto the garden.

It was in the dining room that I was forced to confront my daily dose of cod liver oil. Mother tried giving it to me straight, in a tablespoon, but I gagged on it repeatedly. As an alternative, she measured it carefully into my orange juice. It floated clear, on top of the juice, but as my mother stirred vigorously, the thin layer of oil dissolved and the beautiful freshly squeezed juice, always a favorite part of my breakfast, was filled with oily globules. I would take a deep breath and prepare to gulp it down, but always there was a pause before I could bring myself to down it. The small oily globules then merged into larger ones and soon floated back to the surface. Mother stirred again. I took another breath and downed the glass obediently. But for years after the cod-liver-oil-period of my life, even the thought of orange juice was anathema to me.

The study was on the right side of the house across from the dining room. It was there that our family gathered on winter evenings. Mother, or sometimes my father, read to us aloud from books like *Aesop's Fables* and Kipling's *Just So* stories. Luther and I sat at their feet on the large white bearskin rug that lay in front of the fireplace. The most coveted spot was on the bear's head. The minute dinner was over, there was always a mad race to see who would get there first. The loser often sat on my father's lap. He was second best to the bear.

Across the back of the house, from left to right, were the guest bedroom, my parents' bathroom, and their bedroom. All three had windows looking onto the small center courtyard. I remember the excitement of preparing the guest room for the visit of my Aunt Mildred. My mother wanted everything to be perfect for the visit of her youngest and prettiest sister. She bought a lovely silk nightgown with a matching dressing gown for her first night in China. She laid them on the bed, imagining how thrilled Aunt Mildred would be. Aunt Mildred's husband was a building contractor in Peabody, Massachusetts. Though he was doing well, Mother knew that Aunt Mildred had never known this kind of luxury. The nightgown and dressing gown were hung in the wardrobe, but they were not enough. Each time Mother was out shopping she would see some other item she wanted to add. Brocade slippers were bought to accompany the nightgown. In the weeks before Aunt Mildred's arrival Mother thought of more and more things she wanted to buy for her sister. The embroidered jewelry box bought for the dresser must have a piece of jewelry in it. The dresser drawers must have handkerchiefs; the bureau must have lingerie.

When Aunt Mildred arrived, she found a gift in every drawer: a sandalwood fan in one; a small brocade purse in another; a delicately embroidered slip in a third. And in the jewelry box a ring, which I, a little girl of eight, had been allowed to choose. Her birthstone and mine were the same: amethyst.

Mother sat on the bed as Aunt Mildred unpacked her suitcases and I hovered close by, hardly able to contain myself with excitement. As she opened each drawer and discovered each new gift, her eyes welled up with tears. "Helen, you shouldn't. It's too much.""

"And why shouldn't I? You're my sister, my prettiest sister, and I wanted to make this visit special for you."

"But it's special already." Aunt Mildred insisted. "Just coming to see you is special, and having a chance to come to China is special." She dabbed at her eyes.

I couldn't wait. It seemed she would never get around to opening the jewelry box. "Aunt Mildred, Aunt Mildred, you haven't opened everything yet. There's more." I was twitching with anxiety. "Look in the jewelry box. There's something in there too. It's from me. I mean, it's from Mother, but I chose it."

I had chosen the ring with guidance from my mother, a small amethyst stone in a delicate silver filigree setting. When Aunt Mildred saw the ring she gave me a big hug and her eyes welled up again. "Marguerite, of all the beautiful things your mother has given me, this is the most special and is my favorite." She put it on her finger. I think I was as happy as a little girl could possibly be.

Aunt Mildred stayed for several months, and during her visit she used my parents' bathroom, between her room and theirs. The bathroom had windows on one side that looked onto the ivy-covered inner court, and on a long shelf beside the bathtub was a cut-glass bowl filled with colored bath salts. As a special treat I was sometimes allowed to bathe there and to sprinkle the pastel crystals in my bath water. Nonetheless, I had many unhappy evenings in that bathroom, for it was there that for a brief period I had to endure the weekly agony of having my hair curled in rags. Despite the curly hair on my father's side of the family--he, two of his brothers, and one sister all had kinky hair--when I was small, my hair was absolutely straight. Mother wanted me to have curls, not simple curls, but long ringlets. Once a week, before bedtime, she set me on a bench in that bathroom and wound my hair around cotton rags. First she wrapped each swatch of hair around a length of rag, then wound the rag back up to cover the hair, and finally tied the two rag ends together securely in a knot. It felt as if my hair was being pulled out at the roots and the entire curling session was punctuated by my intermittent cries of "ouch." In bed at night the knotted rags made it miserably uncomfortable to sleep. I hated it. And I hated the resulting curls. Blessedly, the curly-hair period of my life could not have lasted long, for among the many snapshots that my parents collected of us children, there is not one in which I have ringlets. For years my hair remained straight, but in my teens it started to wave and soon became almost kinky. It was as if the hair itself had belatedly decided to bow to my mother's determination to have a curly-haired Chinese child.

The last room in the main house was my parents' bedroom. It too had a large window looking out onto the small center court. It was there that I watched my mother brushing her long hair as she sat at her triple-mirrored dressing table. Sometimes she let me brush it for her, but I could never get the bristles to go through to the depth of her thick hair, and soon she would take the brush away from me.

Sometimes I hovered about as she dressed for a formal evening dinner party. I remember particularly a white lace dress that she wore when she was inducted as Worthy Grand Matron of the Peking chapter of the Eastern Star. It had been specially ordered from America for the occasion, a blend of lace and tulle, the fitted bodice of lace flaring into a skirt of tulle with inserted lace gussets. I thought it the most beautiful dress I had ever seen. But even more than that dress, I admired the white fox coat that she wore over it. It was so bushy and soft, and I loved to bury my face in it and snuggle up against it. Mother had other furs too. She had a full length coat of sable, another of mink, and still another of gray caricul, all of which were for daily wear. But for formal evening occasions she always wore the white fox. Then there were also her two fox stoles, one white and one a silver fox, the kind where the fox's mouth clamped onto its own tail and the front and back feet snapped together. It gave the appearance of a real fox draped around the shoulders. In those days they were considered very elegant.

Those furs have a special place in my memory. Apart from picturing my mother swathed in her white fox coat, I also picture my own children some fifty years later in America wearing those same coats. In their college years it was quite the thing to scour the thrift shops for clothes from a bygone era, and some of my daughter's friends had unearthed some real gems among their mothers' old things. Kathy had been despondent. "I don't suppose you have anything but Chinese dresses," she said hopefully.

"No, that's about all I have," I answered. *I hadn't worn anything but Chinese sheaths for years.* "But I *do* have some old furs of Grandma's."

"Furs? You have *furs? Real furs?*" Kathy could hardly contain herself. "What are they? Coats? Jackets? Where are they?"

"Yes, yes. Of course real furs. I know there's a white fox coat and some others. I can't even remember what. They're all down in one of the trunks in the basement." *I had never been able to bring myself to discard them even though they were worn and out of style.*

Nothing would do but to go down to the basement immediately to search for the furs. The first trunk we opened was full of table linens, all beautifully embroidered, some with fine cutwork, all representing untold hours of handwork. The second trunk was filled with brocade bedspreads and antique Mandarin robes. Just seeing them once again brought back memories. *All these beautiful things, reminders of days long past, lost in the bowels of a trunk. I should get them out and use them, or display them. But who will wash and iron them? I can't even think about it. There's no time for reminiscing.*

Finally we come to the furs. Amid shrieks of "Look at this one!" and "Wow! This is just great!" "What about this one!" my three children plowed through the furs. My oldest, Eric, claimed the white fox, slightly yellowed but still gloriously bushy. His friends at college labeled him "the abominable snowman." Kathy got the gray caricul and was the envy of her college friends at Duke. My youngest, still in high school, had to settle for a jacket of long-haired brown fur. I don't know what the fur was, something nondescript. It was silver-tipped and somewhat worn at the elbows. I don't know what happened to the sable or the mink. They probably had seen too much wear to have been worth keeping. The white fox stole we sold at a local flea market in Maryland many years ago. We let a young mother have it for mere pennies and were delighted to see her little girl, all of three or four years old, winding it around her neck and running off happily, the bushy tail trailing behind her. *The silver fox is still in that same trunk. I don't know what to do with it. Who would dare to wear it and invoke the wrath of some animal rights activist? Yet I can't bear to throw it away.*

I seem to have wandered off to another time and place. I return now to the house and another memory, a less happy one, of my parents' bedroom. It is vivid in my mind. I can see my mother lying in bed fighting the agony of a migraine headache. During those periods, the drapes were drawn and the room kept in total darkness. In hushed tones the servants passed the word around that *T'ai T'ai* had a headache. We were cautioned to keep our voices down and banished to other parts of the compound, usually to our own quarters behind the main house in the last two remaining courtyards of the property.

The first of these was *our* courtyard and Mother always referred to it as "the children's court," but I always thought of it as "the laundry court" because that is where the laundry was hung. The bathroom Luther and I shared bordered the left side of the courtyard. For some reason it was sunken an inch or two below the other rooms. It was almost as if it had been an afterthought, built just to tie the main house to the rooms behind. I disliked that bathroom because the floor, unlike all the other rooms, was of concrete, and cold underfoot. I hated walking in it in my bare feet. Once, we found a scorpion lurking in a corner, its jointed tail curving upward into the air. After that, I refused to get out of the tub until the amah had first examined every inch of the concrete floor.

Behind that bathroom, going across the width of the courtyard, were Luther's and my bedroom and Lois's bedroom and bath. The laundry room was sandwiched between the two bedrooms. A covered walk-

way running from my parents' room to Lois's room divided the courtyard in two.

All I can remember of Luther's and my bedroom is the two
rather ugly and utilitarian brass beds. Though its windows looked onto
the courtyard, that side of the courtyard was reserved for hanging the
laundry, and the many lines of sheets, towels, table-linens, and clothing
hanging out to dry kept the sunlight out, making the room dark and
dreary. I can still see my mother's corsets, flesh colored, their laces waving in the breeze, hanging beside my father's silk Chinese undergarments.
Looking back, I can't help thinking how unappealing our room was.
Nonetheless, I have warm memories of it because it was there that
Mother would sing to us before putting us to bed. To me she sang songs
about little girls, about dollies and rolling pins, all songs that I continued
to sing to my own daughter in later years. The words and melodies repeat themselves in my head. *I don't want to play in your yard. I don't
like you any more. You'll be sorry when you see me, sliding down our
cellar door. You can't holler down our rain barrel; you can't climb our
apple tree……..*

That was my favorite. It was a song about two little girls,
neighbors, who quarreled, then made up, and remained friends throughout their lifetimes. I had never seen a cellar door, or climbed an apple
tree, but as I drifted off to sleep, I dreamed of one day having a friend
like that. I could see us together climbing our jujube tree instead.

When Mother had tucked me in she would move to Luther's bed
and sing to him songs of little boys and sailing ships. *There's a ship sails
away, at the close of each day. Sails away to the land of dreams.
Mother's little boy blue, is the captain and crew, of the wonderful ship,
called the White Pillow Slip.* These songs are long forgotten, but once in
a great while, at the senior day-care center where I sing, it warms my
heart when a woman in her eighties or nineties will remember the same
songs, the ones *her* mother had once sung to her. My mother would have
been one hundred and twenty-two if she were alive today.

The jujube tree was on the other side of the courtyard, outside
Lois's room, which in contrast to Luther's and my bedroom, was filled
with sunshine. I loved Lois's room and could hardly wait until I could
stop sharing with Luther and move in with her. The room was decorated

in cream and old rose, the furniture cream colored, the curtains of rose damask, and the bedspreads of the same rose damask covered with see-through natural-colored crocheted spreads.   On the floor were thick Tientsin rugs of pale beige with clusters of rose-colored lotus flowers and their platter-like green leaves in each corner. Windows stretched across the length of the room and looked onto the right side of the courtyard which was dominated by the large jujube tree. I had always assumed these jujube were dates, for that is what we called them. Even now we refer to them as Chinese dates. Despite the concern of our parents, we used to climb up on the roof of Lois's room, and squatting flatfooted coolie-style on the roof tiles, eat as many of the crisp apple-textured fruits that we could reach. For children, there were distinct advantages to the courtyard style of living as we were not always under the eyes of our parents.

On the far right side of the courtyard a passageway led to a final small elongated courtyard that held my older brother Richard's suite--he had his own bedroom, sitting room, and bath--and a row of rooms used for storage. The back gate of our house opened from this courtyard onto the street.

Chapter 4
Home: The Garden Side

THE RIGHT SIDE OF OUR COMPOUND had no courtyards and was what I think of as the garden side. In the front part of the garden was a house occupied by my grandfather's concubine and her daughter Mabel. The family always referred to the concubine as *Yi Tai Tai,* a euphemism for concubine, the *"Yi"* meaning Mother's younger sister. Mabel, being my father's half-sister, was my aunt. When we were small, we called her *Hsiao Ku Ku,* or youngest paternal aunt, but as we grew older we didn't hesitate to call her by her English name. Neither she nor her mother raised any objection despite the generational difference between Mabel and ourselves. She was the same age as my sister Lois and often joined us in our garden. Yi Tai Tai, however, kept to her own quarters and I do not recall *ever* having seen her in our part of the garden or in the courtyard side of the property. We children, on the other hand, were frequently in her house.

My grandfather had died long before I was born, but after his death his concubine and her offspring, according to Chinese custom, became the responsibility of the Ch'ien family. As a child I never questioned why Yi Tai Tai lived with us rather than some other member of the Ch'ien family. She was just *there,* and as I grew older I supposed it was because my father was the most affluent of his siblings that he was the one to provide a home for her and her daughter..

Clementine Hoo, one of my best friends, was the only one of my contemporaries who, like me, had a concubine in her family. However, the position of their concubine within their family was a world apart from Yi Tai Tai's status within ours. Both concubines lived within the family compounds and both were maintained in comfort. Neither was maltreated as were so many concubines in tales of China's feudal culture. However, there the similarities ended. *Our* concubine was my grandfather's, whereas the concubine in Clemy's family was her father's. She always addressed Clemy's father as *Lao Yeh* (Master), and her mother as *T'ai T'ai* (Mistress). She called Clemy's brothers *Shao Yeh* (Young Masters), and addressed Clemy as *Hsiao Chieh* (Young Mistress). The concubine and her children, Clemy's half brothers and sisters, definitely held subservient positions within their family.

Our concubine on the other hand was not in the least subservient. She did not refer to my mother as *T'ai T'ai*--she always said *"ni ti ma ma"* (your mother)--or address us children as Young Masters or Young Mistresses. Instead, she called us quite freely by our first names. Though she spoke no English, for some reason she used our English names, I suppose because my father did. Her voice was sharp and shrill, and I can still hear her calling out to Luther or me in her strong northern Chinese accent, "Loo-sir! Mah-go-ray!" I don't know how she addressed my father. When speaking to us she certainly never referred to him as *Lao Yeh*. Instead she said *"ni ti pa pa"* (your father).

She had been a servant girl in my grandfather's household when she became his concubine, and I assume that her selection had been made personally by my grandfather rather than by his wife. If she had been chosen by the wife, as was often the case when a woman no longer wished to service her husband's physical needs, the choice was often of an unattractive woman. Yi Tai Tai was a good-looking woman and had no doubt been a very pretty girl. Perhaps the knowledge that she had been my grandfather's personal choice accounted for her peremptory manner with us children.

She had the coveted melon-seed face with small features and an exceptionally high, wide forehead. Her hair was combed straight back, away from her face in a bun in which she often wore jasmine flowers.

Jasmine and another kind of white fragrant flower were sold at some of the market places strung onto small wires and arranged on a stickpin for the hair or in the form of a brooch or pendant. They were lovely to look at and very fragrant. Occasionally Yi Tai Tai would buy an extra one for me. I would pin it to my dress and pull it up to my nose throughout the day until the flowers had turned brown and their fragrance stale.

Yi Tai Tai with daughter Mabel

Yi Tai Tai's house had a large living room, a dining room, a parlor, and a bedroom and bathroom for herself. At the side, at right angles to the house-proper, but separated from it by a stone patio, was another room with its own private bathroom for Mabel. In the "L" that was formed by the concubine's house and Mabel's room was their own private garden. Though much smaller than our garden, it was equally well tended by the family gardener. On either side of the double doors that led into her garden from the main entry court of the compound stood a pair of cassia trees. Their pale yellow flowers were small and unassuming, but their fragrance lingers today in my memory. I remember too the hosta at the back of her house. My mother always called them August lilies, and it was in that month, when other flowers were beginning to lose their luster, that the lilies emerged from their broad striated leaves with their spectacular show of sweet-scented blossoms. Entering Yi Tai Tai's garden from the front there was the fragrance of the cassia blossoms; exiting from the back of her house, the fragrance of the August lilies. And as I write these words, I find myself irked that so many fragrant things surround my memories of this woman whom I did not particularly like. But as a child I was not conscious of either like or dislike. She was simply a part of our household and her house a part of our lives.

It was in the living room of Yi Tai Tai's house that the monthly reassembly of the bedding quilts took place. The bottom layer of the quilts, the layer touching the body, was always of white cotton; the top, the *pei mien*, usually of colorful silk or satin embroidered with some decorative motif. Since no protective sheets or quilt-covers were used, the only means of keeping the quilts clean was to disassemble them completely so that the white cotton underlayer could be washed. The entire quilt then had to be reassembled. This was done once a month without fail. I would sit on the floor and watch the amahs at their work. They spread the large cotton bottom layer of the quilt on the living room rug. On top of that went the cotton batting, which often had to be painstakingly replumped with prong-like instruments. The quilt surface was then placed in the center and the bottom layer folded up and over the batting so that the white cotton completely overlapped the embroidered quilt-face, with a four-inch border of white to spare. Then, all was sewn in place, by hand, of course.

It was also at Yi Tai Tai's house that we were able to enjoy Chu Shih Fu's incomparable Chinese cooking. For dinner, four hot dishes followed by a soup were standard. A pot of rice congee stood on a side table for those who wanted it. It was supposed to help the digestion. Desserts were not served except on special occasions, but the meal concluded with a platter of whatever fruits were in season, already peeled, cut in pieces, and skewered with toothpicks.

The dinner dishes were too numerous to mention, but the breakfast dishes served at Yi Tai Tai's were special. We sometimes had the more common breakfast of *hsi fan*, (rice congee), accompanied by *shao ping, yiu t'iao* (baked sesame-flavored bread and crispy deep fried crullers). This was almost a standard breakfast for Northern Chinese. At our house it was often supplemented with *he pao tan*, fried eggs cooked like folded lotus leaves. Each egg was fried over a hot fire so that the edges were sizzled and ruffled, and then folded over to form a half-round. After some soy sauce, a dash of vinegar and a touch of sugar had been added, the egg was simmered gently until the white was firm but the yolk still soft. I always chose to put my egg into my bowl of rice congee where it flavored the thick, bland porridge. Other times we had deep fried slices of *man t'o*, the steamed bread that might have been served with dinner the night before. These were served with a sprinkling of moist white Chinese sugar.

Though these were delicious breakfasts, Chu Shih Fu's morning offerings often went beyond the normal. Of his many specialties my favorite was his *ts'ung yu ping*. These bore not the slightest resemblance to the flat scallion cakes that are served in Chinese restaurants in this country and that are in fact served in most of North China. Instead of flatbreads, Chu Shih Fu's scallion cakes were the size and shape of cinnamon rolls, layer upon layer of flaky pastry filled with chopped scallions. The dough was made of plain flour, mixed with boiling water. Thus the dough was partially cooked by the boiling water even as the dough was being formed. It was rolled out into a paper-thin sheet that was then spread with lard, a generous sprinkling of chopped scallions, and salted to taste. The sheet was then rolled up into a tight cylinder, the cylinder in turn curled into a snail-like form, and then deep-fried to a crisp golden brown. Just before serving, Chu Shih Fu would squoosh each one between his fingers so that they came to the table semi-crumbled and flaky. *Delicious, delicious cholesterol-laden bits of heaven!* Surely, cholesterol or not, heaven would have opened its gates to Chu Shih Fu and his culinary masterpieces.

Years later, after Yi Tai Tai had moved to Shanghai, my mother rented the concubine's house with all its furniture and Chinese antiques to Anna May Wong for several months. Anna May Wong was at that time the only Hollywood movie actress of Chinese origin that we knew of who was given billing. I believe she was actually American-born and I don't believe she could speak Chinese--at least she did not speak Mandarin--but her distinctly oriental features made her ideally suited for portrayal of the oriental mystique. My recollections of her were always as a dragon-lady type in some Chinese opium den, though I'm sure she played other roles.

Among the local population in Peking, American movies were very popular and movie stars much admired. Therefore, her presence in our home drew a great deal of attention and even envy. I was excited and proud that a movie star was actually staying at our house. Imagine my mother's indignation, however, when soon after Anna May had returned to America, an article appeared in one of the popular American movie magazines of the day showing a picture of her "in her lovely Peking home," and another "surrounded by her beautiful Chinese antiques." My mother conceded that a rented property could still be construed as Anna May's home but resented our prized antiques also being ascribed to her.

At around the same time that Anna May was staying at our house, I also had the chance to meet another movie star. I was in the lobby of the Peking Hotel with my mother when someone said that Charlie Chan was in the dining room. I went running to the entrance of the dining room to see if I could catch a glimpse of him. One of the waiters pointed him out. He and another man were seated at a table at the far end of the dining room. He had his back to us so I couldn't see his face. I asked my mother if she would get his autograph for me, but she said that if I wanted it I should get it for myself.

"What shall I say?"

"Just ask him if you can have his autograph. I'm sure he won't mind."

It didn't seem so difficult. I thought I could do that. I was already excited at the prospect of showing the autograph to my friends and imagining how envious they would be. They were quite impressed that I knew Anna May Wong. Now, imagine, I would have met *another* movie star! Mother gave me a piece of paper from a notebook in her purse and I got a pen from one of the waiters—Mother only had a pencil and I wanted the autograph in ink. As I walked the length of the dining room I was silently repeating to myself, "Please may I have your autograph....please may I have your autograph....please may I have your autograph." I was nervous; I could feel my heart beating as I approached his table. But when I stood before him and could see his face, it was not Charlie Chan at all that I saw, but some foreign gentleman with brown hair who didn't look in the least bit like a Chinese detective. I don't know what I had expected. I knew that Charlie Chan was not a *real* Chinese; had even been reminded by my mother that his name was Warner Oland. Major Chinese roles in those days were always played by reigning Caucasian stars. I remembered Luise Rainier made up with slanted eyes playing in *The Good Earth,* and Paul Muni in some other movie in which he was made up as a Chinese, but somehow I had thought Charlie Chan would look at least *something* like he did in the movies. I was so surprised and dismayed that I stood there, momentarily speechless.

He must have sensed my confusion. Looking slightly amused, he came to my rescue. "And what can I do for you, young lady?" he said. And I, recovering at last from my stupor, managed to untie my tongue enough to get out the words I had been rehearsing all the way to his table. At the same time I thrust the pen and paper forward tentatively.

"Of course you can have my autograph," he said. Would you like me to sign my real name, or Charlie Chan? That *is* why you wanted my autograph isn't it? Do you know what my real name is?"

"It's, it's ---," I stammered. *By then I had forgotten what it was.*

Again he rescued me. "My real name is Warner Oland. How would you like it if I signed both names?" And without waiting for my reply he scrawled both names diagonally across the page. The next day I was proudly showing off the two signatures, embellishing shamelessly the account of my meeting with Charlie Chan. Still, meeting him had been a disappointment. I did not feel I had really met Charlie Chan at all.

As I look back on those early years in the North City house, I realize that my life was divided into two distinct and separate halves. On the left side of the property, the courtyard side, my mother's side, I lived the western half. On the right side, the garden side, where Yi Tai Tai's house was located, I lived the exclusively Chinese half.

On my mother's side, the language spoken, except to the servants, was always English; at Yi Tai Tai's we spoke only Chinese. On my mother's side I knelt each night beside my bed and said my prayers to God and Jesus. On the other side, at Chinese New Year and the spring festival, I bowed three times--but never kowtowed-- to our ancestors' portraits. On one side we ate western food, on the other, Chinese. On the western side, we had bedding of sheets and blankets, whereas Yi Tai Tai and Mabel slept Chinese style, with no top sheets, only cozy quilts, folded under at the sides and the bottoms to form a cocoon-like *pei t'ung*. How I wished that I could snuggle up in one of those at night instead of the smooth, cold sheets of our western-style bedding!

I also learned two sets of table manners, western on one side and Chinese on the other. In our western dining room I learned how to hold my knife and fork; in Yi Tai Tai's dining room I learned to hold my chopsticks correctly. My father insisted on this. Not to do so was as bad as holding a fork in one's fist. I was not allowed to eat unless my chopsticks were held properly. I remember many a time when my father would lean across the table and rap my chopsticks sharply with his own. It always seemed to me that this happened just as I was selecting a choice morsel from the dishes at the center of the table. He was reminding me in no uncertain terms that correction was necessary. I shudder to think what my father's opinion would be of my three children, wielding their chopsticks like most Americans, incorrectly.

In the western dining room I was taught that soup bowls were to be tipped away from the body, that dinner bread or rolls were to be broken into bite size before buttering, but that morning toast could be cut in half with a knife. On the Chinese side, everything was already cut in bite-size pieces; there was no need to break or cut. On one side of the house, bowls must never be brought to the mouth; on the other side, the rice must be pushed into the mouth directly from the bowl. On the western side eating was to be done quietly. On the other, we could slurp our noodles noisily. On the western side we were never to reach across another person but should always ask politely to have things passed, the request always prefaced with the mandatory "please." On the Chinese side, reaching was not only permissible, it was expected. I always remember once asking my father to give me a helping of some dish at the center of the table--this before the lazy Susan had reached Peking. His reply, "If you're not even able to reach for your own food, you will never be a success in life." I reached.

The games played on the two sides of the property were also different. It was on the western side that I was first exposed to bridge. When there were not enough players for a foursome, I was corralled into holding one hand and instructed on what to bid. "Do you have any extra long suit?" I was asked. "Yes." "Any aces, kings, or queens in it?" "Yes." "How many?" "Three." "Then bid that suit." When the bidding was over, I was allowed to go off to play until the next round of bidding. But it was in Yi Tai Tai's house that I saw mahjong for the first time. I was much too young to be interested in the game, but I hovered about the players, mostly waiting for the servants to bring noodles or other tasty snacks for Yi Tai Tai and her companions that I was allowed to share in. The food was often served at the side of the mahjong table, and play stopped only long enough for the players to have a quick meal.

Sometimes it is hard to imagine that two cultures so widely divergent, so distinct and separate, could be melded so readily within one household, but they were. We children were totally unaware of the unusual circumstances; we enjoyed the benefits of both. On Christmas Eve our stockings were hung on the mantelpiece awaiting the arrival of Santa Claus; presents awaited us on Christmas morning under the glistening tree. On New Year's Eve we were allowed to parade through the rooms and courtyards banging on pots and pans, but on Chinese New Year we celebrated Chinese style.

Chinese New Year was so much more exciting for children than the western New Year. On Chinese New Year's eve my father always bought a plentiful supply of fireworks that we set off in the front courtyard. Luther was always allowed to light the rockets that soared into the

sky and seemed to take forever to finally erupt in a deafening explosion. I was too timid to light the rockets but had fun with the little snail-like things that lay on the ground and when lit became wriggling, sparkling worms. There were also hexagonal boxes called *ho tze* with six or more tube-like firecrackers set in them. Each one would go off in turn, first sending out

a beautiful spray of sparks, followed by a loud explosion. The ones I liked best, though, were the *hua*, the "flowers," which did not explode at all, but sent forth spectacular sprays of sparks. My father always bought several of these, but always one extra large one for the grand finale of the evening. I watched in delight as the sparks went higher and higher, spraying across the rooftops, and wider and wider until the entire courtyard was filled with a shower of golden light.

Though Mother always dressed us in western clothes when I was small, for Chinese New Year's day, we put on our Chinese best. For us children the best part of New Year's Day was the red envelopes filled with money that we received from the older generation. The envelopes had a good luck symbol or some characters denoting good fortune printed in gold on the outside, and inside were usually two Chinese silver dollars. *In China, good fortune always came in twos.* We hoarded the silver dollars from year to year to see who could accumulate the most. I remember feeling sorry for Richard and Lois because they were considered too old for red envelopes. They were for the small children only.

Luther and me,
dressed for Chinese New Year

The older ones received small gifts instead. One year Lois was delighted with a ring she was given, but I felt the ring far inferior to two brand new silver dollars.

The new year also brought wonderful things to eat. In every Chinese household a tray of sweetmeats not usually served at other times of the year appeared in a sectioned lacquer or porcelain container. Sticky rice-flour dumplings filled with sweetened white or black sesame paste were also served on New Year's Eve. Highly indigestible, but oh so good! And over the New Year period we always had *la pa chou*, a sweet porridge-like soup made from a variety of grains and filled with Chinese jujube, lotus seeds, raisins, apricot seeds, red and green beans, bits of chestnuts, and water caltrops. A great pot was made, to last for days afterwards. Here in America I make a simpler version for cold winter evenings using only rice, red beans, dried red jujube, and lotus seeds. It doesn't compare with the real thing, but it suffices.

Also at Chinese New Year, boughs of delicate plum blossoms filled the rooms because they signified prosperity for the coming year. In America, the blossoms of the flowering quince strongly resemble the Chinese plum blossoms, and for years after we settled in America I cut branches from our quince bush to force it into bloom for the Chinese New Year.

There was one more room on our property that I have not yet touched upon. That was my father's personal library; it stretched across the back of the garden. It was his special room, where he pursued his particular interests. It was there that he practiced his brush painting and calligraphy, and it was there that he displayed his most prized antiques.

On the left side of the room a couch backed up to the windows to give ample light for reading. A carved marble-topped table stood at the center, surrounded by four matching stools. The set was similar to the one in the western library, but instead of random markings, the marble surface of this one showed a distinct scene of mountains and water with clouds drifting overhead. It was as if a painter had set his brush directly to the smooth marble surface. These scenes in marble were highly prized and most often displayed in frames for the wall, or mounted onto screens.

Against the back wall stood two tall curio cabinets in which were displayed some of my father's most prized "curios." *That's what we called them in those days.* My favorite was the small crystal teapot no more than three inches high and about as wide. Its cover was attached to the teapot's handle with a chain. Teapot, cover, and chain were all carved from a single piece of crystal, not a join anywhere. Etched in my memory too is a bowl of white eggshell-china that was so thin it seemed translucent. Other pieces included a jade paint-mixer in six sections on an ornately carved wooden stand; a pair of figurines of white bisque; and I vaguely recall a few pieces of *T'ang* pottery. *I never liked these; they seemed so crude and out of place beside the other delicate objects.* All the pieces were antiques of great value, the choicest piece being a gold-colored bowl of the *Hsuan Teh* period, circa 960 A.D., which, though of porcelain, rang like a metal bell when flicked with a fingernail. I was never allowed to handle any of these curios, but sometimes to keep me happy my father would hold the gold bowl in his palm and let *me* be the one to produce its bell-like ring with a flick of *my* fingernail. Or he would hold the white egg-shell bowl up to the light and let me wiggle my fingers behind it so that I could see my flickering fingers through the translucent porcelain.

On the right side of the room was my father's black lacquer kneehole desk, and against the back wall on that side stood a large cedar

chest--it must have been fully six feet long and three or more feet high—
in which he stored his most prized paintings. Browsing Peking's many
antique shops and fairs for paintings by famous artists was one of my
father's favorite pastimes. Each time he found a new treasure he would
unroll it proudly for the family, but then it would disappear into the
depths of the cedar chest, never to be seen again except by special friends
whom he knew to have a true appreciation of Chinese art and whom he
deemed worthy of a private viewing.

My father's desk was positioned at right angles to the window
so that the light fell on the left side. The large desk was intended for two
people to sit across from each other, but my father sat at it alone, with his
painting equipment spread before him. The center of the desk was always
left clear to allow room for the lengths of rice paper on which he practiced his painting and calligraphy to stretch across its depth and fall to the
floor on the other side.

I was always fascinated by the many and diverse objects that he
used for his painting. Most impressive was his inkstand, which seemed
enormous when compared to the small ones of our schoolroom. Many,
many ladles of water were needed to make enough ink for his calligraphy. A stacked set of small round dishes held the different colored
paints. Most of these were little chips no more that a quarter-inch square
and came wrapped in small packets of rice paper. The exception was the
yellow color, which was a cylindrical chunk about an inch in diameter
and about as thick. This was put in a small cup rather than a flat dish.

Then there were the separate dishes for
mixing colors: one, a round sectioned
dish with its own cover; the other a very
flat dish with six petal-like sections radi-
ating from a round center. It was called a
plum blossom dish, actually a misnomer
since the plum blossom has only five
petals, not six. There was also an array of brass ruler-like weights for
holding down the paper. Some were etched with large Chinese character,
others with flowers or scenery. And finally there were the two brush-
holders: a large cylindrical porcelain one on its own carved wooden stand
for my father's large calligraphy brushes, and a smaller one made from a
hollow section of old bamboo which held the finer brushes for "hills and

water" landscape paintings. Some of the large brushes were as much as an inch in diameter. They were themselves things of beauty, their bamboo stems mellowed with age to a soft rich brown, their tips rimmed with black and topped with ivory-like beads through which were threaded red-corded loops. My youngest son said to me when he was no more than ten, "Mom, when you die, can I have grandpa's brushes?" Even then he had an eye for beauty.

Little did I realize then that in later years much of my father's painting equipment would become mine. Today I have some of his seals, each cut from a different stone. A few are absolutely plain, but they show off the infinite shades of coloring in the stones themselves. Others are carved with animals at the top: a tiger, ox, ram, or other animal from the Chinese zodiac. I also have the round covered porcelain box holding the sticky vermilion stamp-pad. From the *Ch'ien Lung* period of the mid-eighteenth century, it is of white unglazed bisque. Two dragons in high relief wind themselves around the box's sides and cover, meeting head to head at the top. The dragons' tongues float free within the dragons' heads. If I shake the box, the tongues dart in and out. The stamp pad inside is as moist and usable today as it was when my father died, over thirty-five years ago.

Today some of my father's ink sticks, a couple dating back to the nineteenth century, are in the Freer Gallery of the Smithsonian Institute in Washington. Several years ago they were put on display as part of an exhibition of old Chinese painting materials. With some pride I noted that on the descriptive plaques my name had been listed as donor. I could not help wishing, though, that some of my father's best pieces had been among them. I remember in particular the small wooden chest with specially fitted drawers in which he stored his most prized ink sticks, each nestled in its own quilted compartment of gold-colored brocade. One was shaped like a Chinese lyre. Tiny seed pearls adorned another. Still another was set with rubies. All lost today.

As a child I loved being in that room with my father. Sometimes, when he was feeling particularly indulgent, he would let me ladle the water from the deep, triple-sectioned water container into his ink stand. Then he would let me grind his ink for him. I would use one of his ink sticks and carefully grind it round and round to the tune of re- peated questioning, "Daddy, is it ready yet? Is it ready yet?" It seemed

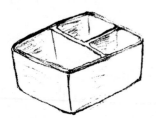

to take forever, but gradually the clear water turned murky and thick, and my father would give me a sign of approval. It was a slow process since a large amount of ink was required to fill his extra-large inkstand, but what might have been thought of as a chore by a young student became a privilege conferred on a small child by a loving parent.

Once the ink was ready I would then stand patiently and watch my father make his preparations. Before taking up his brush, he sketched the bare outlines of his proposed painting with the burnt end of a paper spill. (*I am not sure if this was considered cheating, because in later years when I took painting lessons myself, my teacher never pre-sketched his landscapes.*) This he twisted himself from a piece of rice paper. When he was through with his sketching he would let me have the spill and would give me some paper on which to make drawings of my own. I sat at the blackwood table on the other side of the room, happy in the company of my father.

Chapter 5
Childhood

LUTHER AND I race through the compound, he in his new red car and I on my tricycle. Starting in the concubine's garden at the front end of the property we pedal furiously through the paths around her flowerbeds, then through the long corridor that runs between her house and the Chinese kitchen. We thread our way through the roses, the zinnias, and the red, the pink, and the white flowers in formal beds in our garden. I am far ahead of Luther who has a hard time maneuvering his car around the flowerbeds. He clips the edge of the rose bed and Mother cries out, "Luther, watch where you're going. You'll run over my roses!"

Luther has no time to answer because he is too busy trying to catch up with me. I am already well on my way past my father's library and into "the children's courtyard." By the time he catches up, I have gone through Richard's courtyard as well and am resting just inside the back gate by the storerooms. From the front of the house to the back gate that opens onto the street behind, we have ridden a short city block. I am ready to start back again, but Luther is not interested in racing anymore.

The car is a beautiful thing, his birthday present, ordered especially from England. It is very grand, a bright shiny red. It has rubber tires, a door that opens on one side, and a steering wheel with a horn in it. But it is heavy and cumbersome. In small spaces it can't turn around and

Luther has to get out and lift one end to turn it. I am no longer envious as I was when we first opened the wooden crate and beheld this magnificent thing.

I pedal back slowly to join Mother where she is sitting on the terrazzo porch that faces the garden. She has on her dark horn-rimmed spectacles and is trying to read a book. In a pale flowered dress she is silhouetted against one of the two moongates behind her. The porch is entirely shaded by the wisteria vine that covers it. The flowers are in full bloom, their purple clusters part of the leafy ceiling. Though it is mid-summer and hot, the wide terrazzo railing is cool. It is lined with red geraniums, and I must push one aside to make room for myself.

Luther pedals his car around the flowerbeds once more, this time taking it slowly, not pressured by trying to keep up with me. He parks at the edge of the porch and comes up to join Mother and me. He has barely sat down when he is up again. He cannot sit still.

He starts running up the inside of one of the moongates at the back of the porch. "I bet I can run farther up the sides than you can," he challenges me.

"I bet you can't." I take the challenge and get up to run up the sides of the other moongate. "Mother, Mother, watch us," I cry. "See who gets up higher."

Mother puts her book down and turns to watch us. She puts on a serious look and mediates, "I think it's a tie." For the moment all is settled. Tired, I flop down on one of the rattan chairs. I am four. My world is beautiful.

My world *was* beautiful, and my life was beautiful. I wanted for nothing. Within the four walls of our compound was everything a little girl could want. I had a luxurious home and servants who provided for my every need. I had all the toys that girls of my age in China had ever dreamt of: a baby doll with a porcelain face whose eyes could open and close, a doll house full of miniature furniture, paper dolls, cards for cross-stitching, and coloring books and crayons. There was nothing I longed for. I already had everything. Best of all was a tiny tea set of fine bone china from England. With my little friends I had tea parties, not with homemade mud pies, but with miniature cakes and sandwiches made especially for me by our cook. As I had heard my mother do, I asked each guest, "Would you like cream or lemon?" as I placed a tiny wedge of lemon on each saucer. We held our little fingers in the air as we sipped our tea. We were so very elegant.

My father took Luther and me everywhere with him--to visit his friends, on shopping trips, to the fairs, and to the Chinese opera. Sometimes he took us to *T'ien Ch'iao*, the fairgrounds outside the city's main gate. Though I call it the fairgrounds, it was actually a kind of combination flea market and fair. The wide, open space was teeming with every imaginable form of life. Blind fortunetellers occupied a space beside itinerant barbers and child contortionists. Silk-robed gentry moved among the various stalls while ragged beggars hovered nearby looking for easy handouts. We loved watching the magicians, the wrestlers, the musicians, and the many other performers. My father browsed among the antique stalls, and Luther and I, accompanied by our rickshaw boy, watched one performer after another. Though we had a car and driver, I don't recall my father using it when out with us. Instead, he rode in our private rickshaw, and Luther and I in a hired one. Luther always knelt facing backward with his knees spread to outside edge of the seat. I sat between his knees facing front, my back to his back. I don't know who had devised this method of seating, but it was highly satisfactory. I could see everything as we approached; Luther could see everything we left behind. I would see other children in their rickshaws squeezed uncomfortably together side by and feel quite pleased with our arrangement.

Though my father always rode in the private rickshaw when we were out with him, normally it ferried us children about. Our rickshaw coolie was a fast runner, faster than the coolies of most of our friends. When we went out in a group, the coolies would race, and we were quite smug about being consistent winners. Our rickshaw was kept immaculate, its black lacquered fenders shining and the two brass lamps that hung on either side polished to a brilliant sheen. The seat cushions were laundered to a blinding white, and the one loose cushion at the back had a ruffled border. In the winter, a fur-lined robe covered our legs. Moving deftly through the bicycles, carts, and ordinary rickshaws—most of them quite shabby--that moved along the streets of Peking, our rickshaw boy streaked past them all, head held high, proud of his speed and the vehicle he pulled. It was a Rolls Royce; the other rickshaws all old jalopies.

On the Moon Festival, celebrating the eighth lunar moon, my father took us to the lantern shops and let us choose the ones we liked. All were made of paper on frames of stripped bamboo. I almost always chose one in the shape of a lamb because I loved the fuzzy look of the curled paper wool that covered it. We then went to *Pei Hai*, the North Lake Park, which was one of the three lakes in what we called the Winter Palace, to share in the excitement of watching other families each with their own candle-lit lanterns enjoying the late summer festivities. The most common and cheapest of the lanterns were the lotus flowers. They looked like enlarged versions of the real flowers, their ridged petals shaded from dark pink at their base to almost white at their tips. Cheaper still, for those who could not afford lanterns, were the real lotus leaves. The well in the center of the broad round leaf made a perfect nest for a candle. In retrospect, the natural leaves and inexpensive lotus-flower lanterns were really the most beautiful, for when the evening was over and families left for home, some were left behind to float on the water's edge. Then the lake's edge glittered for a time with the glow of the candle-lit flowers and leaves.

In the winter months my father took us at least once, sometimes twice, for a family meal of Mongolian barbecue at Tung Lai Shun, famous for its Mongolian barbecues and hot-pot meals. The restaurant was one of many located inside Tung An Shih Ch'ang, the Eastern Peace Market. The second floor opened onto the rooftop where individual tables were set up for the barbecues. Each table had its own large brazier at its center, and the fire was always blazing hot before the waiters summoned us to our table. Around us were other tables with smoke and flame rising from each. Though the tables were always surrounded with benches, these we usually pushed under the table, preferring to eat standing up. Peking winters were bitterly cold, and wrapped up in our winter coats and hats and gloves, standing gave us the necessary freedom of movement to do justice to the meal before us. For Mongolian barbecues in Peking bore not the slightest resemblance to what passes for a Mongolian barbecue in America.   Instead of mixing up our meat and sauces together in a bowl, handing them to a restaurant chef for cooking, and returning to our table with a bowl of cooked meat, each of us did our own cooking. We mixed our own sauce from the condiments at our table, into which we then dipped only a few pieces of meat. Using our individual chopsticks, almost two feet in length, we then cooked the meat ourselves on the center brazier. We watched the meat sizzle and brown to just the degree we liked; then scraped it off the brazier directly into the piping hot *shao bing* (sesame buns) that the waiters replenished constantly. Before each mouthful had been swallowed, we were already busy mixing the second, sometimes making changes to our seasonings, a bit more chili pepper, a bit more vinegar. Then back onto the grill. Every mouthful was hot, as were we by then. By the time the meal was over, hats and gloves had been shed and collars loosened. We went home, our stomachs full, our spirits happy.

In those childhood years, sometimes our whole family went for sledge rides on the canal outside the city walls. There was one stretch

Sledging on the canal: Daddy, Lois, me, coolie, and Luther.

several hundred yards long where we hired a sledge coolie to pull us along the canal. The sledge itself was no more than a low platform with four legs on each side. This sat atop two strips of wood to which iron runners had been affixed. Though its surface was rough, we always carried our own longhaired fur blankets with which we covered the sledge, making it quite comfortable. The sledge was big enough to seat five or six people. At the front end was a leather belt that was harnessed over the coolie's shoulders. Though the startup was slow and labored, once in motion, the coolie was able to hop back onto the sledge and join his passengers on the ride. When the momentum gave out he had to get off and pull again, but successive efforts were far less exhausting than the initial startup, and often Richard or Luther would get off the sledge to help. If Richard was not with us, Luther would often berate me for not helping him in the pulling, but buttoned up in my fur coat and nestled snugly among the fur blankets, I was much too comfortable to think of dislodging myself from the sledge.

Luther and I both wore our fur coats when out on the canals. His was of a nondescript fur that I think was some kind of cat. Mine was nicer and was of baby leopard, its spotted markings much smaller than those on full-grown leopard skins. I also had a gray fur coat of land otter, and a white one that was reserved for Sunday school, church, and parties. It, the white one, was of squirrel belly, an inexpensive fur that needs no further description. However, by the time I got to high school it had been discarded in favor of a white ermine cape for evening dances. The baby leopard was later remade into a short skating jacket that I wore with a circular wine-red skirt. Outfitted so smartly, one would have thought I was at least capable of doing simple figures so that my skirt would twirl around me, but not so. Despite no lack of enthusiasm, I was a plain skater, forward only.

In those early years in Peking, Luther and I were inseparable. We were only thirteen months apart so it was natural that we should be playmates. As small children we were constant companions, not so much because of our "real" blood relationship—we knew that we were born to the same parents--but because we were so close in age. Richard and Lois were there, in the same house, but they were so much older and had their own friends and activities. Besides, they were at school during the week while Luther and I were home. I knew that my father loved us, and if he sometimes took Luther out without me, it didn't bother me. After all, Luther was a boy, and in those days it was understood and ac-

cepted that boys had more privileges than girls. Certainly they got to do
more things with their fathers.

Luther enjoyed a special place within our family. He was kind
of the young prince around whom my small world revolved. Mother too,
because of concerns for his occasional childhood convulsions, seemed
more attentive to Luther than to the rest of us. If he cried at night, she
took him into her bed. If he was hurt, she seemed to be more concerned
with his wounds than with ours. While I was growing up, my father was
in Nanking much of the time and Richard had left for college in Scotland
when I was only six. Luther became the "little master" of the household
and the servants catered to his every whim. He was the heir apparent to
the Ch'ien family throne.

The world I shared with Luther was within the walls of our
property, and though friends often came to visit, most of our days were
spent with each other. I tended to follow where Luther led. Together we
played at Chinese opera-style fighting, not cops and robbers or cowboys
and Indians American style, but with wooden swords and Chinese spears
with collars of long fringe around the spearheads. We bought little replicas of opera figures, usually warriors, that were four or five inches high
and had rings of horse hairs protruding around the hems of their skirts.
We placed them on a large brass tray that sat on top of a carved wooden
stand--this was in the living room of Yi Tai Tai's house and served as a
coffee table--and when we beat the sides of the tray, the figures moved
around, battle flags twirling at every beat. When I think about the horrendous din this must have created, I am amazed that Yi Tai Tai didn't
complain. I'm sure that my mother would have had something to say
about the noise, not to mention the vehemence with which we banged
away at the handsome brass tray. It was a beautiful piece, fully thirty
inches in diameter with a finely etched floral design covering its entire
surface. It made a fine arena for our battling opera figures, but I am sure
we left many a dent along its polished edge. But I suppose that even
though Yi Tai Tai was not in the least subservient, her subconscious may
have told her it was best not to offend my father's children.

Luther had a Chinese warrior headpiece mounted with fuzzy
pompoms on wire antenna that jiggled when we did our make-believe
fighting. When he shook his head, the whole headpiece quivered. I was
envious, but even without the trappings of a warrior I played at battle

anyway. We stuck the double flags of battle into the backs of our shirt collars and whirled round and round mimicking the battle style of opera performers. When supposedly on horseback I swooped about with the tasseled stick that represented a horse--*the tassel suggesting a horse's tail?*--all to my own rhythmic cries of "t'ing, t'ing, t'ing, t'ing, t'aang

t'aang!" meant to sound like the clanging of the stage cymbals. I liked most to imitate the sweeping measured walk of the warriors and high officials, again to the slow rhythmic beat of "t'ing, t'ing, t'aang!" Though we never bought any of the big hoops that encircled the waists of the important figures, I consciously held my elbows in fixed position away from the body to accommodate these supposed symbols of rank and power. Neither did we ever wear any of the elaborately painted masks that were

Luther in opera gear, dressed for battle with sword and "horse."

available in the stores, but we had several false beards that we hooked over our ears. Because Luther was the leader in this play-acting--as he was in almost all the games we played together--it was the male parts on which most of our attention was focused; I never acquired any of the female headdresses. Still, I often affected the mincing, pigeon-toed gait of the female roles. I imitated their expressions of deep woe, raising my arms to eye level, elbows out, fingers slightly in front of eyes, fluttering them in a downward motion to simulate the falling of tears. This I combined with a shrill falsetto wailing. I thought this hilariously funny, and even when not play-acting with Luther, would often wander through the garden with mincing steps, shrieking "eee-ah, eee-ah" in high falsetto.

In later years, Luther became quite an aficionado of Chinese opera and learned to sing many of the better-known opera solos by heart. Even today, in his home in New Jersey, he spends many of his leisure hours watching videotapes of his favorite operas. I, on the other hand, had not the slightest interest in the operas themselves but was always thrilled nonetheless when included in my father's opera outings. For me these occasions were excursions into an exciting world. Chinese operas were not dignified affairs like those in the west. Both the performances themselves and the audience were noisy and active. Food vendors sold their wares along the aisles; attendants moved deftly in and out of the aisles filling and refilling empty teacups. The shells of watermelon seeds littered the aisles and crunched beneath our feet. Frequently a hot wet towel went flying through the air as one attendant hurled it to another in a distant aisle. Added to this was the ear-shattering din of the Chinese orchestra whose cymbals seemed to clang incessantly. Then too there was the frequent applause of the audience when the singer executed a particularly fine passage. Cries of "*hao, hao!*" (bravo, bravo!) came from all corners of the audience.

With almost no stage props, a knowledge of the on-stage gestures of the performers was essential to a full appreciation of Chinese opera. The singing too was hard to understand, as the tones of the Chinese language itself were often lost in the overriding tones of the singing. To lovers of Chinese opera this was no obstacle as most of the stories came from familiar Chinese historical tales. For me, however, the show meant nothing. When a particularly magnificent costume appeared, or when actors were engaged in furious fighting, or when acrobats were tumbling spectacularly on stage, I focused momentarily on the performance, but most of the time I was not even watching. I had no idea what was going on. While my father and Luther were engrossed in the performance, I occupied myself instead by running up and down the aisles eating watermelon seeds and cajoling my father into buying me *t'ang hu lu*, the delicious skewers of candied fruit that were a popular snack in Peking during the winter months.

It was not until recent years, long after the days when Chinese opera was readily accessible to me, that I learned the meaning of many of the symbolic stage gestures. Then, though I knew that a tasseled stick served as a horse, I had no idea that throwing it down meant the actor had dismounted. Neither did I know that a character walking between two yellow flags was riding a carriage, or that his moving his extended hands apart meant he was opening a door. I couldn't help admiring the long graceful pheasant plumes that adorned some of the male headdresses and the way the actors made them wave to and fro with a simple flick of the head. But I was totally unaware that waving them one way symbolized anger; another, surprise. Neither did I know that there was purpose to the yards of sleeve that covered the hands of both male and female characters; that flicking them up to expose the hands meant one thing; that waving them about meant another. Even the positions of the hands and fingers had particular meanings, all of which were lost on me. Had I known these things, I might at least have learned to appreciate Chinese opera if not to like it. But even today, I find the singing jarring and unmelodious to my ear, which has always been attuned to western music.

At home it was not only at playing at opera that I followed Luther. Though I was every bit a girl, and happy to be one, it always seemed to me that his activities were more exciting then mine. Whenever I could, and whenever he would tolerate me, I tagged along after him. Because of the occasional convulsions he had had as a small child, Luther was watched over carefully by my parents and by all the servants. Lin, our rickshaw coolie, when not involved in other duties was assigned to accompany Luther in all his activities outside the house. Thus he became Luther's personal overseer and companion. Luther, with his own personal servant, was able to do many things away from home completely independently of the rest of the family. In fact it was with Lin in tow, or rather, with Lin towing him, that he was able to attend so many Chinese operas and to develop a taste for them.

When Luther became interested in kite-flying, it was also Lin who accompanied him. He and Luther went often to the large open field near Peking's eastern city wall, which was an ideal site for launching kites. I tagged along whenever they would let me.

Chinese kites came in all shapes and sizes and were much more elaborate than any kites I have ever seen in the west. As with so many things in China, the frames were made of strips of split bamboo. The bodies were of paper but often had cloth appendages. Luther's prize kite was a goldfish with large googly eyes that spun around and made a whirring noise when the kite was aloft. The body was painted in the brilliant goldfish colors of orange and assorted reds, but the twenty-foot tail was made of cloth. The kite, not counting the cloth tail, was five feet tall. Because of its size and awkward shape, it was all we could do to carry it on our rickshaw. Though we had always flown some of the smaller kites ourselves, this one, Luther's prize, was almost entirely launched by the coolie. Once skyborne, Lin used all kinds of intricate maneuvers to make the kite soar and dance. Once aloft, its pull was so strong that Luther and I together could not hold it. So it was really Lin who flew the kite. He gripped the spool and played the line while we ran along at his side, making a show of helping. It was Lin who launched the kite and Lin who flew it, but we who delighted in the fact that *we* were flying the biggest and grandest kite in the air.

Often when he needed a rest, Lin would tie the line to our rickshaw, which the kite would jerk forward several inches at a time with each gust of strong wind. Once I was sitting in the rickshaw when this happened. I had a moment of panic when the rickshaw started its jerking forward movement, sure that I would be pulled up into the air, rickshaw and all. Lin for the moment was nowhere to be seen. I yelled desperately for Lin. "Lin, Lin, where are you?" Luther tried to help, but the kite's pull was too strong for him. The rickshaw kept inching forward. What a relief it was when Lin came running back from across the field. He had gone off to relieve himself. He quickly grabbed the spool and all was well again, but in his absence the rickshaw had moved all of three or four feet.

Proud as I was of our goldfish kite, what I really longed for was a centipede. The centipedes were made of many separate round discs joined by strings at a given distance from each other. They could be as long as fifteen feet, and when aloft and buoyed by strong winds, seemed to be writhing and wriggling with each shift of the wind. They were supposed to be very difficult to fly, but I was sure that we, that is, Lin, could have mastered it. Besides, Luther was not interested in a centipede, and whatever Luther did not want, we did not get.

When I look back on those days I can't help thinking what a joy Lin's job must have been to him! Though he had his job of pulling our rickshaw, and of course keeping his eye on Luther, and on me, he also had a chance to engage in all the recreations that people of his class could not normally hope to enjoy. Rickshaw coolies were among the lowest class of humanity in China's cities. Their lives were hard, their life spans short. In rain or shine, scorching heat, or bitter cold, those who were not privately employed spent their waking hours on the streets waiting patiently for a poorly paid fare. In winter, in temperatures well below freezing, they stood by their rickshaws throughout the day, arms hugged

around their bodies in their efforts to keep warm. Lin was among the
fortunate few who were privately employed, and who, when not actually
hauling a rickshaw, could sit in the comfort of a gatehouse and share in
the household gossip of the other servants

Apart from his early convulsions, Luther was actually a very
normal, healthy young Chinese boy. I don't recall exactly when his convulsions stopped, but know that years after his last one--they didn't continue in his adult life--Lin was still playing the role of baby-sitter *cum*
companion for Luther. However, not all the activities that Luther shared
with Lin had the approval of my parents. I think it was mostly because
of Lin that Luther spent so much of his time in the front gatehouse,
which was the servants' gathering place between chores. Across one
wall of the gatehouse stretched a *k'ang*, a large brick platform that served
as a bed for I don't know how many of the servants. In the summer it
was cool, and in cold weather, coals inside it were lit and the *k'ang* itself
as well as the room was kept warm. Passing through the front entry
court, I would often see Luther sitting cross-legged on the *k'ang*, either
playing chess or listening to their gossip. They showed him some pornographic pictures, never realizing that he would show them to my mother.
She was of course furious and told them off in no uncertain terms. The
servants then labeled him *Hsiao Mo Ku* (Little Mushroom), an affection-
ate term for "little troublemaker," and in private they always called him
that. Otherwise they continued to address him as *Erh Shao Yeh*, Second
Young Master.

Other than the pornographic pictures, there were other areas
where the servants' influence, particularly Lin's, caused my parents some
concern. I recall an instance when I overheard them talking. It was obvious they were talking about Luther. I heard my mother say, "The doctor said it was just a rash, but the silly child thought he had some venereal disease." And my father, clearly upset, replying, "I'll have to have a
talk with Lin and find out just what's been going on." I could hear the
anger in his voice.

Just days before that, while looking for something in Luther's
dresser drawer, I had come across some odd looking small rolls of
quilted bandages tucked at the very back of the drawer. They were pink
colored and had a strong medicinal smell. I wondered what they were.
But when I asked Luther, he just snapped back at me, "It's none of your

business." When I had heard my parents talking, somehow, though I didn't even know what a venereal disease was, I was sure their conversation and the bandages were in some way connected with Luther's "goo-goo." Lin disappeared from our household a few days after that. Luther had lost his companion and it was high time he did. He was a child no longer.

Chapter 6
Mother

WHEN I THINK OF MY MOTHER it is hard for me to see her other than as she was at the end of her life, a small woman, her fine hair thinning and not quite held up by hairpins that were always half in half out. When she was younger it had been a beautiful auburn, a rich brown with reddish highlights, and even when she died at eighty-five, it had not turned completely gray. The straps of her slip would often have slipped down her sloping shoulders. "Gibson-Girl shoulders" she used to say. As a result, her slip often hung down on one side or the other below the hem of her dress. The heels of her shoes were always somewhat worn down on the outer edges. They caused her to slip frequently and she had some near-serious falls. Her glasses always seemed to need cleaning and I often marveled that she could see at all through the foggy lenses. Looking at her, one would not have thought that she had once been in the upper echelons of official Chinese society. But in China there had been cobblers to repair her run-down heels, sewing amahs to hand-sew slips to conform to her sloping shoulders, and her auburn hair, whether in place or not, had crowned her head with a rich lustrous sheen.

I never thought of my mother as beautiful or brilliant, though in her way she may have been both. She wore no makeup and despite her dark auburn hair, her eyebrows and lashes were pale and gave a pale look to her face. Her eyes were large, hazel, flecked slightly with green, but when I was small they were often hidden behind horn-rimmed spectacles, and later by rimless glasses. I knew she was clever--she had been valedictorian of her high school class--but not in an intellectual way. Ours was not a family that discussed literature, art, world events, or social issues at the dinner table. My mother was a doer more than a thinker. Her thoughts were on what could be done in the small world immediately around her. If there was a task to be done, a problem to be tackled, she would do it and do it well.

Mother's greatest attribute was her capacity for making friends, and keeping them. When she sold her home in Cambridge to live with my brother Luther in the small New Jersey town of Pitman, she was over seventy, not an easy age to break into an established community. Yet within a year streams of younger women were coming to the house regularly to pick her up for church, for bridge, for tea, and for any other activity in which she was interested.

She had always been a "joiner," active in community activities. In Pitman she participated in a flower-arranging competition and came home with a blue ribbon for her miniature arrangement of wild flowers. She had a passion for flowers, and even when none were blooming in Luther's garden, she would somehow manage to find some little wildflower or even a few sprigs of feathery grass, to arrange in a demitasse cup or an interesting looking bottle. As a girl she had taken lessons in elocution, and this had carried through to an interest in acting. In Pitman she became involved in the local drama club and took first prize for best director at the annual drama festival in the region.

One year Luther gave her a round trip airplane ticket to the West Coast to visit some old friends. She promptly traded it in for a Greyhound bus ticket that permitted unlimited travel within a ninety-nine day period. She went to Florida, California, Vancouver, Nova Scotia, New England, New York, and many points in between, all in response to repeated invitations from her many friends. She returned to Pitman on the ninety-ninth day. She was over eighty at the time. It was in the sixties, a time when seventy was "old" and eighty was an age that many would not live to see.

Mother was born Helen May Court in England in 1879. Her mother, Clara Court, my grandmother, was from a well-to-do family from the south of England. The family had not been happy when my

My mother (on right) with her three sisters, Aunt Margaret, Aunt Irene, and Aunt Mildred.

grandmother chose to marry a young man of a lower social class with little education and no visible talents or skills. I am not sure when my grandfather immigrated to America but know that he went alone to seek his fortune and sent for his family later. It was not till my mother was thirteen that the whole family left England to join him in the small town of Peabody, Massachusetts, where my grandfather had found work as a tanner. Though the fortune he sought eluded him, his new trade provided adequate support for his family of six children, two boys and four girls.

My mother was the oldest. Then came Aunt Margaret, Uncle Norman, Aunt Irene, Uncle Harvey, and Aunt Mildred. I know little of my mother's childhood except that it was a happy one and that she and her brothers and sisters had a warm relationship with each other and with their parents. Mother was the acknowledged smart one in the family. She was the only one in her family who attended college—Boston University—but dropped out after only two years to help support her family.

At the time she met my father, she and Aunt Irene were running a rooming house in Cambridge. When I first learned of the rooming house, I found it hard to understand how my grandparents could have permitted two young unmarried daughters to live alone away from home. Not only were they single women living alone, but they were renting rooms to young unmarried men. Surely that must have raised a lot of eyebrows!

Not until I was in college did my mother give me some explanation, and then only a partial one. "You see, I was not a young unmarried woman. I had been married before, and divorced. And I was not so young. I was already in my thirties and considered mature enough to oversee Aunt Irene. Though she wasn't that young either. She was all of twenty-four, not that young by standards of that day."

This was one of the few serious conversations I had with my mother about her past, and even this barely touched on the years before China. Mother, a divorcee? The word had in my mind unfortunate connotations. Divorcees somehow did not seem totally respectable. It was hard to believe that Mother was one of *those*. I voiced my surprise. "I thought divorce was practically unheard of in those days."

"It was. But I really had no choice. It was either divorce or stay with a husband who drank heavily. When he was drunk he'd strike out at me."

"What do you mean, 'strike out at you'? Did he actually hit you? Did he hurt you?"

"Not at first. He was insanely jealous and if I so much as smiled at another man, even the minister, it would infuriate him. At first he just hurled insults at me, told me I was a useless human being, called me a slut. Then he started slapping me, hard, again and again, first on one side of my head and then the other." Mother paused. "There's no point in

talking about it now. It's all in the past and it's over." She would have
stopped at that, but I pressed on.

"But did he ever really hurt you?"

"Yes, he hurt me. The slapping turned to shoving, first with one
hand and then the other. He pushed me so hard that I would fall against
the furniture or the wall. I got some bad bruises but was never seriously
hurt. It was all so long ago and somehow I've put it out of my mind. But
it got steadily worse and I knew I couldn't stick it out."

"Did you have no idea he was a drinker when you married
him?" I asked.

"No, no inkling at all. No one else knew either. He didn't drink
in public; never went to public bars. But when he came home, the first
thing he did was to pour himself a drink. Then he would have another,
and another. When I tried to stop him, he'd snap at me, 'Leave me alone.
What I do is my business.' I couldn't understand why he did it. It wasn't
as if he had any problems in his life. He had a good job, and when he
wasn't drinking he didn't seem to be unhappy. He and I sang together in
the church choir. He was the soloist, had a beautiful tenor voice. And he
was a handsome man with a lot of charm, considered quite a catch. Everyone thought me lucky that he had singled me out. But it was only a
few weeks into our marriage that I realized what I was in for. Except for
my family, no one knew, and I doubt that anyone would have believed
it."

How long did you stay married?" I asked.

"Only a year and a half. I would have ended it earlier but I got
pregnant and then I was locked in."

I had always thought Mother was unable to have children, and
that was why we were all adopted. "But that means you *were* able to
have children." I said. "It must have been Daddy then who had the problem."

"I was quite sure that it was, but he never would go to see a doctor, so that was that. But I've never regretted for a moment that we
adopted all of you." With those words, her eyes started to water.

"But what about your baby? What happened to the baby?"

"It was stillborn, and I've never regretted that either. As soon as
I recovered from the birth I got the divorce, even though it was socially

unacceptable at the time. I was lucky that my family stood by me through it all. None of them even tried to talk me into sticking it out."

I was still trying to absorb everything my mother was telling me. I knew that life had not always been easy for her during the years she had been in China, but she had always been such a strong woman. With my father away much of the time, she had carried the burden of bringing up us children most of the time on her own. Still, it was hard for me to even imagine the troubles she had endured before her China years.

"So you see, Marguerite. I was not exactly a giddy young girl living a free and easy life away from home. When Daddy and I were married I was already thirty-three years old. I had already been divorced for eight years." She asked me, "Do you have any idea how old I am now?"

I had never known her exact age but ventured a guess. "Fifty-five? Fifty-six?"

She smiled. "No, I'm a lot older than you think," she said. "Sixty-six. I'll be sixty-seven on my next birthday."

I was incredulous. She had always been so busy, so active. Sixty-six was *old*. I was about twenty at the time and in my mind she had not many more years to live. I could feel the tears welling up in my eyes. Mother put her hand gently over mine. She couldn't help smiling. "I'm not headed for the grave just yet, Marguerite." We both laughed; but for the first time I became aware of her mortality, that she would not be with me forever.

During the time that Mother and Aunt Irene were running the rooming house in Cambridge, they had four roomers, all students at Harvard. One of them, Dennis Liu, was Chinese, and my father was among the friends who often visited him. According to Aunt Irene, it was she, and not my mother who first drew his attention.

"How come he ended up with Mother then and not with you?" I asked her.

"Oh I liked your father a lot. He had a wonderful sense of humor, and he and I laughed and joked. I admit that I flirted with him—I was quite a flirt in those days--but I wasn't the slightest bit interested in him in a romantic way. I was still looking for a rose-covered cottage with a picket fence, and not even the promise of a mansion would have lured me half way around the world to a country as strange as China." Aunt Irene laughed. "I think your mother found the way to his heart through his stomach. Your mother was a wonderful cook--you know that

of course--and she would often ask if he would like a piece of pie, or cake, or sometimes we would invite him and Dennis to have a meal with us. She always did the cooking. Your mother gave both of them their English names, you know. At first she named your father Earl, but Dennis kept on pronouncing it Erh-luh—he couldn't get his tongue around the "rl" sound-- so she changed it to Chauncey. When we were all together your mother was full of questions about China. Neither or us had ever met a Chinese before, and your

My parent's wedding picture

mother was fascinated by the life they described. Actually, that may have had a lot to do with why your father turned to her, because she was so interested."

They were married in July 1912, two years after they first met. Despite her having been married before, Mother wore white. Her head was covered with the traditional veil and she carried a bouquet of garden flowers. I don't know who attended the wedding or where it took place; surely not in Peabody where her past divorce would have been well known and probably had been the subject of much local gossip. I often wondered if she had told my father before their marriage about that part of her life. If she did not, how did she conceal from him that she was not a virgin? Was she aware of the great emphasis the Chinese place on a bride's virginity?

Or perhaps he did know and did not mind. Perhaps he conspired with her to keep it from his family. I do know, however, that she never told him of the stillborn child from her first marriage, for when she had not conceived in three years of marriage, he assumed that it was her fault. Having been pregnant once before, she felt otherwise, and was sure the fault lay with him. According to her, neither followed up by seeking medical help. I know that together they lied about her age. I never knew my father's exact age but guess he was seven or eight years younger than my mother. Neither one wanted his family to know that his new bride was so much older than he.

Other than the little I learned from Aunt Irene when I first came to America, I know nothing of my parents' courtship. Whether it was a romantic courtship, a slowly evolving friendship, or a stiff and formal relationship. Did they draw odd looks when they were seen together, this American woman and Chinese man? Was my mother embarrassed by the critical looks of others? Or did she and my father try to avoid public scrutiny by confining their meetings to the parlor of the rooming house? Was he scorned because of his race? Was he called a Chinaman, or worse, a Chink? Somehow I cannot imagine my father having been looked down upon. He was no immigrant laborer; he was a Harvard student, obviously from a family of stature. Nor can I imagine my mother being scorned because of her association with him. Whatever the case, knowing my mother, I doubt that she was daunted by any criticism, either of her, or of my father, or of their relationship.

One of my American cousins, Dorothy, close to ninety now and living in a nursing home, once stated to me bluntly that she thought my mother had married my father for his money. It was true that my father came from a wealthy family, and this must have been obvious to my mother. However, I find it hard to accept that she was motivated solely by his wealth. She was a thirty-three-year-old divorcee with no prospects for the future. How much longer was she to be locked into running a rooming house? She was fascinated by her introduction to a foreign culture seen through the eyes of my father. She longed for a different life. She had the opportunity and she seized it. I would hope that love played its part, but I don't know. Certainly, as a child, I lived in a happy, harmonious home that suggested the presence of love and affection.

Many people have asked me through the years if my mother's family disapproved of the interracial marriage. Given the times, I would have thought they would have had strong objections, not only to her marrying out of her race, but also to her having chosen a life so far from home. But when I came to know my mother's family in later years, they showed nothing but affection for our Chinese family. In fact, I often felt they loved us more *because* of our differences. And far from believing themselves to be racially superior, I detected always a note of deference to my father. They were working class; none except Mother educated beyond high school. Yet they seemed devoid of the strong racial prejudices that existed at the time. I wonder too if my grandfather's acceptance of my mother's marriage came in part from his own experience. He had come from humble origins. In England he had seen no future for himself and had left his family and all that was familiar to him to try for a new life in America. He had crossed an ocean to find that new life. His daughter's marriage to my father was *her* chance to make a new life. He would not try to stop her.

My first contact with our American relatives came when I was only three years old. My parents brought our whole family to America for a visit. My grandfather had died a few years before that so I never met him, but my grandmother was still alive. I loved my grandmother; and after that visit I wrote to her regularly, at first childish drawings accompanied by a few words copied in a four-year-old's unformed hand from my mother's lettering; later, accounts of my school activities in longhand. She always replied. She was an accomplished tatter and to the day she died was still sending me handkerchiefs and other small items that were trimmed with her tatting. She was much loved in that small community and was proud of the more than two hundred cards she received on her eightieth birthday. It was on that visit that my parents bought for her the small house in which she lived until she died. Little did she, or my parents, know then that the proceeds from the sale of that house would one day provide seed money for our resettlement in America some seventeen years later.

When the house was sold, there was none of the squabbling over individual entitlements that so often accompanies the death of a parent who dies without a will. All agreed that the proceeds "should go to Helen." I don't know how the money was kept or who was responsible for it. I know only that it was there for my mother when she needed it.

Mother was indeed lucky in having the family she did. I remember them all with love and affection. At some time in my life I had stayed at the homes of them all. Uncle Norman had a "way" with animals. He had trained his dog Topsy, a nondescript animal, a mix of many breeds, to do all the usual dog tricks, rolling over, playing dead, barking on cue, and sitting up and begging. He brought Uncle Norman his paper in the morning and his slippers at night. To me, who had never had a pet of any kind--my father did not like animals--these were marvelous accomplishments.

Aunt Irene was my favorite aunt. She found her rose-covered cottage in Detroit and the man of her dreams in Uncle John. The two were obviously devoted to each other throughout their lifetimes. He worked in a factory that made parts for General Motors, not a job of great prestige, but he supported his family comfortably. They were two of a kind; they laughed a lot and joked a lot, two happy people in a happy home with three happy children. It was a joy just being with them. It was hard not to be envious of them, and when I saw them together in later years I often wondered if my mother, despite the luxurious life she had experienced, didn't feel a twinge of envy at not having had the kind of life that Aunt Irene enjoyed.

Aunt Mildred, the youngest of my mother's sisters, was probably the least favorite of my aunts and uncles. I will never forget how wonderful she was to our family when we finally resettled in America, but she was on the prissy side and extremely fussy about her housekeeping. Whereas at Aunt Irene's we could be totally relaxed, I always felt I should tread gently in Aunt Mildred's meticulously ordered household. She was a marvelous cook and fed us sumptuously, but even she admitted that Mother's pies were better than hers. Mother was an exceptionally good cook, but a tidy one she was not. She was the kind who wiped her doughy hands on the dishtowels, dripped flour into the kitchen draw-ers, and left flour on drawer handles and oven doors and all over the floor as well. When Mother made a pie, or several pies, Aunt Mildred fol-lowed after her in a frenzy, cleaning out the drawers, wiping up the han-dles, and sweeping the floor, trying desperately to keep her immaculate kitchen immaculate.

Uncle Irving had his own ideas on the proprieties too. He was a contractor, and a successful one, building houses from basement to roof-top with his own hands and the help of an assistant when required. At the end of the day he came home hot and sweaty, and dirty from his la-bors. He always went upstairs immediately for a bath and within the hour was down again in full suit and tie. He expected to sit down at the dinner table at precisely half past six. The table was always set formally with white linen cloth and napkins and the family silver. None of this eating-in-the-kitchen-in-shirtsleeves business for him. He might labor with his hands during the day, but at home he was a gentleman.

Both Aunt Mildred and Uncle Irving doted on me. She, I think, because I was as tidy as she and was almost as meticulous in picking up after Mother; he, because I was the daughter he had always wanted. They had no children of their own but had played a large part in raising my Uncle Harvey's three boys--his wife had left him before the boys had reached their teens. But they were boys, and it was a girl that Uncle Ir-ving had always wanted. During the months that we stayed with them, I was that girl. He loved me without reservation. Uncle Irving, despite his rigidity on how his house was run, was prone to telling off-color jokes. Not seriously off-color, and certainly not even remotely "dirty." And I, just twenty at the time, and never exposed at home to any stories that even hinted of sex, thought I was at last privy to a sophisticated adult world. As for Mother, she usually gave Uncle Irving a reproachful look, at the same time trying to smother her own laughter. It was important that I know she didn't quite approve.

I was never in the home of my Uncle Harvey and am not sure he really had a home. He was single, a janitor for some office building, and I assume he may have had a room at his work place. Instead, once we had settled in Cambridge, he was in our home frequently and it was al-ways fun to have him visit. He was the youngest of my mother's family and had a temperament much like Aunt Irene's, funny, and with a happy outlook on life despite his circumstances. Yes, Mother had a wonderful family and I felt close to them all.

Of greater importance than the approval of my mother's family of her marriage to a Chinese was the reaction of my father's family to his bringing home a foreign bride. In those days the Chinese disapproved strongly of marrying outside one's race, and even today, among the more tradition-minded, it is frowned upon. I cannot forget my first husband, Chinese-American, saying when our daughter was still a little girl, that if she were to marry a Caucasian he would disown her. That from a man who had been born in the U.S. and had lived much of his adult life here. I am happy to say that with the passage of the years his views on this subject changed, and I'm quite sure he would have forgotten that he ever uttered those words. In fact, he probably would have claimed never to have said them.

It always pleased my mother immensely when acquaintances who thought I was her daughter by birth remarked on my resemblance to her. Despite having no blood connection, I probably had acquired expressions and mannerisms that accounted for the resemblance. But back then, the stigma carried by children of mixed blood was so strong that whenever the possibility arose that someone might think I was half Caucasian, I always immediately denied it and clarified further by stating that I was "all Chinese." I remember one instance of which I am particularly ashamed to this day. I had already graduated from college and was working in Washington as social secretary to the wife of the Chinese ambassador. On one of my mother's visits to Washington, Madame Koo had been nice enough to invite us for lunch at the Embassy. During lunch she remarked on my resemblance to my mother. She was complimentary. "I can see where your daughter gets her good looks," she said. But before my mother had a chance to acknowledge the compliment I had already jumped in with a denial. "Oh, but she's not my *real* mother!"

I will never forget the look of hurt on Mother's face. It was as if I had slapped her. She then had to explain that I was an adopted child. I know now, and I must have known even then, how hurtful it was to her when I denied her as my true mother, but I was mindful then only of my own immediate social status.

When my father brought his American bride back to China, *his* mother was no longer living. Thus my mother was spared the oversight of what might have been a dominating and controlling Chinese mother-in-law. My father had told her of the subservience that was normally required of a new Chinese bride to her mother-in-law; among other things, that a Chinese bride was expected to kow-tow to her new parents.

Mother insisted that she would do the same. She was determined to fit into the family and to perform all the duties of a Chinese daughter-in-law. But when she was brought in to be introduced to my grandfather and knelt to begin this humbling act of obeisance, he stepped forward immediately and raised her to her feet. In English he told her that he did not wish her to kow-tow to him, but in Chinese he reprimanded my father, "You should have told her that I did not expect her to kow-tow."

"I did tell her," my father said. "I told her that a foreigner would not be expected to kow-tow, but she insisted that she wanted to show her respect for you."

"She will be a good daughter-in-law," my grandfather concluded. "But it is not because she is a foreigner that she should not kow-tow. It is because she is a Christian." Though not a Christian himself, he had a genuine respect for the beliefs of others.

My mother was touched by her father-in-law's understanding, and he in turn was appreciative of her readiness to embrace the customs of her new family. They became friends. He not only showed no signs of disapproval of his son's taking a foreign wife, but accepted her willingly. She got on well with him from the start and often said that during the years that he was alive her life within the Chinese family was a happy one. Still, I cannot imagine that she did not have many moments of longing for the familiar things of home and other moments of regret for having adopted this strange new world.

My parents lived in the family compound and had their meals with the family. They did, however, have their own private courtyard, which gave them some degree of privacy. Another courtyard was occupied by my father's older brother, the second son in the family. The oldest son had died shortly before my parents' marriage. According to my mother, her sister-in-law made no effort to welcome her into the family or to ease her way into the Chinese culture. It did not help that my grandfather often favored my mother with generous gifts. When he

Left to right: **Mother (with Richard in her lap), Second Aunt, my father, Second Uncle, and Grandfather**

bought her a sewing machine without giving a comparable gift to his other daughter-in-law, the jealousy displayed by the other woman was blatantly apparent. Their relationship was less than perfect.

I don't know how long my parents lived in the family compound or when they built the North City house for themselves but suspect it must have been shortly after the death of my grandfather. I know that in 1918 he had a massive stroke and was paralyzed from the waist down. I am guessing that he died a few years after that.

In 1923, my father was appointed chief of the Central Salt Gabelle, responsible for the administration and collection of salt revenues for the entire country. In ensuing years he also served intermittently as Vice Minister of Finance. How my mother, an unsophisticated woman from a lower middle class American family, coped with her new status is hard for me to imagine. Mother had worked hard at becoming a part of her new Chinese family and her first priority had been to learn the language. Though she received no formal tutoring, she never stopped asking, "how do you say this?" or "how do you say that?" And she asked these questions of my father, of her new Chinese friends, of her servants, and of anyone else with whom she came in contact. It was not long before she had learned enough "kitchen Chinese" to instruct the servants, to converse with shopkeepers and sales people, but with Chinese officialdom? Was she exhilarated by the challenge? Or was she overwhelmed by feelings of insecurity? Was it stress that accounted for her migraine headaches? Were social conversations in her presence conducted in English? Or did she sit mutely by while Chinese was spoken across her and around her? If so, she strained to grasp at meanings, and sometimes she understood more than was intended.

On one occasion she was quite sure that she heard one of their dinner guests compliment my father on his wife's beauty. Her pleasure, however, was only short-lived when she understood my father to reply that she was only *kuo teh ch'u* (passable). Later in the evening, when she asked my father if she had heard correctly, he was surprised that she had understood the conversation but also somewhat chagrined.

Mother couldn't help feeling slighted, and her words were a reproach, "It would have been nicer if you had just agreed with your guest, and certainly more complimentary to me. But I suppose I should be pleased that you consider me at least passable."

My father tried to explain. "Helen, you mustn't be offended. Of course I agree with our guest completely, but no matter how beautiful *I* think you are, it would appear immodest of me to say so. You have to understand; it's not the Chinese way."

"You mean to say that if someone should tell me my children are good looking or smart, I should say they are not, or that they are just passable?"

"Well you certainly shouldn't agree. You don't have to say they are *not* good looking, but you shouldn't agree and say that they *are*. *That* would sound immodest, as if you were boasting. You can simply avoid accepting the compliment by saying they could do better in school by applying themselves more, or that they are not as smart as *their* children. There are any number of things you can say." He went on to say, "Helen, it's hard to explain. But don't you see that if someone told you that you were beautiful and you just accepted their words, it would be as if you had said 'Yes, I am beautiful.' Surely you can see that."

Mother didn't really see, and felt that it was all carrying the semblance of modesty to a ridiculous extreme. Still, she learned to accept these small cultural idiosyncrasies and on occasion to adopt them herself. As for me, even after being in America for years, I consistently went the Chinese way. In the years that my husband and I were stationed abroad in an official position we led a very active social life. In Taiwan, many Chinese were already switching to western dress, but I habitually wore *ch'i p'ao*, the slim Chinese sheaths, which were both becoming and economical. A yard and a quarter of fabric was enough for the simple sheath, and tailoring was cheap. I usually bought fabric for six dresses at a time and had them made up all at once. I had many truly beautiful dresses—in Chinese brocades, in Indian sari fabric shot with gold or silver, in Italian silks, and in fine British cottons and wools—and received many compliments on my clothes. One American friend in particular always admired my dresses. I never thought of how I was responding, but one day when I was wearing something she found particularly attractive, she said to me, "I just love that old rag you're wearing," and followed that immediately with, "Do you know why I said that?" Without waiting for me to reply, she explained. "It's because every time I admire a dress of yours you always say, 'Oh, I've had this for years,' or 'I'm afraid the fabric is really poor,' or 'The colors have faded badly.' Can't you just accept a compliment the way it was intended and just say thank you?"

She had made her point. These days I acknowledge with gratitude every nice word that comes my way. And I do say "thank you."

I was always grateful that my mother didn't try to "go Chinese" in her dress. Mother did wear Chinese clothing on occasion when she first arrived in China, but it was a time when short loose tops were worn over long skirts and the *ch'i pao* was also straight-cut and loose. Both styles were comfortable and becoming. Once the *ch'i p'ao* had metamorphosed into a form-fitting sheath, she wore only western clothing, which was much better suited to her full-bosomed figure.

When I was living in Hongkong, in the mid-fifties--my husband had been assigned to the American Consulate General there as a political officer--it seemed to me that almost every newly arrived American woman would immediately hie herself to a Chinese tailor to be fitted for a *cheong sam* (Cantonese words for *ch'i p'ao*). Chinese tailors had not mastered the art of cutting for the fuller-bosomed western figure. The only way they could get a dress to fit was to take a tuck here, a tuck there, and yet another tuck. The dress got tighter and tighter. The results could be unfortunate. Thus, many a western woman ran the risk of having every bulge, every line of panty or bra, made blatantly visible in her Chinese sheath. My husband would often raise his eyebrows at the sight of yet another Caucasian woman appearing in a Chinese dress. "Looks like a Cantonese sausage," he would remark. (Cantonese sausages, unlike hotdogs with their smooth surfaces, were full of lumps and bumps where fat and lean were stuffed into the sausage casing in large chunks.)

In Hong Kong, a British social acquaintance described quite aptly the reason the Chinese sheath was not suited to western women. I quite liked Paula Carter, a down-to-earth person who always said what she thought and hang the consequences. She was considered "common" by many of our other British friends, but common or not, her observation and reasoning were quite sound in this case. "It's not because of our boobs. It's because of our bums," she maintained. "*Our* bums are on the same plane as our stomachs, so we have a double bulge at the same level, both front and rear, whereas Chinese bums are lower down. This makes *their* stomachs look flatter--which they usually are anyway--and their rears too." Ever since she made that statement, I have noted without fail how right she was, and have noted other "bums" as well. *Chinese bums are low; African bums are high; Caucasian bums are usually in between.*

But back to my mother: Having been born English, become a naturalized American citizen, and married a Chinese, Mother took part in activities sponsored by all three nationalities. She was a natural club-woman and enjoyed her participation in various international women's groups. She was most heavily involved in the Eastern Star--of which she later became a Worthy Grand Matron--and the British Women's League, which did a great deal of charitable work in the city. During her years in China she was distressed by the poverty she saw all around her, and when a group of Chinese returned students started an orphanage, she enthusiastically joined in supporting and working in it. For twenty-five years she was also on the executive boards of two old ladies' homes, one run by the British and Americans, and the other by the Chinese. In addition, she was constantly caring for the sick children and elderly parents of our servants. My sister Eva, the one who arranged my adoption, recalls that during her visits to our home, my mother would rush out to a servant's home regardless of the hour if a child or aged parent was seriously ill. If she could not help herself with some simple home remedy, she would see to it that the patient was taken to a doctor.

I recall most vividly the weekly clinics she ran at our country home in the Western Hills during the summer months. It had not been her intention to start a clinic. She was down at the foot of our property watching the coolies who were unloading bricks for the well that was being dug. I was just a child at the time and was the one who noticed the nasty sore on the arm of one of the coolies. I pulled on Mother's arm and called her attention to the man's open wound. I couldn't help screwing up my face and showing my revulsion, "Mother, Mother, look at that man's arm. It looks awful."

She moved closer to get a better look and evidently agreed with me, for without a second thought she beckoned him to follow her up to the house. Poor man. Not knowing why he was being summoned, he was somewhat intimidated at being singled out by *Ch'ien T'ai T'ai*, the mistress of the house, but he relaxed when Mother pointed to his arm. He then realized he wasn't being reproved for some misdeed. Mother had the cook bring her a basin of hot water and sent me running to the bathroom for the Lysol and some bandages. She sat him down on the low stone wall behind the kitchen, gently swabbed the open sore clean of putrid matter, applied some antiseptic ointment, and bandaged his arm. A few days later, wound on the mend, he was back at the house with two friends, one with a boil on his leg, the other with a nasty cut on his head. She treated them both. Within days the word had spread and *Ch'ien T'ai Tai*'s clinics began.

Though she had no medical training whatsoever, in the Chinese countryside where there was no medical care at all, her ministrations were like a gifts from the heavens. To the poor peasants who lined up outside our gates to seek her help, her treatments must have seemed like miracles. On clinic days some twenty to forty people would stand in line waiting to see *Ch'ien T'ai T'ai*. Sometimes she wasn't able to see them all and they would return to stand in line another day. But she worked until she was exhausted or until darkness fell rather than turn anyone away.

Most of the problems were matters of simple hygiene that could be taken care of with Lysol, iodine, hot water, and soap. Boils were most common, often festering and threatened with infection. She would lance them, clean and wrap them, and give instructions on keeping the wound clean until the skin had healed. In children, worms were commonplace. Small tots with enormous bloated stomachs clung to their mothers' legs as Mother dispensed mild doses of worm medicine.

Sometimes the problems were more serious. I remember watching Mother treating a severe dog bite. The bite was so deep I could see the leg bone. Again, hot water and disinfectant. Somehow she cleaned the wound. It healed. The gratitude of the peasants for these simple cures was shown by the steady supply of vegetables, eggs, and live chickens they brought to the house. They had no money, but these were the payment they could provide. Mother accepted them all with thanks. Why? We certainly had no need of their offerings. I'm sure we ate the eggs and the chickens, but the vegetables? We had our own well-tended vegetable gardens that supplied us with more than enough to feed our family and our servants, but Mother said that to have rejected them would have made the givers feel their gifts were unworthy. She was always considerate of the feelings of others and conformed always to her own standards for being a lady.

Throughout my childhood and teenage years the one thing my mother impressed on me more than any other were these criteria. *A lady is one who at all times and in all places is mindful of the feelings of others.* Hardly a week went by that she did not make this statement to me at least once if not more. She had an almost compulsive obsession with making me into a lady. If I was overbearing with a servant, it was "A lady would not behave that way." If I was short with a salesperson, it was "A lady would have shown more patience." If I did not acknowledge a favor or a gift adequately, it was "A lady would have shown more appreciation." If I gave an order in an overly peremptory way, it was "A lady would have been more gracious." It was always, "a lady this" or "a lady that." Somewhere along the line she must have gotten the message across, for whether or not I became a lady on the inside, I have managed to give the impression of being one on the outside. And I know which fork to use, and in which direction to tip my soup bowl.

Through the years it has often irked me that the one word used most commonly to describe me is "a lady." Prim? Proper? Refined? Reserved? Correct? Those are the adjectives I attribute to the word "lady." How much I would have preferred being thought of as something less restrictive and more down to earth. In my adult life, when I was working at the CIA, I was often called upon to participate in experimental programs. Being bicultural (Chinese *and* American), I was in essence a two-dimensional guinea pig. In fact, I was a three-dimensional guinea pig because I was also female at a time when there were still relatively few women officers actively involved in clandestine operations. At an office-sponsored sensitivity session, one of those things sometimes referred to as "touchy feely sessions," I was housed with seven other participants for a full week of total togetherness. All our waking hours were spent together. One of the early exercises required us to identify our own "façade" as well as the façades of the other participants. *What was a façade? I didn't think I had one. What I appeared to be was what I was, or so I thought.* Each of us was to describe the others in a few short words. In their evaluations of me, one said I was "a perfect lady." Another said, "a real lady." A third described me as " very ladylike." And the one that topped them all, "I can imagine her presiding at the White House." If I had been in high heels and the Chinese sheaths that I habitually wore at the office I could have understood somewhat that impression--*Chinese dresses did have a formal appearance--* but here at this training locale I was wearing blue jeans and sweatshirt. I couldn't have looked more sloppy. These people had never seen me otherwise. There was no question as to the façade I projected. I could not get away from the "lady" image. It bothered me. *Had my behavior been aloof? Had I seemed unapproachable?*

In another instance, a memo originating from another office described me as "a lady of quality." The words had been included in a proposal for a very special assignment and the writer had obviously intended it as a strong recommendation, but far from appreciating his words, I was only discouraged at other people's perception of me. Among my own office mates the memo provoked much amusement at my expense, and I had a hard time living it down. In the next few days I was often greeted with, "How's our lady of quality today?" or "Is our lady of quality free to look at this draft?" How I would have preferred to be seen as something else, to come down from that artificial "lady" pedestal and to join the rest of the world. *Oh, Mother, Mother, what have you made of me! You've taught me well to look like something I have no wish to be.*

But apart from her instructions on ladylike behavior, her other teachings often came in the form of well-worn cliches. When I behaved badly, it was "Pretty is as pretty does." When we spent too much time with children she disapproved of, it was "Birds of a feather flock together." When a task was poorly done, it was "Do it right or not at all." Whenever we were unkind in some way, it was "Do unto others as you would have others do unto you." If we made a nasty comment about someone, it was "If you can't say something nice, don't say anything at all."

All these phrases stuck with me throughout my lifetime. I still remember how conscience-stricken I was the first time I made a gratuitous comment that a particular woman was a troublemaker. I was so disturbed at having said something "not nice" that I lay awake for hours that night examining my behavior. In the years since then, without a qualm I have lapsed into speaking ill of whomever I please, whenever I please. My mother is no longer here to censor my behavior or my speech.

As I look back on the things my mother taught me, I am not surprised that she never told me any of the "facts of life." Even now I cannot imagine her talking to me about sex, and I certainly cannot imagine broaching the subject myself. She did, however, tell me about menstruation. I remember vaguely something about a woman's "womb" and about bleeding every month if an egg wasn't fertilized. No mention at all of how that fertilization took place. It really didn't matter, whatever it was that she said. I had learned about "the curse" long ago from older friends and was eagerly awaiting the day when I would share their experience. *It never occurred to me what a nuisance it would be.* At the time, though, it was as if Mother were divulging some great secret of life, a great secret that *her* mother had never told her. It seems that she had been told nothing about what to expect until it actually happened. "I was in the backyard chopping wood when I first felt the wetness in my underpants," she explained. "When I went into the bathroom and saw that I had been bleeding, I just thought I had overstrained myself. I changed my pants and went back to chopping wood. When I felt myself wet again, I put on another pair of clean pants. Finally, I had gone through all my own underpants and also Aunt Margaret's and Aunt Irene's— Aunt Mildred's were too small or I would have gone through them too-- before Grandma came home and told me that it was something that it was a part of a girl's growing up and that from then on it would happen every month. She never told me any more than that."

My mother was the one responsible for giving us children an early start in our religious upbringing. She attended Sunday morning services once or twice a month at the Anglican Church located inside the British Embassy compound, but the whole family went regularly to Sunday evening services at The Union Church. I couldn't have been more than two or three when my parents were taking me to church services there. It was an interdenominational church attended by most of the English-speaking Protestant community of the city. Dressed in my Sunday best, hardly able to see above the pews before me, I would sit beside the rest of the family. Mother always gave me a pencil and a program and I would while away the hour of the service drawing pictures on the program or doodling over and around the printed words. I was also allowed to search out the correct hymn in the hymnals well in advance of actual singing time. Sometimes, depending on where we happened to be sitting, I would spend some time keeping an eye on Mr. Hoose to see at what point he would fall asleep. Mr. Hoose was the head of the American Bible Society and a well-respected citizen of the community, but he habitually fell asleep during the church service. Sometimes, even on his arrival, he would appear to be walking in something of a daze as Mrs. Hoose gently guided him to his seat. However, even when awake at the beginning of the service, he would invariably be asleep by the end. I had no idea at the time that Mr. Hoose had sleeping sickness; I had never heard of the disease called narcolepsy. I thought he fell asleep out of boredom. I was always quite bored with the sermon, so it did not surprise me that Mr. Hoose shared my opinion.

As soon as I was old enough, in addition to attending evening church services, I was enrolled in morning Sunday School. At both church and Sunday school I loved the music. I knew the words and music to the Doxology when I was no more than three years old. Children's hymns like "All Things Bright and Beautiful" and "Jesus Wants Me for a Sunbeam" remain with me today. As I grew older I participated in all the church activities: sang in the choir, took part in pageants, joined youth discussion groups, and helped at all church functions. It was therefore a surprise and disappointment to my parents when I refused to join the church. This came as a complete surprise to my father, who had become a Christian not so much because of his beliefs, but simply because my mother wanted it so. It surprised him that I was not willing to do the same, for no other reason than to please my mother.

As a child I had wanted very much to be a sunbeam for Jesus. I had believed with all my heart that God had created "each pretty flower and each bird that sings." But as time went by, the doubts began to creep in. I could not reconcile *that* God, the one who had created us all and who loved us all, with the God who was by his own admission jealous and vengeful. I could understand that there must *be* a God. I could understand that Jesus *might* be his son. But the Holy Ghost? I could not grasp that concept at all. I had no doubts that the Holy Ghost was a good spirit, but he, or it, was almost as nebulous as the ever-present evil spirits of China. No, I had sung the hymns joyfully, studied the Bible dutifully, said the prayers, and mouthed the Apostles' Creed, all with steadily increasing doubts about what I believed and what I did not. *I believe in God the Father, Maker of Heaven and Earth*--------------. I moved my lips but could not bring myself to speak the words. I told my mother that I was not ready to join the church. I could feel her disappointment, but she never pressed me.

One of the biggest regrets in my life is that in my mother's last years I so seldom accompanied her to church. During those years I was abroad most of the time with my husband and children. We came home on leave only once every two years and stayed only two months. It would have meant so much to her if I had gone with her to church on those Sundays I was home. It was so little to ask. If she had asked, I would have gone, but I was always relieved that she didn't. She hoped I would *want* to go with her, but she showed no signs of reproach. Two months of Sundays, eight hours over two years, when she could have at her side the daughter she had spoken of so often to her friends. But I went once or twice at most. I was much too busy with the trivialities of my own life to be concerned with my mother's disappointments.

When I was a small child I had looked to her always for love and protection. But as I moved into my teenage years, I no longer clung to her as a means of support; I had less need of her. I no longer needed her help with homework, with the choice of clothing, or with such problems that I had; and I had few. I had become so self-sufficient that she could no longer mother me. And as my need of her diminished, she tended to defer more and more to *my* wishes, to *my* whims, allowing me to dictate the direction of my life. She never pressed me to continue with things that I had simply tired of: scouting, in which I never progressed beyond Second Class; piano, at which I was too lazy to practice; voice lessons because they were no fun. Throughout my school years I was a good student and she brimmed with pride when I consistently brought home straight-A report cards. She was the proud mother who expected the best from me, and I the daughter who could do no less than meet those expectations. I thrived on her approval, and she, doting mother that she was, reveled in my successes and set aside my deficiencies. She excused my every fault, overlooked my thoughtlessness, my selfishness and my preoccupation with self. She built my self-esteem at the expense of other failings.

Mother died in 1964 at eighty-five. She was the dominant force in my life. For much of my life she was my only parent. Today I have few material possessions to remind me of my mother: an antique wormwood cabinet, a few small pieces of ivory, a small red lacquer box, and a beautiful set of Chinese dishes, her wedding present to me, all gifts to me during her lifetime. But I need no material things to remind me of my mother. I am myself a daily reminder of all that she gave to me. In giving in to me too much, in ignoring my faults too often, she would not have been judged a *perfect* mother, but there is no other mother I would have chosen. She loved me unconditionally. By her example she showed me what kindness is, what courage is, and what responsibility is. Most of all, she showed me that life, whatever it brings our way, is what we make it. Along the way I learned some, but not all, that she taught me. Today I know that everything that is good in me was a gift from her. Everything that is bad, I acquired on my own.

When she died she had few physical possessions to leave. Having lived so much of her life in luxury, it was sad that at the end, totally dependent on her children, she lived in the basement apartment of Luther's house in New Jersey. The windows of her living room were above ground, but barely. They looked onto the concrete driveway of his carport. What view she might have had was blocked by Luther's car, by parked bicycles, by the lawn mower, by garden refuse and garbage cans, a world removed from wisteria in full bloom seen through Chinese moongates. But through it all she made a new life for herself. She never complained about her reduced circumstances. I never heard her, like Eva, bemoan the loss of her glory years. She did not dwell on or live in the past. Her life was in the present and she made the most of it. And she had friends. Wherever she was, she always had friends.

Chapter 7
Father

MY FATHER WAS so very, very Chinese. Sometimes I find it hard to believe that he had ever studied in America and been married to an American woman. His English, both written and spoken, was excellent. He had the faintest trace of an accent, but his grammar was beyond reproach and he never made the mistakes in usage that are so common in those who learn English in adulthood. Other than acquiring the language, however, he made few concessions to the West. He did become a Christian, or at least paid lip service to Christianity--to please my mother. He even became an active Mason. But in every other way he remained totally Chinese and never gave up his Chinese ways.

During the years we were in China I never saw him in western clothing. He always wore a Chinese silk gown, white in the summer, or dark in the winter, dark blue or gray with a *ma kwa* vest of darker color. In winter he wore the traditional Chinese skullcap, six-gored black satin, topped with a black Chinese knot. His feet were always shod in soft-soled Chinese shoes, cloth, not leather. In his library he wore loose-fitting long pants wrapped with a band at the waist and a short mandarin-style top buttoned down the center with silk frogs. They were the undergarments worn under his long robes, but in the privacy of his personal library he often went without the outer gown. When he finally moved to the United States for good in 1957, he still enjoyed wearing his Chinese clothes and his soft Chinese shoes, but the children in the small New Jersey town where he lived with my brother laughed at him and revived the old refrain, "Chink chink Chinaman." In resignation he finally switched to western-style sport shirts and loafers.

During the China years, it upset my mother that my father refused to bathe at home. Though their bathroom was large and luxurious and its windows looked onto the lovely ivy-covered inner courtyard, he preferred to go to a Chinese bathhouse. The bathhouses in Peking could always be recognized by their tiled walls. To this day, whenever I see a building with a tiled front, I think of a Chinese bathhouse. Though I have never been inside one--they were for males only--I can understand why my father preferred them to bathing at home. There, he was thoroughly scrubbed by a bath attendant and could enjoy a bowl of steaming hot noodles or a dish of spicy dumplings while luxuriating in his bath. He went religiously once a week and always came home invigorated and in good spirits.

My father was a true gourmet and was known to be quite a connoisseur of Chinese cuisine. One of his favorite dishes was eel, cooked in a variety of ways. The best of these was *sheng ch'ao shan yu sse*, shredded eel sauteed at high heat in large amounts of oil, spiced heavily with white pepper, and topped with generous amounts of fresh coriander. Two others, which I have never had except when out with him at his favorite Peking restaurant, were octopus eggs and ducks' testicles. Each was gently cooked in its own delectable sauce, and both were laced with a touch of vinegar. Each of these esoteric dishes, however, he had the good sense never to force upon his foreign friends. In fact, being more sensitive to foreigners' tastes than some Chinese, he never even ordered for foreign visitors some of the dishes commonly included at standard Chinese banquets such as sharks' fins or bird's nest soup. When I was living in Hong Kong in the fifties I recall with some amusement attending a dinner where the host, a Chinese businessman intent on impressing an important visitor, had ordered up an extravagant meal. When the bird's nest soup appeared, the guest looked dubious, whereupon our host began to explain that the nests were not made of twigs or straw or other unappealing and possibly unsanitary refuse, but were really made from the secretions of birds. Our host went on to describe the entire process in great detail. "You see, the birds spit out their saliva which then hardens into gelatinous threads, so the nests are really made from the birds' saliva." I could see an ill-disguised grimace on the face of the guest. He took a single token sip of his soup, but no more. By that time even I was beginning to find the soup less appealing.

My father loved his Chinese food, and he liked to eat it in the Chinese way. On one occasion at Luther's home in New Jersey, he disappeared from the table for the entire duration of a meal. We were eating Chinese soup-noodles when he had quietly left the room. We all assumed he had gone to use the bathroom, but when he returned he had his chopsticks and empty bowl in hand. When Mother asked what had happened to him, he explained, "I took my noodles to the basement because I can only really enjoy them when I can slurp them Chinese style. You know you would have frowned on that."

How right he was. Western manners did not approve of slurping at the table. But I could understand his feelings. Every Asian will agree that noodles from a bowl taste better when slurped. As I write, I am reminded of my niece's experience at the home of the Japanese Consul-General in Hong Kong. Noodles were served, and Patsy was eating them in the genteel fashion of the western world, quietly, when the Consul-General leaned toward her, and with a considerable show of solicitude, whispered, "Please, please, make noise!" Solid evidence that even in this modern multi-cultural world, there are some instances where East remains East and West West.

My father was the kind of man who was impossible not to like. Everyone with whom he came in contact took to him immediately. He was relaxed, jovial, comfortable with himself, and comfortable with others. He had a marvelously wry sense of humor that would creep out at the most unexpected times. From Kao Kao, a sister from my birth family, whose existence I was unaware of until I was over thirty, I learned that during the war years, when he was living in Chungking, he was a popular figure not only with his many men friends, but also with a bevy of younger women. When the Sino-Japanese war began he had still been a government official and had moved to the "interior," to free-China, with the government, but at the time, he was no longer in the official world and was instead managing a small bank. Nonetheless, despite his less impressive status, the small house that he occupied was constantly full of visitors. Many of these were the young women whom in his letters to us in Peking he spoke of as his goddaughters. My mother would occasionally refer to these "goddaughters" as if there were something questionable about their relationship with my father. However, when I questioned Kao Kao in later years about these relationships, she actually laughed at my doubts. "No, your father was just such a wonderful, likable person. We all enjoyed his jovial personality. All these young women, including me, used to go over to his house and spend whole afternoons. Your father loved to eat so we'd go in the kitchen and cook special dishes for him. We competed for his approval, and he would pass judgment on our efforts and give us suggestions on how this or that could be improved."

I don't believe my father had ever cooked a thing himself--I cannot imagine him soiling his hands with the menial tasks of chopping a cabbage, slicing meat, or stirring a pot of soup--but he prided himself on his knowledge of cooking, believing that eating and cooking went hand in hand. He often said in Chinese "to cook well, one must know how to eat well." He was one who knew how to eat well. To this day I recall his instructions on making "*shih tze t'o*," the North China dish known as "lion's head." The meatballs of pork are first browned and then simmered for hours in a "sandpot" casserole together with nappa cabbage. He always said "*ch'ieh hsi, chan sung,*" (cut finely, but chop loosely) to ensure that the meat remained tender. Today I take the lazy route and use ground pork from the supermarket and know that my father would say that grinding has made the meat stringy.

Even in later years in America, he expected excellence, both in flavor and in presentation, in the Chinese food served to him. Mother occasionally made a Chinese dish for him, but though he did not complain directly to her, he found her dishes lacked *kuo wei erh* (flavor of the pot). *"She adds soy sauce and thinks she has produced a Chinese dish."* During our visits to New Jersey on home leave from abroad I too would cook Chinese dishes for him. I had taken numerous cooking lessons while living in Taipei, considered myself quite good, and thought I would surprise him with my expertise. *Foolish girl, to think I was good enough to please my father's demanding palate!* I will never forget how upset I was when he was critical of my *cha chiang mien*. *Cha chiang mien* is what these days I call Chinese spaghetti. It is made of ground pork instead of beef, and the sauce made of sweet bean paste rather than tomato sauce. In our Peking days it was always served with four top-pings: shredded cucumber, shredded radishes, bean sprouts, and shredded egg. On this occasion, when I served it to my father I had decided to omit the egg—too much extra work--which I hoped my father would overlook, but I was not to be so lucky. My father looked at the three small dishes of cucumber, radishes, and bean sprouts with approval and then reminded me, "You've forgotten the shredded egg." I then had to beat the egg, heat the wok, pour in several batches of the beaten egg to form thin crepes, and then shred it finely on a chopping board. More work and more dishes to wash, and no servants to do the job, but I should have known that my father was not one to settle for mediocrity.

My father was the third son in a moneyed family from the Ch'ang Chow area of Kiang Su province, ninety miles northwest of Shanghai. Throughout my childhood years, when he held an official position, he always went by the name Ch'ien Fang Shih and among Eng-lish speakers was known as F. S. Ch'ien. My mother always called him Chauncey, the English name she had given him. All the males of his generation carried the same generational character of "Fang." His broth-ers' names were Fang Ming, Fang Tu, and Fang Ting. I never knew my oldest uncle, Fang Ming, who had died before I was born. The genera-tional character for the next generation of Ch'ien males, my generation, was "Chao." Richard's name was Chao Sun; Luther's was Chao Lin; and our cousins' names were Chao Yuan, Chao Chun, and so on.

I never knew how these generational characters were chosen un-til my Cantonese father-in-law explained it to me. According to him, originally the generational character was from a Chinese eight-character couplet selected by a family elder. Each character within the couplet became in turn the generational character for the family. Thus a single couplet would provide the generational character for eight successive generations. My father-in-law knew his family couplet and took my chil-dren's generational character from it. My grandchildren should use the next character in the couplet, but unfortunately none of my generation know it. These days many Chinese seem to arbitrarily choose a genera-tional character for no other reason than that its meaning appeals to them. The old tradition has been lost. In our family's case it is possible, and probable, that the couplet from which the character is chosen was recorded in the Ch'ien family records. These were housed in our family temple in Hangchow, but unfortunately were destroyed during the Cultural Revolution. My cousin Helen in Shanghai believes the temple itself

Left to right: **Second Uncle, Fifth Uncle (husband of my father's fifth sister), and my father, holding fan.**

itself is now a historic site, but I am unable to confirm this. None of us who remain know either the temple's name or its exact location.

My biological father, Fang Ting (throughout this memoir referred to as Fourth Uncle), was the fourth son in the family. I was unaware until well into my adult years that he, like me, had been adopted as an infant *out* of my grandfather's immediate family in the traditional *kuo chi* adoption arrangement. A cousin of my grandfather had died without any offspring. His widow desperately wanted, and needed, a male heir to carry on *her* husband's family line. She selected my biological father from the many children of that generation on the basis of a fortune teller's readings of his *pa tze*, his "eight characters," and hers. This system was based on the year, month, day, and hour of birth, much like the reading of a horoscope. The two readings combined to make an auspicious match and the *kuo chi* adoption was arranged. My grandfather's cousin, though deceased, now had a son to carry on *his* line of the larger Ch'ien family. Thus it was that my biological father, Ch'ien Fang Ting, the fourth of my grandfather's sons had been adopted *out of* my grandfather's line, and I had been adopted back *into* it.

At this point I expect the reader to be somewhat confused. Even my first husband (Chinese, with degrees from both Chinese and American law schools) never had the patience to sort out the who's who of my family members. He simply shook his head when I tried to explain. I should say that I debated long and hard before deciding to include the above explanations in this memoir, but decided in the end, that the details, however complex, provide some insights into the traditional Chinese system of adoption and the importance the Chinese place on the maintenance of a family's lineage and bloodline. (See Chart of Ch'ien Family Relationships on Page 298.)

All this transferring of children from one branch of the family to another was assuredly recorded in the Ch'ien family records but is now irretrievable. My oldest cousin, now deceased, was the only one who was able to give me any information about earlier generations in our family. According to him, our great grandfather was a lowly apprentice in a pawn shop. The family wealth, acquired in our grandfather's generation, was from the ownership of textile mills. Presumably this giant leap was made in my grandfather's generation. All remaining relatives agree that our grandfather raised his status by passing the arduous Ch'ing Dynasty imperial examinations at the highest level. As a result he was awarded a high-ranking official position in China's northeast. According to my cousin, he was the first chancellor of Pei Yang University in Tientsin, later to become Nankai University. Still later he was appointed Ambassador-designate, responsible for establishing the borders between Russia and China.

I never met my paternal grandfather but thought of him as a person to be admired. All I know of him was learned through my mother and not my father. According to her, he was kind, considerate, and forward thinking. Though not a Christian himself, he was sympathetic to Christian causes. His picture hung at the head of the stairs in Peking's Salvation Army headquarters because it was he who had donated the funds to start the Salvation Army's first soup kitchens in Peking.

For years I gave my grandfather credit for what I regarded as an almost visionary experiment in the education of his four sons. I had been told by my mother that he had sent each of his sons to a different country for their advanced education: the oldest to England, the second to Germany, the third (my father) to the United States, and the fourth (my biological father) to France. I thought this showed foresight and an early awareness of our shrinking world. It was therefore something of a disappointment to find out in my middle age that the fourth son had in reality been sent not to France, but also to the United States where he studied at the University of Maine. Perhaps France had been an unrealized intention.

That my fourth uncle had studied in the U.S. was a total surprise to me as I had never known he even spoke English. During the eighteen months I was in Shanghai during the war, though I had Sunday lunch or dinner with my natural/birth family frequently, not a word of English had ever been spoken. Not only had Fourth Uncle studied in the U.S., it seems he had fallen wildly in love with an American girl whose photograph and lock of hair he kept for years.

Though my father was the most successful of the four Ch'ien brothers, he was not the brightest. That honor went to his second brother, my Second Uncle. My father, by his own admission, had been something of a playboy during his college days and had not spent much time on his books. In those years many Chinese students who went to America were financed by Boxer Indemnity funds. These scholarships had been set up by America with the money received from the Ch'ing Dynasty government in reparation for damages inflicted during the Boxer uprising. My father failed to pass the first round of exams to qualify for these government-administered funds and consequently, the cost of the first year of his Harvard education had to be borne by his own family. Thus it was obvious that he came from a wealthy family and he was soon labeled a *kung tze ko erh*, loosely translated as "a young princeling," with added connotations of big-spending playboy. Later, he did pass the second round of exams, but by then the label had stuck. However, from then on his studies at Harvard, room, board, and tuition, were covered by Boxer Indemnity funding.

Both he and Second Uncle returned to China in 1912, the year after China became a Republic. Second Uncle returned from Germany with an advanced degree in chemistry, and my father from the U.S. with a business degree from Harvard. My father's first job was with the Bank of China. In those days, students who had been educated abroad, and particularly those returning from the U. S., enjoyed a special status as "returned students" and were much in demand. It was not long before he was appointed manager of the Hankow branch. In the early years of the Republic, when the new president was making attempts to set up a central government, China's shortage of funds forced it to take out foreign loans. The collateral for these loans was to be the proceeds from China's salt revenue. A central salt administration was set up under the aegis of the lending countries. This came to be known as the Salt Gabelle, or colloquially as "the Salt." At its head was a senior British official. Under him were three departments: Chinese, British, and Accounting. My father was appointed to head up the Chinese Department. When in 1923 the British gave up their supervision of the Salt, my father became chief of the Central Salt Gabelle, responsible for the administration and collection of salt revenues from the entire country. While in this position he was called upon twice to serve as Vice Minister of Finance, once under H. H. Kung, and once under T.V. Soong. He also served for brief periods as Acting Minister of Finance. Unfortunately, he did not get on well with T.V. Soong, and his tenure in the Finance Ministry was short. However, he had some fifteen years of plenty when he held the position of Chief of the Salt. During those years he enjoyed the prestige the Salt gave him and the affluence that went with it. When those years ended, he remained with the government for many years, but never again held a job of great consequence. At the time the government moved to Nanking he was head of the Opium Suppression Commission, a job without the exalted standing of the Salt Gabelle.

Several of my father's family must have lived in Peking during at least some of my childhood years. I have vague memories of cousins, the children of my father's oldest and second sisters. There are also photographs that include Amy, daughter of my father's fifth sister. However, I believe that other than my father's oldest sister and her family, the others moved to Shanghai very early in my childhood. Consequently, I did not really get to know most of my father's side of the family until I went to Shanghai to study many years later. Up until then, the only aunt I remember knowing was *Ta Ku Ku*, my father's oldest sister. She is clear in my memory, a cheerful woman with kinky hair and thick glasses who was always good to small children. However, my only memory of my uncle, her husband, was not of him while alive, but of his death. I was a small child when he died.

I don't remember attending my uncle's funeral but do recall going to the house with my father and Luther to pay our respects immediately after his death. Where my mother, Richard, and Lois were, I don't know. At the front gate was a man kneeling on a mat and at the same time beating a drum to announce our arrival. As we stepped through the front gate into the courtyard, I was surprised to see it had been totally transformed into what appeared to be a closed room. A scaffold had been erected to support a temporary ceiling made of straw matting so that the entire front courtyard was enclosed. It seemed that the court was enveloped in silk, all dark-colored, gifts from friends and relatives. The lengths of silk hung from the scaffolding, each length with large Chinese characters of paper pinned to its surface. The open coffin sat in the center of the courtyard supported on each end by two wooden benches. Mourners, wailing loudly, knelt on both sides, facing the coffin. A small mat was on the ground in front of the coffin, and visitors in turn stepped up to pay their last respects. Some bowed three times. Others kowtowed. My father took his turn, kneeling on the mat and kowtowing three times. *It was the only time in my life that I have seen my father kowtow.* I was in a panic lest I have to do the same--I had never done it before-- but my father told Luther and me to make three bows. Together we stepped up and bowed three times. Before turning away I stood on tiptoe trying to peer into the coffin, but I was too short to see into it from where we stood. I was given a small flower made of white yarn to wear. A servant than ushered us into the dining room in another court where several tables had been set up, each laden with food. We sat at a few places that had just been vacated and helped ourselves to the dishes in the center of the table. Others who had been eating when we arrived left when they had finished. Other new arrivals took their places. No effort was made to converse. People came and went.

I have no recollections of the funeral ceremonies themselves. Days before, however, I remember sitting at the dining table at Yi Tai Tai's house folding little squares of gold "tea-paper" into replicas of *yuan pao..* Each of the shoe-shaped silver ingots was supposed to represent fifty ounces of silver and was to ensure that my uncle was well provided for in the afterlife. I was told only that they were for the funeral. I never saw them being burned, or any of the many other paper replicas of things that were to accompany my uncle to ease his life in his onward journey. My aunt must have left Peking after my uncle's death as neither she nor her two sons were a part of my school years.

Many years later I experienced another family death. This time of my father-in-law in Hong Kong in the late fifties. The family was Christian, not Buddhist, but I was surprised that in this modern cosmopolitan city the family adhered so closely to traditional Chinese customs. The women in the family were required to wear only black rough cotton for one hundred days--even a black-on-black design was deemed inappropriate--no nylon stockings, only cotton. No patent leather shoes or fabric with the slightest sheen; no jewelry of any kind. And for one hundred days we could not indulge in any kind of public entertainment. No movies, concerts, sporting events. For one hundred days we could not enter the homes of even the closest friends. That would have brought our grief, our association with death, into their homes. Close to the end of the hundred-day period, my husband and I did drop in on some close Chinese friends who lived nearby. We were denied entrance even though we knew our friends were home. Even the servants had been alerted. When the hundred days were over, we wore only dark colors for the rest of the year.

When I think of my father, it often saddens me that as an adult I knew him so little. I was only seven when his job took him to Nanking and he was no longer a part of our day-to-day life in Peking. But I remember so well how as a small child I loved being with him and how favored I felt when he took me with him on his outings. I don't recall his ever speaking harshly or even raising his voice to me. He gave me kernels from his pomegranates, popping them into my mouth one by one. He tore off shreds from his pomelo sections especially for me. I never doubted that he loved me; and he was always kind and gentle.

My father died in America in 1965. He was buried beside my mother in a small cemetery in New Jersey instead of the country that was his own. There were no drums beating, no mourners wailing; there was no one bowing or kowtowing to his resting body. I am sorry that he, who was so Chinese, died with no Chinese tradition to mark his passing.

Chapter 8
Chinese School

IT WAS NOT UNTIL I was nine years old and Luther ten that our paths started to diverge. It was then that my parents decided it was time we joined the outside world and went to a proper school. Both Richard and Lois had attended the Peking American School from first grade through high school. In their case I suspect that it was my mother who had made the decision to give them a western education, and that my father, without serious thought, had simply gone along with her wishes. However, too late, he regretted the decision that resulted in his children being uneducated in their native language. Now he was insistent that Luther and I have a Chinese education.

There were many Chinese schools in the city, some of the best being the missionary schools that had been started by the American missions and continued under their sponsorship. Luther was sent to Yu Ying, considered one of the best of the boys' schools. The tuition was higher than most of the Chinese-run schools. Therefore, its student body was made up of children from relatively affluent families. Still, its students came from a much broader range of economic and social levels than our family was accustomed to. It was big by the standards of that day, its twelve grades having about two thousand students. Classes were large, with about forty students in each classroom.

The girls' school that paralleled Yu Ying was Pei Man. It was regarded as one of the best of the girls' schools and was also very large. However, my parents and many of the "returned students" who had been educated abroad felt the need for a smaller school where their children would receive more personal attention. A group of them banded together and started a new private school that they called Ming Ming.. They rented a small single courtyard house and personally selected a principal with impressive credentials, a doctorate in education from a prestigious university in the United States. Under her guidance a qualified teaching staff was put together. Ming Ming was launched. It began with only four grades, first through fourth, with about ten children in each grade. Each year a new grade was added to accommodate those of us who had started in the fourth grade. I began in the fourth and proceeded to the new fifth grade when it was added the next year, and then to the sixth. My class was the first to graduate.

The first day of school was an exciting one for me but mixed with anxiety. Though I couldn't help but be nervous at the prospect of being in unfamiliar surroundings and among so many children whom I didn't know, Mother had reassured me that there would be many whom I *did* know. Still, I was apprehensive. Luther had always been my security blanket, and for the first time he would not be with me. I realized now I was going to be on my own. I would be leaving the small world that he and I had shared.

When Mother and I arrived at the school, I was dismayed to see several of the boys chasing another boy around the courtyard and raining blows down on his shoulders. One kept trying to hit him on the back of his head. The victim was ducking as best he could but was at the same time laughing, apparently unperturbed by the attacks

"Why are they hitting him?" I asked one of the girls. "What did he do?"

She looked at me oddly, surprised that I couldn't see for myself. "Can't you see? He's just had a haircut. Everyone gets to *ta san kwong*, to hit him three times."

I digested that piece of information which was totally new to me, and hoped that no one would notice that I too had just had my hair cut. I was unaware then that the "hit three times" custom applied only to boys.

As I stood in the courtyard beside my mother, I looked around at the other students. Some were already in their respective class rooms, and through the windows I could see them examining the books that had been set on each desk and looking tentatively at each other. Others were standing alone in the courtyard looking quite forlorn, probably waiting to be told where to go. A few other parents were there, all waiting to introduce their children to the principal. I didn't think I was going to like her. She was standing at the door to her office, all smiles, welcoming each parent and child in turn. The smile on her face was so rigidly fixed that it appeared to have been glued on. I thought her quite ugly. Over sixty years have passed since I last saw her, but I can still see her myopic eyes squinting through glasses so thick that her pupils seemed to be swimming in pools of concentric rings. Her lips were thin, and on her upper lip were vertical wrinkle lines. Her hair was meticulously marcelled, the flat exaggerated waves clinging to her head like a tight skullcap.

Actually, Dr. Soo Yi Wang proved to be a most competent principal and not the ogre of my imagination. However, she was very strict and did not hesitate to impose her rigid standards of behavior on all her students. In particular she was a fanatic on personal hygiene. To this day I recall the weekly assemblies at Ming Ming when she would ask the entire student body en masse:

"Have you brushed your teeth this morning? All who have, raise your hands."

Every hand went up.

"Have you washed your face and hands?"

Again every hand went up.

"Did you wash your hands before eating? Did you wash them after using the toilet? Did you bring a handkerchief to wipe your nose?"

To all these questions most of us raised our hands and answered, "*Yo,*" yes, we have.

And then, "Have you had your bowel movement this morning?"

Back then most of us had been trained to a morning program and routinely raised our hands to indicate yes. But one poor unfortunate soul, Kwan Kwei Hwa, whose older sister Shang May later became my best friend, would confess that she had not. So frequently did she respond "*mei yo*" (have not) that our conscientious principal took it as her personal mission to make sure that Kwei Hua had her daily bowel movement. After posing her questions to the student body, she would then address her question directly to the poor girl. "Kwan Kwei Hua, have you had your bowel movement today?"

And the doleful shamefaced response, "*Mei yo.*"

To this day, when I think of Kwei Hua I can see her at our school assemblies, a shy little girl, mortified by her own inadequacy and completely intimidated by the stern unrelenting disciplinarian who was our principal. The whole school was aware of Kwei Hua's dilemma and none of us could understand why she didn't simply lie to escape Soo Yi Wang's weekly interrogation. But Kwei Hua, whose parents had apparently instilled in her the importance of being truthful at the expense of bowel training on schedule, continued to endure the weekly interrogations. When the day finally came that she was able to answer yes, "*yo,*" the whole school breathed a sigh of relief. The beaming look of pride on Kwei Hua's face lit up the room and there was no doubt in any of our minds that she was not lying, that she had truly been successful. Soo Yi Wang's personal interrogations of Kwei Hua stopped shortly after that.

I was a model student and was never subjected to the public humiliation that Kwei Hua endured. However, I was not to escape Soo Yi Wang's vigilant eye. One morning she summoned me and my then best friend to her office. Neither of us had misbehaved in any way so we were totally unprepared for what was in store. It seems we giggled too much and acted "silly" in the presence of boys. Soo Yi Wang cautioned us to mend our behavior and to model ourselves after her favorite girl student. Though totally chastened while in her presence, no sooner were we out of her sight than we reverted to our silly selves. Both of us had just discovered boys, and though we tried to maintain straight faces in their presence, the effort itself only sent us into more paroxysms of giggling.

Besides discovering that for boys a new hair cut was cause for being hit three times by anyone who felt inclined, at Ming Ming I learned more of Chinese children's ways. No more "eenie meenie miney moe" or "one potato, two potato, three potato, four" to decide who was "it." Now it was "*sh'o shin, sh'o pei.*" (palms up, palms down). While speaking the words in unison, we all thrust a hand forward with either the palm up or down. Whichever child's palm differed from all the others, that child was "it." At Ming Ming there was no more western-style hopscotch, throwing the stone in successive squares of an airplane-shaped grid and hopping around the squares to pick it up with one's hands. Chinese hop-scotch required that the stone be kicked from square to square of an eight-square grid while hopping on one foot. Neither stone nor foot was to touch a line. Hands were not used at all except in the initial throwing of the stone.

It was also at Ming Ming that I first discovered that the ink for our calligraphy could be bought in bottles, already made up and ready for use. Though I had never minded the laborious process of grinding the ink by hand, still it was a joy to find it already done. There was no question that it was more efficient and certainly less time-consuming than the manual way. Each student had his own brass box filled with a kind of batting over which the bottled ink was poured. We bought the boxes at school supply stores. They came in various shapes, some round, some oval, some square, and some oblong. All were less than four inches across and etched with either Chinese characters or a floral or landscape motif. At the beginning of the school year there was much comparing of the brass ink boxes among the girls to see whose was the nicest. Mine was oval and had a chrysanthemum design. I had chosen it with great care and thought it by far the best.

Most of the girls disdained the use of ordinary pencil sharpeners, instead using a chisel-like tool with a very sharp blade to whittle their pencils to a wickedly fine point. It was also common for the girls to wrap the covers of their books with brown paper to keep them clean. I never saw a single boy take the trouble and suspect he would have been thought a sissy if he did. The books in Chinese primary schools always had only soft paper covers, so this book-wrapping went a long way to preserving the flimsy covers. The more industrious girls also took great pains to wrap each corner individually. I adopted all these practices eagerly, and despite my initial concerns, settled happily into the routine of Chinese school.

Classes were of course all in Chinese, but my mother taught the English language classes. We had English three times a week and it was the only time that English was spoken. Mother also put on the annual English school play. She not only directed the play but created the sets, designed the costumes, and took responsibility for the entire production. One year she put on a production of Cinderella. I played Cinderella, complete with ringletted blonde wig. I wonder if any of the other girls felt that my mother was showing favoritism in giving her daughter the lead part, but there was no question that my spoken English was better than most of the other girls, so I believe it was excused.

The next year Mother put on Sleeping Beauty. This time, regardless of how good my English was, I could not again be given the

Cinderella. I am at center with blonde curls.

lead. Instead, I was to play the bad fairy. After the other fairies, in their white tutus and golden wands, had bestowed their precious gifts on the newborn princess, I was to emerge from the wings, an old crone, hobbled and bent with age. Mother described the costume she had in mind for me, a dreadful black cape over a long dreary-looking black skirt. If a broomstick and pointed hat had been added, the bad fairy would have looked much like a Halloween witch. I complained bitterly. "Mother, do I have to? I don't want to look like that. I'll be ugly."

And her answer, emphatically, "Yes. You have to. The bad fairy is not supposed to look good. She's wicked and evil and she's supposed to *look* the part. Remember, you're playing a part. It's not going to be *you* on stage, it's the bad fairy, and she's supposed to look bad."

"But Mother, bad people don't always *look* bad," I argued. "Sometimes bad people can look good too."

Mother would have none of that. "No arguing, please. It's already decided. You'll wear the costume I've chosen."

Of course I knew that Mother was right, but in the weeks before the performance I whined and wheedled non-stop. Few days passed that I didn't pester her with new suggestions for improving my costume. I was a vain little thing and my good opinion of myself had been reinforced throughout my childhood by the many compliments my parents' friends bestowed on me. "What a pretty child you are! What a sweet little girl! What a fair complexion!" My mother deplored this almost habitual Chinese way of lavishing compliments on a child. She always made a point of countering these remarks later in the day with her standard "pretty is as pretty does." But was it any wonder that I thought so highly of myself? I had no doubts at all that I was pretty. What a rude awakening it was when in my adult years I came across a picture of myself and a little English girl performing a hula dance. The picture showed an adorable Caucasian girl, her head a mop of blonde ringlets, a dazzling dimpled smile on her face. She could have given Shirley Temple some solid competition. Beside her, a quite ordinary-looking Chinese girl, with one ear protruding awkwardly from her straight black hair. Yet at the time I had thought myself the pretty one. Certainly I had not been lacking in self-esteem.

At the performance, the bad fairy appeared on stage not as an aged crone, but as a sprightly fairy in pert ballet costume with black net tutu. I must simply have worn my mother down with my daily unrelenting complaints. My costume was every bit as pretty as the other fairies' costumes, even prettier because it was one of a kind. The other fairies, the good ones, were all alike, in white, whereas I alone stood out in my all-black costume. Later there were veiled complaints that the bad fairy should have been made to look drab and ugly. I know that Mother was sorry that she had indulged me.

Ming Ming was a good experience for me. Weekdays, school was school, like any other I suppose, but on Saturdays, which were also school days, we had special non-academic classes. Art classes were on Saturdays, as were lessons in the use of the abacus. Pushing the beads up and down was far more fun than adding and subtracting on paper. Physical education was also on Saturdays. We had classes in Chinese boxing, single swordplay, double swordplay, and in Indian clubs. I was quite good at Indian clubs, good enough to be chosen as one of the two students to perform at one of the school functions. The tips of the Indian clubs were lit with flame and the two of us put on an impressive display with our twirling maneuvers. I was immensely pleased with myself.

Saturday was also the day for field trips. At the cloisonné factory we watched the painstaking process of making cloisonné. Fine copper filaments were woven into intricate designs and then filled with layer upon layer of enamel coloring. We visited glass factories to see the glass blowers creating bowls and vases in the beautiful blues and greens for which "Peking glass" had become famous. Best of all were the visits to the silkworm farm. We were encouraged to try our hand at raising the worms ourselves. This was a popular hobby for girls, and many would start raising them from the egg stage, nurturing them until the eggs hatched. The baby worms were fascinating to watch. Cute little things of a brilliant green, they often seemed to be standing up vertically while waving their heads about. I put them in a large flat uncovered box and lined it with mulberry leaves. For me it was an astonishing sight watching the silkworms grow. It took only about two weeks, and several sheddings of skin, for them to be as long as three inches. By then they were no longer cute. Their skin became a pale, dirty looking gray-green and their bodies fat and puffy. I was tempted to poke them with a pin to see if they might pop. They consumed unbelievable quantities of mulberry leaves that had to be replenished daily. Unfortunately I was not as conscientious a caregiver as I should have been for I often found my silkworms inert and looking almost dead in an empty box. I kept them in the sewing room with Yu Ku Niang who often had to take over because of my neglect. However, she was no more enthusiastic about caring for the worms than I, and neither of us was grief-stricken when they died. I had been told that if the worms were put on a piece of paper when they started spinning, the spun silk would form a web that could then be used as a powder puff. At that stage of my life I had no use for face powder and it did not bother me that my worms had died before they could make me a powder puff.

By the time I graduated from Ming Ming the school had moved from the single courtyard property to a large western-style building with extensive grounds. The house was the property of the Salt Gabelle and my father had arranged for its use. It was actually a residential house, but was more than large enough to serve as a school for its fifty-odd students. It had a beautiful wide sweeping staircase; the living room made a fine assembly hall; and the library, dining room, and bedrooms made generously sized classrooms.

Graduation from Ming Ming. I am fourth from left.

Graduation from the sixth grade was a grand affair. All the boys in blue blazers and white flannels, the girls in long Chinese dresses. We felt very grown up. The first leg of my formal education had been completed in Chinese.

Soon, however, I was to be switched from a totally Chinese education to an American one, but Luther, at my father's insistence, remained in Chinese school. Today I fault my father for not taking a stronger stand with regard to my education. Through my adult years, again and again I have regretted that my father did not insist that I first complete my high school education in Chinese before switching to English. Though I continued to take Chinese language classes in high school, and also had home tutoring for many years, my formal Chinese education was sketchy after the sixth grade.

Luther, on the other hand, had a much better grounding in Chinese. When I was reading stories like *The Bobbsey Twins* and *The Wizard of Oz* in English, Luther was reading in Chinese, not *The Hardy Boys*, but tales from *The Three Kingdoms* and other legendary stories from Chinese folklore. Today I envy Luther's language capability. Not too many years ago, well after his retirement from Dupont where he spent his working career, he was invited by the Chinese government to conduct a series of lectures at the Chinese Academy of Sciences in Nanking. He was justifiably proud to find that after fifty years of non-use, he was able to deliver his lectures in Chinese.

His longer attendance at Chinese school and his mingling more with non-westernized schoolmates also increased his interest in some of the more traditional Chinese hobbies in which he had only dabbled before. One of these hobbies was cricket-fighting, and I recall going one evening with Luther and Lin--months before Lin had been fired--to a field outside the walls of the Temple of Heaven to trap crickets. It was dark, and armed with flashlights, we waited patiently in the tall grass for the sound of a cricket chirping. Then, guided by its sound, we crept ever closer, parting the deep grass with our hands, until we found its hole. Over this we placed a cone-shaped net. More patient waiting until finally a cricket would emerge only to find itself trapped. From the ones that we trapped we culled the largest. *Luther has no recollection at all of this outing, but I remember it quite clearly and am quite sure it happened because there is no other way I would have known of it.*

After Lin had been fired, Luther turned to his new schoolmates at Yu Ying for company. By then he had become more knowledgeable in the ways of fighting-crickets and became completely engrossed in this new activity. Self-caught ones were no longer good enough for him. Instead, he and his Yu Ying friends went to the fairs and markets where fighting-crickets were bought and sold at prices gauged to their demonstrated fighting abilities. Still anxious to be a part of Luther's activities, I tagged along with them once, and though his friends were nice to me, Luther was clearly irritated at being saddled with a little sister. Feeling very much unwanted, I followed meekly behind the boys as they moved from vendor to vendor evaluating and haggling for the crickets they wanted. Some of them, the ones in individual containers, seemed terribly expensive. According to the vendors, these were the ones with proven fighting abilities. I spotted some in a large baskets that were marked at much reduced prices, but Luther was scornful of my discovery. "But some of them are really big," I insisted.

"Size doesn't have anything at all to do with it," Luther retorted, sounding very superior. He was clearly irritated with my injecting myself into his activities. Meanwhile the vendor was touting the merits of his prize fighter. "I guarantee you this one will fight to the death," he claimed. But seeing that Luther was still reluctant, he said, "Of course, if you can't pay the price, you can choose yourself from the ones in the basket. Who knows? You may be lucky enough to get a good one." There was much more haggling on price, but finally the boys settled on the ones they wanted. Luther bought two of the supposedly good fighters, and despite his earlier dismissal of the cheaper ones, did choose one of the larger ones from the basket. The vendor then put the crickets into individual little paper tubes that he made of newspaper. These he folded at the ends so that the crickets could be taken home securely.

Once Luther got absorbed in this hobby, one corner of our kitchen courtyard became filled with an array of little pots and other equipment. There was a large pot which served as a fighting arena, and small pots for holding individual crickets. Some were of clay, some of bamboo, and one made of a small gourd. There were also tiny little dishes for food and water, and bamboo sticks with stiff hairs protruding from one end that were for tickling the crickets to prod them into fighting. Luther's new friends from Yu Ying came to the house frequently with their own crickets to challenge Luther's. Groups of boys would be huddled around the fighting arenas, each loudly cheering on his own cricket. The courtyard would be buzzing with the excitement of the fights, and the servants would often stop in their mid-day chores to peer over the boys' heads for a glimpse of the battles. As for me, I squeezed in among them on a few occasions but had no real interest. I was ready to go my own way. My days of being Luther's shadow had come to an end.

Chapter 9
American School

BY THE TIME I GRADUATED from the sixth grade at Ming Ming my father's job with the government had already taken him to Nanking when the capital was officially moved to that city. Though he came home for frequent visits, he was no longer a full-time part of our household. It was understood that both Luther and I would eventually go to America for our college education, and feeling it important that I receive my high school education in English, my mother enrolled me in the Peking American School, commonly known as PAS. What role my father played in allowing me to make this early shift from a Chinese education to an American one is questionable, but I suspect he once again gave in to my mother's wishes. However, in Luther's case he had remained adamant that Luther continue for at least a few more years in Chinese school.

Despite my regrets today that my formal Chinese education stopped so soon, at the time I was happy with the move. Since Ming Ming was ahead of the American school in most subjects, as are most Chinese schools, I was able to skip seventh grade and go directly into the eighth. The whole tenor of my life underwent a radical change. It was a total shift, from a Chinese environment to an American one, and from the Chinese language to English.

My first day at PAS was full of excitement. I felt I was moving into the big time, from a tiny school of fifty children into what I then thought of as an enormous one with all of two hundred students. This time there was no apprehension. I was already accustomed to sharing a classroom with others, and several of the students from my Ming Ming class were also moving on to PAS. Mother had wanted to take me to school herself, but the last thing I wanted was to be seen hanging onto my mother. I was twelve, old enough to be independent.

It was only 8:30 when I arrived on my bicycle, but already the school compound was teeming with activity. On the first day of school everyone else was early too. Rickshaws carrying small children, some alone, some with a parent, were pulling into the gates. Older students on bicycles were riding in and parking their bikes in the bicycle racks. The Marine bus with its canvas roof and side-flaps pulled up just inside the gate and disgorged its horde of students from the American Embassy and Legation. Almost simultaneously the children from the British Embassy arrived in their mule-drawn army cart. A few chauffeur-driven automobiles pulled up with students from some of the other embassies. And then there was the closed horse-drawn carriage in which Victor and Oliver Yang arrived. They had once been Manchu princes, and the family still retained some of the trappings of their past. The carriage, attended by coachman and groom, was something of an anachronism even in those days, and always drew stares and comments from the foreign students who had only recently arrived in Peking.

Though some students were going into the large, pink brick building, their arms loaded with supplies, others were rushing out. They wanted to get into the game of prisoners' base that was already going full swing in front of the building before the school bell rang. Others were swinging on the double rings and climbing on the monkey bars. It was obvious that all were happy to get back to their friends and the familiar environment of school.

There were many American schools in China, all established for the express purpose of providing an English education for the small number of American children in China. Among them were the Shanghai American School (SAS), the largest of the American schools, and TAS in Tientsin. Many of these American schools also admitted other foreign nationals, but among them all, PAS was the only one, which as a matter of policy, admitted Chinese children. The Board of Trustees was made up of representatives of the foreign embassies, the local business community, the Christian missions, and the Peking Union Medical College (the PUMC), established by the Rockefeller Foundation. Many of the Americans in Peking had professional and social contacts among the Chinese, particularly with those who had studied in America, and it was only natural that the children of those families be admitted to PAS if they so wished. The board made the decision that one third of the school's student body should be Chinese.

During the years that I attended PAS, though the main student body was primarily American--and one third Chinese--there were also students from England, Australia, Russia, Greece, France, Germany, and India. At our weekly assembly gatherings, the flags of all these nations stood at the head of the hall. We stood and recited our pledge of allegiance, each to his own flag. "I pledge allegiance to the flag and *to the country for which it stands*." We all--Chinese, Americans, and other nationalities--benefited from the interracial, intercultural mingling.

PAS had twelve grades, plus kindergarten. The total student body numbered about two hundred. Classes were small; the average class size about fifteen.. The high school curriculum met all the standards for U.S. college accreditation, and the school's scholastic standing was high. Each year PAS students received several of the four-year full scholarships that were awarded annually to a student in China by each of the American Ivy League colleges. In my class of thirteen students, three of us were awarded scholarships: one from Radcliffe, one from Bryn Mawr, and mine from Smith. Luther, a class ahead of me--he rejoined me at PAS in his sophomore year--had a scholarship from Harvard.

Credit for PAS's high standing must go to our principal, Alice Moore. Loved and respected by students and parents alike, she was the school's guiding force from its beginnings and through at least twenty years of its life. Miss Moore was not only principal, but also teacher, administrator, and high school counselor. She steered us ably through our College Board exams and guided us through our selection of colleges. We could not have asked for more.

Miss Moore also played a major role in the selection of the teaching staff, most of whom were recruited from the U.S. However, occasionally Peking residents who had particular qualifications were also enlisted. Our Chinese teacher (i.e., teacher of Chinese language) and French teacher were both Peking residents. Chinese and French were the only foreign languages--that is, *living* languages-- that were taught at PAS. Both were introduced in the first grade. In high school we had Latin.

I can still see our French teacher, Madame Woo-Moray--she was French, her husband Chinese--with her flaming red hair. The hair went well with her personality. She was highly temperamental and always seemed to have a frazzled look about her. When frustrated in one way or another with her students' behavior or their lack of adequate preparation, she would first throw up her hands in despair, and then clap her hand over her forehead moaning of her *mal de tete*! or sometimes it was her *mal au coeur*. During the winter months she habitually wore the same black wool skirt day after day and went to great lengths to prolong the life and appearance of this well-worn garment. Before each class she went through the same ritual while we students raised eyes and brows heavenward. First she opened her purse and from its depths drew out a neatly folded white handkerchief. This she opened up carefully and then spread with great precision over the seat of her wooden chair. Finally, she would smooth down the back of her skirt and seat herself with care on the large white square. If, during the class she had to rise--which she frequently did to write on the blackboard--she would always smooth down the handkerchief again before sitting down. I am sure she did not know that we students took great delight in imitating her daily performance.

Our history teacher was Mrs. Jordan. She was a matronly widow, probably in her late fifties, but who seemed very elderly to us. Her husband had died shortly before she came to Peking and she had recounted to us more times than I care to remember how at his request she had scattered his ashes in Puget Sound. Her ample figure was always tightly and firmly girdled. Before each class, standing before us, she would inhale deeply, draw herself up to full height, girding herself to do battle with us wayward students. With both hands flat against her body, she would then smooth down her dress over her girdle, from bosom to hip. We thought it great comedy to mimic her; her and Madame Woo-Moray.

PAS had no cafeteria; nor was one needed. Since most of the students lived within a mile of the school, they usually went home for lunch. However, others, including myself, often brought food from home. We always ate in the science classroom. We Chinese usually brought Chinese sesame buns, *shao ping*, or steamed Chinese bread, *man t'ou*, filled with spiced pork or beef, or sometimes with shredded meat and vegetables. Often a coolie from home would bring us meals straight from our own kitchens, piping hot in a three-tiered enamel container: rice in one tier and two Chinese dishes in the other two. The foreign students would eye our food with envy and invariably want to trade. To us Chinese, a peanut-butter-and-jelly or a ham sandwich seemed a poor trade for our Chinese food, and there was often much haggling over what a meat-filled *shao ping* would bring in trade. A piece of an American candy bar often sweetened the deal. Despite our reluctance, we often gave in, and I can't begin to count the number of peanut-butter-and-jelly sandwiches I had eaten before ever having arrived in America.

The boys had a locker room with showers in the school's basement, but the girls had only what passed for a dressing room. A portion of the kindergarten classroom was partitioned off for our use, but we had no showers and not even individual lockers. Our clothes had to be piled on benches or hung on hooks on the side walls, our shoes thrown under the benches. What today would be regarded as blatant sexual discrimination, back then was accepted without complaint. Boys' sports were more important than girls' and boys obviously were more in need of bathing than we of the more genteel sex.

By the time I reached my junior year, however, we girls had all become fed up with the lack of a properly equipped locker room. We appealed to Miss Moore. She in turn appealed to the school board, and though all were sympathetic, the funds were simply not available. We decided to raise the money ourselves.

Our first effort at fundraising was to sell ice cream sodas at recess. Local Chinese soda pop, with a scoop of vanilla ice cream, was as close to the real thing as we could get. It served the purpose. The ice cream was made by our servants at home and brought to the school by a rickshaw coolie just before recess. We set up our stand in the main hall, just outside the library. The concept of refreshments during recess created quite a stir and proved to be immensely popular. Students from both grade school and high school stood in line for their sodas while we poured and scooped, poured and scooped, in a frantic effort to keep up with demand. But despite the brisk sales, the profits were minimal. It was also more work than we had bargained for. We looked for other fundraising ideas.

The usual ways in which American teenagers raise funds were not open to us. In a country where everyone had servants and few had cars, car washing was not an option. Nor were bake sales. And it was unthinkable that we should go from door to door soliciting donations. Finally, we decided to put on a play, for which we would charge admission. The auditorium of the PUMC would cost us nothing. The PUMC routinely lent its auditorium to the local community for plays, recitals, concerts, and lectures. There would be the outlay for costumes and sets, but other than that, no other expenditures except our time and effort. That, we were prepared to give. Still, it was an ambitious project for a small group of students. Our English teacher, Mrs. Hill, helped in the selection of a play. She also made suggestions for casting and for direction. The play she selected was James M. Barrie's *Quality Street.* An American classmate, Margaret Krenz, was to direct. I was to play the leading role. For the male roles we borrowed boys from the classes above and below us.

During the weeks before the performance I closeted myself in my room and rehearsed constantly. I was Phoebe Throssel, abandoned by her handsome captain who on his return from the war does not recognize the staid tired spinster that she has become. "I hate him. Oh Susan, how I hate him. He thought I was old because I am weary, and he should not have forgotten. I am only thirty, Susan. Why does thirty seem so much more than twenty-nine? --------Susan, I am tired of being ladylike. I am a young woman still, and to be ladylike is not enough. Was I born to be confined within these four walls? Are they the world, Susan, or is there anything beyond them?" I threw myself into this desperate lament and reveled in my own weeping. My mother would come upon me again and again with tears streaming down my face. In the days ahead the family became accustomed to my coming to the dinner table with red and swollen eyes.

Quality Street was the high point of my high school years. The night of the performance, as the cast-aside heroine, on stage I weep, I rail against the years that have passed me by and left me worn and weary. Looking at myself in as the spinster I have become, I remember the vivacious young woman I once was. I cry out my despair, "I have heard her singing as if she thought she was still a girl. I have heard her weeping; perhaps it was only I who was weeping; but she seemed to cry to me, 'Let me out of this prison, give me back the years you have taken from me.'" And weep I did. The tears I had rehearsed so fervently did not fail me.

But when Phoebe masquerades as her own niece, I *become* the flirtatious, spirited Livvy. I am lost in the performance, totally unaware of spectators, stage, or surroundings. The inhibitions by which I have normally been bound have fallen away. I am free to be another person. I fly; I soar. I am Phoebe; I am Livvy. I am anyone I want to be.

After the performance, Madame Woo-Moray, she of the large white handkerchief, rushed up to me and declared she had cried through the entire dramatic weeping scene. *The Peking Chronicle*, Peking's English language newspaper, proclaimed the next day, "A new star was born on the Peking amateur stage in the person of Marguerite Chien." I was ecstatic. I was convinced that a career on the stage was to be my role in life.

PAS was limited in the non-academic courses and extra-curricular activities it offered, but the school auditorium was made available for dancing classes and music classes, which were given by private teachers. Billie Thunder arrived in Peking when I was in the eighth grade. She was single, a divorcee, with good training in dance. A professional, her reasons for coming to Peking were hard to fathom. But on her arrival, doting mothers eagerly signed up their daughters for classes. Billie was given the use of the school auditorium and once a week my friends and I gathered there for our lessons. "No, no, don't stand straight-legged. Bend your knees. Pretend there is an extension to your spine. It's the third leg of a stool. You're sitting on a three-legged stool." And more. "Arms curved please. No elbows. I want no elbows." The smaller children peeked through the glass doors of the auditorium and giggled at the sight of us placing our feet in the five basic ballet positions and sitting awkwardly on our imaginary three-legged stools.

Dancing lessons were great fun. Whatever we lacked in grace, we made up for in enthusiasm. At our annual recitals, held always at the

PUMC auditorium, we had a remarkable variety in our dance numbers and in our costumes. In perky net tutus we did our arabesques and flitted about the stage as gracefully as we could. In short white toga-like garments we walked about with stately motions and ended with an impressive Grecian frieze that we managed with hardly a wobble. In Indian costumes, feathers in our headbands, we pranced wildly about the stage in a whooping war dance. Best of all was the chorus line in top hat and tails to the tune of "Roll Out the Barrel." We looked oh so smart in our black satin shorts and our sleeveless tuxedo tops with sequined lapels.

Singing lessons also took place in the auditorium. I had always been told that I had a nice voice, so what more natural than that I should have singing lessons. The lessons were not what I expected. "Lay-ee-lo-oh, lay-ee-lo-oh, lay-ee-lo-oh-lay," going progressively up and down the scale, followed by "pa-pay-pee-po-poo, ma-may-me-mo-moo, ta-tay-tee-to-too," supposedly to improve my diction, was not what I had envisioned when I had asked for singing lessons. There seemed no end to the required exercises. *When do I get to sing?* Besides, the lessons were boring and no fun. They lasted only a few months.

Piano lessons were for me the most dismal failure of all. They too were taught in the school auditorium. I had started piano when I was seven or eight years old with a teacher who taught at her home, but I never practiced until an hour before my lesson. With the different rooms in our house widely separated by the courtyards, it was impossible for my mother to know if I practiced unless she sat in the room with me. When she asked me if I had done my practicing, I lied outrageously. "I've already done it." But it soon became apparent--particularly at piano recitals--that I was not making any progress. Mother let me stop. But by the time I reached high school I had developed an interest in music--by then I was singing in the school glee club and in the church choir--and she decided to give it another try.

Mr. Grimes, single, had newly arrived in Peking and was to give piano lessons. He was reputed to be a pianist of concert caliber. At least he gave concerts in Peking. He was good looking in a dark brooding Heathcliff kind of way and his hair was longer than the style of the day. He was highly temperamental and habitually looked angry at the world. Nonetheless, several of the unmarried women cast hopeful eyes in his direction. And I, young as I was, soon had a total crush on him that

lasted well into my high school years. I worked hard at my piano lessons, practiced daily, but I was notably untalented as a piano player.
Even when I thought I had my lesson down pat, I would get so nervous in
Mr. Grimes' presence that my hands would perspire, leaving telltale wet
smudges on the keys. I found this so embarrassing and humiliating that I
finally gave up piano lessons for the second time.

Throughout my school years it seemed there was no end to the
after-school lessons, these in addition to tutorials in Chinese, at home.
There had also been lessons during the summer months. The summer
after I graduated from Ming Ming, when I was twelve, Mother decided I
should learn to draw. I was enrolled in private lessons. The teacher was
very patient with me as I struggled through the basic elements of perspective, but one day he told me that he was putting me into a class with
some of his other students. That suited me just fine, as I did not particularly enjoy being the lone object of his scrutiny as I misdrew lines repeatedly and erased and smudged over and over again.

The first day of my attendance in the class I stepped over the
high threshold of the large hall, curious as to what the class would be
like. I had expected to see children of my own age and was surprised
that the twenty-odd students all appeared to be adults, though in retrospect I believe they were college students. But to me they were adults.
They were seated in a semi-circle, each thoroughly engrossed in his own
sketching of the model at the center of the room. On looking upward I
was momentarily shocked by the sight. The model sitting on the raised
platform was completely naked. None of the other students seemed in
the least perturbed by the nudity before them. The teacher was moving
among them, observing their work, nodding his approval at some and
making critical comments to others. He motioned me to a chair behind
the other students and provided me with a large sketching pad in place of
the small one I carried. Knowing this was all beyond me, I looked at
him rather desperately, saying. "I don't think I can do this."

But all he said was, "Just do your best, do your best," and proceeded on his rounds.

For my part, I was at a loss. Sketching a human figure, a nude
figure, was a far cry from the cubes and other linear objects that I had
finally learned must be drawn larger in the foreground than at the rear.
This was China in the mid-thirties. I had never seen the naked body of

an adult woman in the flesh before. My mother had *never* appeared un-
clothed before any of us children at any time. Even my sister Lois had
never stood before me completely naked even though she and I shared a
room when she was in her early teens. We had all been raised in a culture of modesty that I never completely shook even in my adult years in
America. During the period I was at Smith College I never ceased to be
uncomfortable in the communal showers of my dormitory. (Gillett
House had been occupied by WAVEs during the war and the individual
shower stalls converted to communal ones.) It was not only displaying
my own body that bothered me. I was uncomfortable with the full frontal
views of other naked bodies. Even now, in the locker rooms at the
county recreation center near my home in McLean, Virginia, my friends
are amused that I always turn my back to others when undressing. I also
find myself averting my eyes from the middle-aged and elderly women
with their pendulous breasts and bushes of pubic hair on full display.
Equally if not more disconcerting are several Japanese women who walk
around naked in the locker rooms chatting and laughing and making no
attempts whatsoever to cover themselves with towels. In this day and
age, I know it is I who am the odd one, but it is hard to shed the ingrained
instinctive habits of the more modest culture in which I was raised.

I had never been particularly conscious of my body. As a child,
I had never even played at "doctor" with either Luther or with friends. I
have no recollection of standing naked before a mirror during my adoles-
cent years marveling at the changes that were taking place in my body.
My face I had examined again and again from every conceivable angle in
the triple mirrors of our dressing table, but my naked body, never. Now,
seated behind the other students, and having overcome my initial embarrassment, I was able to take a good look at the model. She was seated
quite decorously on a bench, her knees together, her left foot slightly in
front of her right. She was leaning slightly backward supported by her
right arm that rested on the bench. Her other hand was draped over her
right thigh and concealed her pubic area. No attempt, however, had been
made to conceal her breasts. They were quite small, but I couldn't help
noting the large purplish area surrounding her nipples. *Would mine get
like that when I was older?*

As the teacher had instructed, I did my best. Remembering my lessons in perspective, I even made the right breast in the foreground larger than the left, and the right arms and legs larger than the left. Unfortunately, I only succeeded in producing an odd and somewhat lopsided figure. When the teacher finally made his way back to me, he said not a word about the nude figure I had attempted. "The bench is good," was his only comment. At least my lessons in perspective had not been in vain.

When I told my mother of the day's experience she of course realized that the class was too advanced for me. She suspected that the teacher had found this the best way of extricating himself from giving private lessons to a child who was clearly not a serious art student.

If any other kind of lessons had been available in Peking at the time, I'm quite sure my mother would have enrolled me. But of the many lessons I took, I acquired expertise in none. If my mother had had greater expectations, she did not show her disappointment. She never insisted that I persevere, that hard work would bring success. Instead she steadfastly maintained that she was merely giving me the exposure through which I would eventually develop an appreciation for those particular arts.

In addition to being used for music and dance lessons, and assemblies, the auditorium was also used for all our school parties, of which we had many. The candy party was the first one of the school year, to welcome the incoming freshmen. It took place in the afternoon immediately after classes were over. Taffy-making in the basement kitchen, followed by dancing to recorded music in the school auditorium. Then the Halloween party, a costume affair, and several theme parties. In my sophomore year we did a South Sea Island theme, for which we begged and borrowed every potted palm the city had to offer. Arrivals had to thread their way through a jungle of palm trees to reach the auditorium

The only two dances at which we had live music were the junior prom and the senior prom. These were grand affairs and the music was provided by the U.S. Marine band in full dress uniform. For the other parties we played records on a wind-up record player. Automatic record changers did not exist in those days, and I cannot remember who was responsible for changing the records or winding up the record player. A friend whose memory is no better than mine suggested that "maybe it was the wall flowers," but I think it more likely that one of the boys who was too shy to dance took on the job. At all of our dances except the informal candy party and the costumed Halloween party, the boys wore tuxedos--they all had their own in those days, even the thirteen-year-old freshmen--and the girls wore floor-length gowns. One year my best friend, Shang May Kwan, had her hair swept up and wore a strapless dress, considered quite daring. In those days, though bones were used in corsets ordered from abroad by foreign women, Peking tailors had not discovered them. Throughout the evening I found myself (and other girls too) frequently glancing surreptitiously at Shang May to see if her dress was staying up. It was. And I was envious that I had not come up with the idea myself. But then, I was a late bloomer, had little or no bust line, and probably could not have held up a strapless dress.

The year that *Gone With the Wind* was the hit movie of the year, my mother bought me what was called a "*Gone-With-the-Wind* dress" from the States. It was black taffeta with tiny flocked red polka dots and had off-the-shoulder dropped puff sleeves held on by red velvet bows. The very fact that it came from America and was not made by a local tailor made it something special. In fact, for us Chinese, everything from America was special. A friend, Chinese, once had a dress that an American friend of her parents had ordered from Sears, Roebuck. I can still see it, a navy blue print cotton with a small floral print. What made it so enviable was that it had a shirred elastic waist, something Chinese tailors hadn't yet learned to do.

My *Gone-With-the-Wind* dress made me the envy of all my friends. However, not satisfied with having this choice dress, I wanted to have an eighteen-inch waist, a la Scarlett O'Hara. I have no idea where or how I had acquired a girdle--I suspect it had been left behind by an American visitor--one of those tube-like elastic things with stocking clips at the lower edge. I was sure that this was exactly what I needed. No one had told me that stocking clips required stockings to hold the girdle down. Since I had none, I did without, never imagining what the disastrous results would be. When sitting, I could feel the girdle starting to roll up at the lower edges. When dancing, I was acutely conscious that the whole thing was creeping upward under my almost non-existent bosom. The wasp waist I had hoped for was becoming a bunched up wad around my middle. After each dance I rushed to the girls' bathroom and desperately pulled it down again. Five times? Six times? Perhaps more.

My friends noticed. "What's the matter with you?" they asked.

"Nothing." I wasn't about to explain my dilemma or admit to the vanity that had brought it on. And off I rushed to the bathroom again.

Finally I gave up. In one of the toilet cubicles I managed to wriggle out of the offending tube. Then I had to sneak it through the hall to my classroom and hide it in my desk. Never ever again! *How could foreign women stand these things!* It had not shrunk my waistline and had been miserably uncomfortable.

Refreshments at all the school dances were provided by the parents, and the buffet table was usually laden with a combination of Chinese and western foods. Spring rolls and fried noodles stood side by side with tea sandwiches, cakes, cookies, and fancy desserts. My mother always sent a large layered cream cake. The one time she tried to vary her contribution, there were so many cries of disappointment that she was locked into donating a cream cake to every party through all my years at PAS.

The dances were always well chaperoned by several parents as well as teachers. The only time the lights were dimmed was for the last dance which was always, not "Goodnight, Sweetheart," but "Lights Out, Sweetheart." Nonetheless, in spite of the chaperones, two or three couples, known to be going steady, would disappear from the party from time to time for short intervals. We supposed they were "necking." They were always Americans.

When I look back on those years I can hardly believe how innocent my Chinese girlfriends and I were. We had heard of the games played by the American kids, Post Office, and Spin the Bottle, and knew that they involved kissing, but had never played the games ourselves. We had also heard of "necking" but were not sure exactly what that meant. We thought it was more hugging and kissing. I was a freshman in high school when I received the first inkling of what it was all about. It was at a private dance at the home of my friend Shang May. It was summer and though all the windows and doors of the large living room were open, and an electric fan at each end of the room moved the air somewhat, it was still oppressively hot. I was dancing with an American boy whom I really liked--he had blue eyes and the longest most beautiful eyelashes of anyone I had ever seen--but other than asking me for an occasional dance, he had never paid any particular attention to me. His interest had always been in an American girl whose physical development was well beyond her years. They were not going steady, but the two were among the couples who would often disappear from school dances and who we assumed were out "necking." Tonight, for some reason she was not at the dance and George had turned his attention to me. He had danced with me many times, each time holding me very close, nuzzling my neck, and nibbling on my ear. No one had ever nibbled on my ear before. It was a strange new feeling for me; it sent not unpleasant shivers down my spine, but nothing more. George was a good dancer and as we moved around the floor I was in a dreamlike trance when quite abruptly he suggested, "It's hot in here. Let's get out of here and get some air."

I hated to stop dancing, but as we walked out through the French doors into the garden, my head was full of romance. Despite the heat, it was a beautiful evening and the faint smell of summer was in the air. George steered me by the arm to the gazebo in the center of the garden. We sat down on the bench inside. When George put one arm around me, I was wondering what would come next. For an instant I thought that just *maybe* he was going to kiss me, but no. His other arm went around my waist and before I knew it, his hand was moving upwards to where my supposed breasts were. I pushed his hand down. He pushed up. I pushed down. *Was this what they called necking?*

He kept asking, "What's the matter?"

And my dumb response, "Nothing." I didn't know what to say or do.

More pushing up and down. And finally, he stopped. I literally breathed a sigh of relief. I must have been holding my breath. He took my hand in his and drew it into his lap. I thought all the pushing and pulling was over. But the next thing I knew, he was pushing my hand downward to a place where I knew it shouldn't be. He pushed downward; I pulled upward. He pushed down; I pulled up. *Oh please, please stop. I don't like this at all.*

Throughout this exercise he kept on asking, "What's the matter?"

And I kept on repeating stupidly, "Nothing."

Looking back at that incident, I can hardly believe the state of fright I was in. I was thirteen, an immature thirteen, a child both physically and mentally. I was definitely not yet "awakened," had not even begun to menstruate. I had felt no joy in the experience; I had been petrified and wanted no more of it. It was George, not me, who finally said, "O.K. Let's go back." He sounded disgusted. He did not dance with me again that evening.

The following Monday at school I could not bring myself to look at him. I had been totally enamored of him the Saturday before, but now his blue eyes and long lashes no longer looked beautiful to me. He behaved as usual, did not seem in the slightest concerned. I don't believe he had any idea of the impact his behavior had had on an innocent Chinese girl, or how the experience colored my perception of boy/girl relationships in the years that followed.

Not all Chinese girls were innocent, however. One of them in my sister Lois's class, six years ahead of me, earned herself a bad reputation by going out with some of the American Marines who were part of the American Legation Guard. At the movies, she would sit in the back row of the balcony with her various dates. My group of friends always sat in the front row, but we would look back from time to time trying to see what was going on. However, the couple always sat just below the projector whose beam of light darkened the area just below and gave them some protection from intrusive eyes. All we could see was a double blur of two heads, but once in a while, if one of us happened to turn when two blurs merged into one, we were sure they were kissing. Then we would all turn around in a block. The girls giggled. The boys whistled. It was great spectator sport.

The extent to which the young enlisted American Marines were pariahs to young Peking womanhood was evident in the reaction of some of my schoolmates to my mother's efforts on the Marines' behalf. Mr. Ellis, who was in charge of the Marine Guard YMCA, was a good friend of my mother's. He was well aware of how the young enlisted Marines were locked out of "nice society" and had asked Mother if she would be willing to host an occasional social function where the young men would have a chance to mingle with the more "respectable" citizens of the city. Mother responded immediately and planned a series of afternoon tea parties where groups of Marines could mix with some of the younger members of the local foreign community. She did not include the daughters of Chinese families, as she must have realized that even philanthropy had its limits. Even the more westernized Chinese families would have been reluctant to have their daughters associating with American Marines. Lois and I, however, were always present at these gatherings. Lois was old enough to enjoy the attentions of some of these young men, but never went out with any of them. Nor did I ever hear of any of the young foreign women continuing a friendship with any. In the inter-cultural atmosphere in which we lived, we were without racial prejudices, but class bias was another thing. In a country with a highly classed society such as China, each Chinese was well aware of his own place within this social hierarchy. The foreign community too was all too conscious of these class distinctions. The enlisted Marines were of a different class. We must be nice to them, but our association was to be on a limited, well-defined basis.

Several of my friends knew my mother was going to host these parties, and at school, the day after the first of these, they were full of questions.

"What was it like? Who was there? How many Marines came? Were they in uniform? Did you talk to any of them?"

I described the party as best I could. About ten Marines had come. None of them had been in uniform. I ran through the names of all the local guests, perhaps twenty in all. Most were youngish couples but there had been three or four young single women besides Lois and me. The young Marines had been rather awkward and quiet at first, but once Mother had performed the introductions, the young married couples had taken the lead in engaging the Marines in conversation. The single women were a bit more hesitant but by the end of the afternoon everyone seemed to be talking a lot and they looked as if they were having a good time.

"Yes, a couple of them talked to me. I thought they were really nice," I said. "A couple were really good looking. I don't see why it would be so awful to go out with one of them. I must say, if I were older I wouldn't mind."

One of my classmates was horrified. "You can't really mean that," she said.

"Of course I do." I defended myself. "They were just as nice as any of the guys at PAS and a lot more polite than some."

But Jane couldn't let it go. "Well, I think it's all very well for your mother to be nice to them, but I'm shocked that she let you and Lois associate with them."

"And what was she to do? Make us stay in our rooms till they had gone? I can't get over you. You can be as shocked as you want at my mother, but I'm really shocked at you. You are *so* narrow-minded." It didn't seem like such a horrible thing to say, but after that accusation from me, Jane did not speak to me for three full months.

My mother continued giving her tea parties for the Marines, and though they didn't lead to any dating between Marines and young women of the local community, a few became regulars at some of Peking's local functions. I like to think it was my mother who gave them this entrée. I often think of the episode in the British television program, "Upstairs, Downstairs," in which Lady Marjorie, in an effort to boost wartime troop morale during World War I, agrees to entertain some of the soldiers. She prepares for a massive attendance, only to find that only four appear, and those under orders from their superior officers. Today I wonder how many Marines came to Mother's parties willingly and how many under duress. However, many years later, in Washington, I met one of the Marines who had been stationed in Peking and was thrilled to find that he had been among those invited to my mother's teas. As a result of the years he spent in Peking, he became an avid scholar of Chinese studies. He tells me that he always enjoyed those afternoon teas at our house, so perhaps others did too.

With the passage of the years I find myself increasingly aware of how unique and wonderful the PAS experience was. Its mission was to provide an American education, and that it did admirably. Yet, I cannot help but wish that it had taught us something of the country in which we lived. We were located in a city rich in centuries of history, yet were taught nothing of Chinese history, of Chinese geography, of Chinese religions, or even Chinese culture. We Chinese students absorbed the culture from our families, but what the American and other foreign children learned came by osmosis from their surroundings rather than from the school. We rode our bicycles daily past the Forbidden City without giving a thought to the emperors who had once reigned there or the edicts they had passed. We went ice-skating on the North Lake and played kick-the-can on the park's artificial hills with little awareness that we were playing where emperors and their retinues had once strolled. We swam in the lakes of the Summer Palace, picnicked on their banks, but had been taught nothing of its history. Yet, even as I criticize, I recognize the large part the PAS years played in my life.

Apart from the fine education we received, all of us who attended PAS, Chinese and foreign students alike, emerged from our experience there completely devoid of racial prejudices. We worked and played side by side; we visited in each other's homes, each culture absorbing from the others. I don't believe that the foreign students or the Chinese gave any thought to either race being superior or inferior to the other. It was Miss Moore who, well aware of the discrimination we Chinese might face on the west coast in America, steered us toward the eastern colleges. For my part, it was not until I was a passenger on the American evacuation ship that eventually brought me to America that I was even aware of the racial discrimination that existed outside my sheltered world.

It was not many days into that voyage that I met a young sailor named Paul Lanius. He had never met a Chinese before and took a great interest in me and my little sister Jeannie, then only seven. We were the only Chinese on board. In one conversation he asked me, "Are you prejudiced?"

I was surprised at the odd question. "What do you mean, prejudiced?" I asked.

"You know, *prejudiced*. Are you prejudiced against other races?" He explained. "I'm Indian, you know. Does that bother you?"

I couldn't understand what he was getting at. "Why should it bother me?" I thought he was telling me he was an Indian, from India. "But what do you mean, you're Indian? I thought you were American. You're in the American Navy."

"I *am*, but I'm an *American* Indian."

"You are?" I exclaimed. "You certainly don't look like an Indian." Even as I spoke, I realized how foolish that must have sounded, but he was so unlike my image of the painted and feathered Indians of the movies. It took me a minute to realize that an Indian could look like any other American, but I was really quite pleased to find that Paul was

the real thing and told him so. "But why did you think I might be bothered?" I asked.

"Oh, well, it's obvious you *aren't,*" he concluded. "But in
America a lot of people do discriminate against us, regard us as an inferior race. In some parts of the country they treat us like dirt. Some
places won't allow us in, and sometimes it's hard for us to get jobs. It
makes life pretty rough for us. I just hope that when you get to America
people won't discriminate against you just because you're Chinese and
your skin is a different color."

Until that time I had not even considered the possibility of not
being treated as an equal in America, but now I was getting a faint glimmer of the racial discrimination that some people were faced with. A
second instance, also aboard ship, brought home even more sharply the
racial problems that exist in America.

While everyone else aboard could hardly wait for the day when
we would be sailing under the Golden Gate, one person was dreading it.
Deirdre was a beautiful Eurasian girl who had married a black musician
while both were interned at the concentration camp in Wei Hsien during
the war. In camp, where each person had been judged on his own merits
and not by the color of his skin, the differences in their race had been no
obstacle to their relationship or their marriage. As the days passed and
we drew closer to America, Deirdre became daily more morose. Several
times I noticed that she had been crying. I asked Rachel, her best friend,
what was the matter with Deirdre. "I can tell that she's been crying,"

"She's starting to worry about what her life will be like in America." Rachel explained. "I feel so bad for her. She knows that she'll be
living in a Negro world (that was the "correct" word used in those days),
surrounded by Negro relatives, Negro friends. Her white friends might
not accept her, and who knows whether the Negroes will welcome her or
resent her." As Rachel went on, I was beginning to have some idea of
what Deirdre would soon be facing. For her it would be different from
the rest of us. And so, I learned that everything in America was not all
beauty and light.

As a child I had read *Little Black Sambo* and *Uncle Tom's Cabin*
and *Huckleberry Finn*. We had a cat named "Nigger." He was named
"Nigger" because he was black, just as our white cat was named "Fluffy"
because he was fluffy, and another cat named "Ginger" because he was

ginger-colored. It didn't occur to us that there was anything wrong with the use of the word "Nigger." We spoke of "jewing down" a dealer when we had bargained his price down. I had no idea at the time that the phrase was derived from the word "Jew." Had no idea how offensive it was. It had been a word, just a word. "Nigger" too had been a word, just a word.

Personally, in all my years in America, I never felt any racial discrimination directed against me. Luther had a few insults hurled at him during the war years because he was mistaken for Japanese, but in my own case I found that people bent over backward to be nice, to show that they were *not* prejudiced. It was in Hong Kong, one of the last bastions of British colonialism that I felt for the only time the indignity of being discriminated against because of my race. In 1956, my husband, Chinese-American, had been assigned to the American Consulate General as a political officer. We had just arrived in Hong Kong and had applied immediately to the British school near us for admission for our six year-old son. The children of other new American arrivals were being admitted speedily, but our application was repeatedly denied, as was the application of another Chinese-American child, the daughter of a friend. I made an appointment to see the principal. Her first response to my questions was, "Your son is not old enough." To which I cited the names of several children who were younger. Then, "Your application came in too late." Again I cited the names of several American children who had made their applications after ours. Finally, this arrogant woman said, "Mrs. Eng, I am not obliged to give you any further explanation. Your son cannot be admitted."

I remember being on the verge of tears, whether from the indignity I was suffering or from pure fury I don't know. That evening at dinner I told the family of the humiliating experience. My husband's brother-in-law, at that time a member of Hong Kong's Urban Council, was incensed. He brought the matter to the attention of his law partner, a senior member of the Executive Council. Within days we received notice that our son was to be admitted, as was the other Chinese-American child. I don't know what steps were taken or how much pressure had been exerted. I knew only how fortunate we were to have known the right people!

During the period we were in Hong Kong, from 1956 to 1961, the Hong Kong Ladies' Recreation Club was one of the few holdouts that did not admit Chinese to its membership. I made no attempts to join and did not subject myself to a sure rejection. However, it did seem ironic that though I never experienced any discrimination in predominantly white America, it was in a Chinese city, albeit a British colony, where my being Chinese was held against me.

Chapter 10
Friends

AT PAS I FORMED LIFELONG FRIENDSHIPS with three other Chinese girls. The four of us were inseparable through those high school years.

Shang May Kwan, who became my best friend, I had not known before, but her little sister, Kwan Kwei Hwa, was the one who had endured the frequent interrogations about her bowel movements while at Ming Ming. Their father was a banker, educated in Japan. He was a serious antique collector and their living room walls were lined with his collection. Shang's mother was a sweet woman, but we saw little of either her or Shang's father during the years of our friendship.

Clementine Hoo was the daughter of one of my parents' friends, but I had not known her before either. Her father had been a senior diplomat who had served in Mexico, France, Russia, and Japan. He was many years older than Clemy's mother and had died when Clemy was only ten years old, many years before I knew Clemy. Her mother, also from a diplomatic family, was warm and friendly. She always made us welcome in their home and we all liked her.

Edie Wang was the only one I had known from childhood, as both our families spent our summers in the Western Hills outside Peking. The particular area was called *Pa Ta Ch'u*, literally translated to Eight Great Places, but referring to the eight temples that dotted the hills. The

Wangs rented two courtyards in *Ch'ang An Ssu*, the Temple of Eternal Peace, just below our house. These they furnished as completely as their city home, and with their servants, lived the summer months every bit as luxuriously as in Peking. My mother, when she first came to Peking, found it hard to believe this commonly accepted Chinese practice of renting out parts of their sacred temples. But she soon found that the ever-pragmatic Chinese, including the monks, welcomed the extra income and went about their devotions completely unfazed by the foreign presence.

Edie had also been a student at Ming Ming. Her father, Chinese, was superintendent of the prestigious Peking Union Medical College, spoken of always as the PUMC. Her mother was an American, like mine, a Caucasian American, and so Edie's upbringing and mine closely paralleled each other. Edie was an adopted child, adopted in the more commonly accepted sense, from *outside* the family; not a *kuo chi* adoption from a relative *within* the family. Edie's father had wanted a son to carry on his line of the Wang family, but the *kuo chi* adopted son of a Wang cousin had not worked out. The boy, by then already six, had come into the family after Edie was already firmly entrenched. When the two children could not get along, Edie's mother so doted on Edie that the boy was returned to his birth parents. The continuation of the family bloodline of Edie's father was cast aside and Edie remained, an only child.

Throughout the years at PAS we four Chinese girls did everything together. We often went to *Tung An Shih Ch'ang*, the Eastern Peace Market, to browse among the shops or to have an afternoon snack. The market was a wondrous place, almost a city in itself, occupying a whole city block. Buildings, shops, and stalls, all jammed in together and all bordering four main passages with smaller alleyways tying them together. Merchandise of all kinds crammed the aisles, and the clicking of the abacus could be frequently heard as stall keepers racked up the price of sales. Cameras, used books, cheap Japanese toys, toiletries, fresh fruit, and more were available either at open stalls or in glass-fronted stores. We never failed to stop at the stall that faced the eastern entrance of the market and to eye its display of snack foods. The spiced grasshoppers lay in their dark brown sauce among trays of delicious-looking red-cooked meats, salted fish, and pickled vegetables. "Come on, I dare you to try one," one or another of us would challenge. Edie was always the most adventurous, but even she never took up the dare.

Wonderful smells of garlic, sesame oil, and Chinese spices came from the restaurants within the market. The sounds of waiters yelling out their orders mixed with the click of mahjong tiles that came from some of the private rooms. We had our favorite restaurant where we frequently headed after school. Each of us placed a separate order, one for a plate of fried noodles; another for a plate of *chiao tze*'s, the meat-filled dumplings that have become so popular in America; or for a plate of spring rolls. Infrequently we shared, but mostly we each ate our own. We were poor tippers and it was always an embarrassment when the waiter, according to standard restaurant custom, yelled out in a loud voice the amount of the tip. Our embarrassment, such as it was, was not enough that it caused us to up our tip.

Winter and summer alike, on weekends we went to the movies, most of the time in a large noisy group. Balcony seats, despite the smoke-filled air in the higher regions, were more expensive than those on the ground floor. We always headed for the front row in the balcony and proceeded to make a nuisance of ourselves by throwing paper airplanes at the people below. The airplanes, the boys' whistling when they thought they saw the Marines and their girlfriends kissing in the back row, plus our general boisterousness, did not endear us to others in the audience.

Hatamen Street was the Main Street of our young lives. It was a wide paved street that stretched from one end of the Tartar City to the other with double tramcar tracks running down its length. The street, by today's standard, was uncrowded, but we wove our way through bicycles, rickshaws, and pushcarts, always carefully avoiding the occasional "honey-carts" with the stench of human waste that they carried. A motley assortment of buildings bordered the street on each side. Some were western-style two-story structures that fronted directly onto the paved sidewalk. Others were set back from the road and were Chinese-style with tiled roofs. Mixed in among this medley of mostly commercial establishments was one wide stretch where there was no sidewalk at all, only an unpaved area with makeshift food stalls surrounded by stools and benches to seat their customers. The only building on the street higher than two stories was Glasses Pang's. It was a tall skinny building four stories high with a giant pair of glasses adorning the top of the building and stretching across its storefront. An optician's perhaps? No, that would have been too logical. Glasses Pang's was a shoe store, so named because its owner's name was Pang and of course because he wore glasses. It was there that our family and friends had their shoes made to order. Each of us had our own wooden lasts with our names written on them that were lined up at the rear of the store.

Tung Tan P'ai Lou, a single ornamental triple-arch, spanned the width of Hatamen Street near its southern end, and *Tung Ssu P'ai Lou*, four similar arches, stood at the crossroads of a major intersection a little farther north. It was between the two *p'ai lous* that we rode our bicycles

daily, plying that stretch of Hatamen Street sometimes three or four times a day. The Chen Kwang movie theatre was on Hatamen, as was the YMCA building with its indoor basketball court where we competed sometimes with local teams. There too was the American Bible Society building, presided over by the same Mr. Hoose who slept through our church services each Sunday. The North China Industries where Mother bought all our fabrics was also on Hatamen. From the time I was a little girl Mother used to take me with her when she shopped for fabrics. The salesmen set me on top of one of the cutting tables and treated me to *ch'i shui*, a Chinese soda pop much like Seven-Up, while Mother took her time browsing through the bolts of silks, damasks, and linens. Hsiang T'ai Yi too was on Hatamen, but on the opposite side of the street. It was the general store for imported grocery items, and it was there that we bought our Maxwell House coffee, our peanut butter--when we didn't make it ourselves--our Ivory Soap, Lux soap flakes, and best of all, the crates of Delicious apples and Sunkist oranges that Santa Claus brought at Christmas. Karatsis Brothers too, the Greek bakery that provided our pastries, was on Hatamen Street.

Most of the other places we had to reach were in *hut'ungs* just off Hatamen. PAS was on Kan Mien Hutung (Dried Noodle Street) just off Hatamen, as were the YMCA indoor skating rink, and the YWCA with its lounge rooms and public restaurant/dining room. Also the PUMC buildings as well as the North and South Compounds, the two compounds that held the residences of the American staff of PUMC. The east entrance of the Eastern Peace Market also opened onto a *hut'ung* just off Hatamen. It seems that a greater part of our world was contained within an area barely one mile square, and all either on or just off Hatamen Street.

The Marine Guard YMCA was another that was just off it. Sometimes we went there for our afternoon or weekend snack. The Marine Guard Y had two sections. One was for the Marines posted with the American Legation. It had a soda fountain, a ping-pong table, pool table, a dartboard, and tables set up for other games. The other section was open to the public and was merely a small restaurant. We went there for American hamburgers and for ice cream, but most important, for American ketchup, which was not available on the local market, not even at Hsiang T'ai Yi's. We poured enormous quantities on our hamburgers, often emptying the bottle. Sometimes we were disappointed to find that we had seated ourselves at a table where the ketchup bottle was almost empty, but soon discovered that this was not a chance misfortune, but the result of waiters deliberately conniving to keep us from consuming an entire bottle. Once, quite by chance, we had caught them hastily replacing a new bottle with a partially used one when they saw us coming. Thereafter, for us it became a game, a challenge, to see if we could get ourselves to a table with a full bottle of ketchup before the waiters had a chance to replace it.

Back then in China we were accustomed to three full meals a day plus an afternoon snack. If we didn't go out for a snack after school, we usually had something at home. I remember how hungry I was the first few months at college in America. Cafeterias had not found their way to Smith College, and sit-down meals were served in the dining rooms of each dormitory. Soup and a cottage cheese salad with half of a canned pear, followed by a dessert of cookies or brownies seemed like a meager lunch. Fortunately, there were sandwiches sold on campus, and until I got used to the lighter fare, I bought a sandwich every afternoon.

In the summer, the four of us rode our bicycles to the Summer Palace, some eight or nine miles west of the city, on all-day outings. We drank tea on the Empress Dowager's infamous marble boat, the one built with funds allocated for a Chinese navy. We took our bathing suits and swam in the lake. Our standard picnic fare was fresh bread with a can of corned beef and a tin of sardines, the large ones in tomato sauce that come in big oval tins.

Easter Sundays our church group held sunrise services on top of Coal Hill. The service was always held immediately in front of the center pavilion on the highest of the five peaks. We huddled there in coats and jackets, arms wrapped around our bodies, waiting for that first glimpse of the sunrise. *Christ the Lord is risen toda-ay, A-a-a-a-ah ley-i-lu-u-iah. Sons of man and angels sa-ay...* We sang; we prayed. The expanse of golden rooftops of the Forbidden City stretched out before us. In the half-light of dawn the tiles glistened with morning dew. We were oblivious to their beauty. The roofs of the Forbidden City were no more impressive to us than the *p'ai lous* under which we rode each day on our way to school.

We spent many hours of our free time at what we called the Winter Palace in the center of the city. As children it was at *Pei Hai*, the North Lake portion of this beautiful park, that we played kick-the-can, or sometimes hide-and-seek. The open spaces, the artificial hills, and the pavilions, large and small, made for better hiding places than the square unadorned school compound or the neat foursquare courtyards of our homes. In our teen years we went there just to pass the time and to enjoy the beauty of the park itself. We strolled through its long galleries with their fretted balustrades and coffered ceilings; we wandered along the lakefront enjoying the view of the lotus flowers. Sometimes we bought a bunch of lotus pods from the vendors who carried them on their long prickly stems like so many bunches of balloons. We sat in one of the

small *t'ing tzes*, the oriental-style gazebos that dotted the lakefront to enjoy our lotus seeds. We had to break away the pulpy pods to get to the dozen or so seeds that each pod held. Then the thin outer membrane of each seed had to be peeled away before reaching the delicately flavored edible center. What seemed like a lot of work was as nothing when we finally popped the tiny delicious morsels into our mouths.

One evening, on a moonlit night in summer, a group of us took a portable record player to our favorite *t'ing tze* at the far end of the lake and held a small dancing party. We had always planned to hold a dance one day on the Altar of Heaven but never did. How lovely it would have been, dancing under the moonlight on that circle of gleaming white marble! There were no entrance gates, admission fees, or guards to stop us. It was just there, for us or anyone else who wished to enjoy it.

In the winter, the lakes of the Winter Palace were frozen, and we went skating on its open-air rinks. There were two skating rinks, each of them in front of a large pavilion where food and drink were served. At the foot of the pavilions were seating areas for skaters to put on their skates. Attendants stooped at our feet and laced and tightened our shoes. *It would not have occurred to us to do this menial chore ourselves.* The rinks had temporary walls of straw matting. More often than not we went to the rink that was located in front of *Wu Lung T'ing*, the Five Dragon Pavilion, where the best snacks were served. It was famous for its *shao ping jo mo*, sesame buns stuffed with minced pork. The buns, always piping hot, and the stuffing, deliciously spiced of course, were the perfect end to an afternoon of winter sport.

Though that rink was our favorite, many times we skated across the open lake to check out the other rink. It was always possible we would find other friends there with whom we could join forces. Skating across the open lake was tough going, and we often had to lift our feet in an awkward walk rather than skate most of the way. Within the rink walls the ice was always well maintained and kept smooth and slick, but the ice between the two rinks was rough and wavy where no walls of matting protected it from the harsh winter winds. Tufts of dead grass dotted the surface, as well as occasional dead and shriveled lotus leaves, forlorn remnants of the summer.

Ice-skating at the Winter Palace was not just for the young. Though the skaters included both young and old, for the elderly who did not skate, there were chairs with runners, on which they could sit sedately while being pushed around by sons, daughters, or grandchildren. I have seen many a white-haired old lady beaming happily as she sat serenely on her chair, a participant rather than a mere spectator at this winter sport. No matter that a group of youngsters (usually from PAS) playing crack-the-whip might occasionally hurtle toward her at break-neck speed. Her smile might momentarily be replaced by alarm, but the smile soon returned, evidence of her pleasure at being part of the family activity.

The chairs were also used by children and adults learning to skate. They were a far more substantial means of support than the broomsticks I have seen some beginning skaters leaning on desperately in America. Several years ago, while visiting friends in Minnesota, I got on the ice for the first time in forty years. I was under the impression that, like riding a bicycle, skating was something you never forgot. *What a ridiculous thought!* My friend's skates fit me just fine so I could not blame the skates for my ineptitude. I stepped out onto the ice, only slightly wary, but confident that I would soon regain whatever skills I had had years ago. What a rude awakening that was! I could hardly stand. The broom I had been given to lean on was horribly inadequate. Oh how I longed for one of those chairs from the skating rinks in Peking!

Sometimes we four friends met at one home or another for a game of mahjong. We played for money, each person putting up the amount we would normally spend on a movie ticket. When any one person had lost all her chips, she was allowed to *kwang hua yuan*, to "roam in the flower garden," which meant she could play without chips until she had regained a stake. During these mahjong sessions, we had the servants bring us noodles or dumplings just as the adults did and felt very adult in the process.

We spent a lot of time at each other's houses, just talking. Like most teenage girls we never tired of talking. And we ate. We never tired of eating. Not a meeting took place that we were not consuming some item of food. If we were within earshot of the street, we could hear the street calls or the distinctive sounds of the street vendors advertising their wares. In the winter, if we heard the clacking and whirring sound made by the bamboo sticks of the sweet-potato vendor, we would rush out to the street to buy sweet potatoes, fresh and hot from the vendor's oven. No forks, knives, or chopsticks. Like the rickshaw coolies on the street, we broke them apart and ate directly from the skins. Sometimes we bought large ripe persimmons, fully four inches in diameter, and set them outside on the windowsills to freeze. Later, in the warmth of our dining rooms, we sliced off the tops and scooped out the insides, which had then become a crystallized sherbet. Occasionally one of us would be unfortunate enough to get a persimmon that was not quite ripe. Then it was "puckery." It coated the tongue and inside of the mouth uncomfortably with what felt like a layer of fuzz. It took a long time to wear off and ruined an otherwise delicious dessert.

In the winter too, as soon as it was cold enough for sugar to hold a glaze, vendors of *t'ang hu lu*, skewers of glazed candied fruits, appeared on the streets. We were always eager customers of the *t'ang hu lu* vendor, and when we heard his sound, rushed to the street to make our choices. I usually chose a stick of "red fruit," a cranberry-like fruit the size of a crab apple, too tart to eat alone, but delicious when coated with the sugar glaze. Occasionally I would have a stick of tangerine wedges, or even a whole banana dipped in glaze. We always paid cash for our *t'ang hu lu* but would often watch the rickshaw coolies playing a gambling game for theirs. The vendor had hanging on the side of his display a hollowed-out bamboo tube containing a group of thin bamboo sticks. The sticks were numbered, and by drawing the correct sequence, the player could often win a free *t'ang hu lu*.

It has been so many years since I have heard the sounds and cries of the various street vendors that I have forgotten what many of them sounded like, but back then we recognized each one. Though the sound of the persimmon and *t'ang hu lu* vendors has long since been forgotten, the cry of the steamed bread vendor still rings clearly in my ears. "*San chiao-erh man tou!*" No clackers, bells, or gongs to announce his presence; just a clear cadenced cry calling out the items he was selling. Hot, directly from the steamer, the triangles of steamed bread were filled with either melted brown sugar or with a sweet red-bean paste.

In the summer we sat in our courtyards and if we heard the sound of the radish vendor, we would once more head for the street, either to buy bunches of small red radishes or a single large Tientsin radish. The little red ones were so tender we could peel them with our thumbnails. The Tientsin radishes were as large as grapefruits and resembled large turnips. They were green at the base, fading to white at the tip. The vendor peeled the outer skin to form petals and then cut the radish downward into vertical strips, which he left attached at their base. We broke off the strips as we ate. Sometimes we bought a pound of watermelon seeds--the five-spice ones were our favorites--cracking them with our front teeth and eating until our fingers were black from the soy seasoning and our tongues numb from the salt.

While at PAS, all four of us were on the basketball team and the baseball team. To have "made the team" was no great accomplishment. With such a small student body--approximately sixty in high school-- anyone who was not totally uncoordinated could make the teams. And there were always those who were simply not interested in sports. We also all joined the Girl Scout troop. The American girls ordered official Girl Scout uniforms from America, but we Chinese had them copied by local tailors in a green fabric that came close to matching the real thing. Our scout pins, however, *were* the real thing, ordered from America.

I enjoyed the scouting experience though I didn't have the perseverance to get beyond second class. We must have earned our merit badges in the same way as other scouts around the world. However, I feel that our camping experience was unique to Peking. No hiking for us, and certainly no carrying of heavy backpacks for the young girls of Peking. Even the arduous task of setting up our tents was not for some of us. On the appointed day of our camping trip the Marine bus appeared at the school compound--the same bus that transported the students from the American Embassy to school each day. The camping gear--tents, camp beds, and cooking equipment--had already been loaded onto the bus, all borrowed from the American Legation. We had only to get ourselves and our own personal belongings on board. Then, a comfortable one-hour ride to the grounds of a temple in the Western Hills about fifteen miles west of Peking. Unloading was done with the help of the Marine driver and one other. Some of the girls set up their own tents, but I remember clearly that the one I occupied with a friend was set up by the Marines, as were the camp beds. I suspect they came to our rescue because we may have looked particularly inept at the job. Looking back, I find it a wonder that they were not assigned to help with our campfire and to cook our meals as well. But once all was in order, they drove off. We were left to our own devices. The next afternoon they reappeared. Again, they helped us take down the tents and load us onto the bus. It was not what could be called a typical camping experience, but to me, a coddled and pampered child of the Imperial City, it was high adventure. I had spent the night in a tent, had slept on a real camp bed, and had actually participated in cooking a meal. Best of all had been sitting around a glowing campfire after dark, and closing the day to the tune of "Taps." Our voices rose solemnly in the still night air. "Day is done, gone the

sun.........." It was just like in the movies. I felt myself a true Girl
Scout. *Upon my honor I will try to do my duty to God on high, to help all
other people out, and to live the laws of a true Girl Scout.*

Within this foursome of good friends we tended to pair off;
Shang and I together, and Edie and Clemy together. Shang and I were
the good students, conscientious, industrious, and responsible. The other
two were indifferent about their studies. Though they had no trouble
getting passing grades, they were more concerned with having a good
time than with their books. Of the four of us I was the youngest. Shang
and Clemy were two years older than I; Edie, six months. As their bodies matured physically, mine remained childlike. I envied the swelling of
their breasts and even their complaints about "the curse." Even Edie
arrived at school one day announcing proudly, "Today I've become a
woman." *How I longed to become a woman!* But for me womanhood
was late in arriving. I was well into my fourteenth year.

Shang May always claimed that she was five feet tall, but we all
knew that she was barely four feet eleven. She was smart, cute, and
popular. Though she was not particularly gifted in music or sports, she
participated in both; was in the glee club and on both the basketball team
and baseball team. She was also cheerleader at school games when she
was not actually playing.   Of the seven children in her family she was
the only one who her parents had decided was to have an all-western
formal education. She started at PAS in the first grade and attended
through graduation from high school. At home, however, all was Chinese; not just Chinese, but particularly Cantonese. We had other friends
who were Cantonese, whose families seemed no different from Northern
Chinese families, but Shang May's followed certain customs that the rest
of us thought quite weird. We attributed these customs, perhaps mistak-
enly, to their being originally from Canton. But then again, perhaps they
were just idiosyncrasies peculiar to her family.

The first time I went to her house, I was surprised to find all
three of her brothers in their slippers and undershirts--not tee shirts, but
the sleeveless kind we used to call singlets. Even though they were at
home, I found it rather shocking that their parents permitted them to go
around in this state of undress. As soon as the children got home, shoes
and shirts came off, and they shuffled about the house in a state that the
rest of us found quite slovenly.

Something that *was* definitely Cantonese was the liquid concoction that the whole family drank throughout the day. It was boiled vegetable juice, grayish in color, a muddy looking beverage without a trace of salt. On a small table on one side of the family room multiple thermoses of this drink stood on a tray. Shang offered us some, but one taste, and none of us ever had it again. *How could she stand this stuff!*

"You get used to it. If you had it often you'd like it. Besides, it's good for you."

The health gurus of today would have praised it without end, but to us non-Cantonese it was a dreadful drink and we wanted no part of it.

Shang May's bathroom was another surprise. It had the usual bathtub, washbasin, and toilet, but lined up in a row against the wall beside the bathtub were an additional seven enamel washbasins. I asked, "What are the extra washbasins for? Don't you use the regular washbasin?"

"Of course we do, to wash our faces. But the enamel basins are for *hsi p'i ku*, to wash our bottoms."

I never really figured that out and I never asked. Could bottoms not be washed in the bathtub with the rest of the body? Or perhaps they used the enamel basins like bidets. In any case, I thought it quite strange that each of the seven children had his own basin expressly for washing his bottom. Several years later, while living in my uncle's apartment in Shanghai, I found that others too had an aversion to mixing bottoms with other body parts. And certainly not with faces. During the year and a half that I lived there, making an effort not to increase the workload of the family's only servant, I made it a point to wash my own underwear. When my uncle found that I was washing my underpants in the washbasin, he made it clear that that was not acceptable. He immediately saw to it that I was supplied with an enamel washbasin for that purpose.

Of the four of us, Shang May was the only one who elected to return to China after the Communist takeover, to be, in her words, "a part of the new China." The rest of us--all in America for our advanced education as expected-- elected to remain in America to enjoy the opportunities and benefits this country had to offer. When she returned to China in 1951, Shang May had just received her Master's Degree in economics from Bryn Mawr and had been offered generous fellowships for her Ph.D. at both Bryn Mawr and Cornell. I admired her spirit, her determination, and her patriotism, but in the weeks before her departure, whenever we were together, we argued constantly about the direction China was taking. After her return she wrote me frequently, each letter extolling the accomplishments of the new regime.

"As a natural consequence of my background and training, many of my thoughts and acts are against the happiness and well-being of our people. For instance, individualism--so uncontrolled and so without regard for others--love of material comfort, lack of loyalty toward my own country. I hope that when China's interests conflict with my personal interests, I can forgo the latter without any doubts or hesitation."

What noble thoughts they were! I admired her idealism, wished I could be as selfless, even envied her, at the same time knowing I didn't have it in me to give up the life I had known for a greater cause. But as the years went by, her letters sounded more and more like rote Communist propaganda. "We must clear away all imperialistic influences that are harmful to our unity; we must get rid of the reactionary bureaucracy feudalism and other elements that stand in the way of a unified, democratic, and prosperous China. ------This is very difficult, especially under the threat of American imperialism." The words "American imperialism" appeared again and again, along with repeated references to "our glorious leader, Mao Tze tung." There was a constant denigration of all that was American. It seemed she had become fully indoctrinated to the Communist cause. And yet I wondered at the time if her words reflected her own true feelings or were for the eyes of the censor.

With the passage of time, the Communist persecution of all intellectuals, of so-called "capitalists," and of anyone with ties to America, made it inadvisable to continue communication with Shang May. None of us wrote for fear we would further incriminate her. We did not correspond again until after Nixon's China visit in 1972 and the ensuing "rapprochement" between the two countries.

Shang May's first letter to me after almost twenty years of silence included a snapshot. I was living in Australia at the time, in Sydney. I was in the parking garage of our apartment building when I opened her letter. The garage was only dimly lit. Looking at the snapshot, I thought, "Why she's hardly changed at all." Then, with a jolt I realized I was looking not at Shang, but at one of her daughters. Behind her, a little old lady with gray hair, was Shang.

Shang May came to America for a visit in 1981. We had a tearful and wonderful reunion; and as in our teen years, we talked. She had been labeled a capitalist, sent to the countryside for labor among the peasants. Her family had been stripped of all their possessions. Finally, when she had "reformed" and renounced her capitalist background, her English language capability became an asset. She was made an English teacher in the People's Liberation Army. Her degrees in economics were useless in the communist world. But when I asked if she had any regrets about her return to China, if she would have made a different decision, she maintained steadfastly that she was glad she had returned, glad she had been part of the revolution. She excused even her father's death, six weeks after severe beatings by the Red Guard.

I found it hard to believe that Shang May could rationalize her father's death so readily. When I asked her what he had done that was so bad, that had brought on the beatings, she was defensive. "He fought with them when they tried to take his antiques. He should have let them take the things. They were only material possessions after all. It was really his own fault. If he had not resisted and had given in quietly, they would not have hurt him."

My doubts about whether Shang May had truly been fully indoctrinated, or had been just paying lip service to the revolution, were lessened. We suspected that she was a member of the Communist party but never knew for sure. Shang May is gone now. She died in 1995, not of Communist mistreatment, but of pancreatic cancer. At the news of her death I did not shed a tear. She had not been a part of my life for over forty years. But several years ago, at a PAS reunion held in Denver, during a session of remembrance of alumni who had passed on, I was asked to say a few words about Shang May. Without hesitation I stood up. I was eager to tell the others what I knew of her years since leaving PAS.

I started, "Shang May was my best friend," and with no advance warning broke into uncontrollable sobs. I had seen her only once since she had returned to China more than forty years ago, but I could see her as she had been as a teen-age student at PAS, in her strapless gown with her hair swept up, in her gym shorts leading the cheers for our basketball teams. *Two, four, six, eight. Who do we appreciate!* I could see her as she was in college in America, bright, spirited, idealistic and selfless, everything that was good in a young woman. If there had been any disillusionment with the cause she believed in, she did not, would not, admit to it.

I miss her.

Tuesday's child is full of grace. I don't know if Clemy was born on a Tuesday, but she was a Tuesday child nonetheless. Her body was slender, fine-boned; her walk light; her voice soft and lilting. Incredibly, though it has been more than fifty years since we left PAS, she still retains those qualities.

Despite the death of her father early in her life, Clemy was raised in affluence. The family had a lovely multi-courtyard home very near to our North City house. Two of Clemy's older brothers attended Chinese schools. The third, Eddie, started at PAS at the third grade level. Clemy herself started at PAS in the first grade. Though her school life was conducted in English, at home, as was the case with Shang May, all was Chinese. Eddie, the youngest of her brothers, remembers his mother sending him to *my* mother to learn correct western table manners before leaving China to attend college in America.

Edie, on the other hand, had a lifestyle much like mine. Her mother--her adoptive mother--being American, the language of home was English. But she and Clemy shared after-school tutoring sessions in Chinese. Edie was neither cute like Shang, nor graceful like Clemy. She had an awkward walk caused by the bunions she had developed at an early age, and though she was only five feet five-and-a-half, she was considered "big" by Chinese standards. Chinese students would say, "*T'a hao ta kwai erh*!" (She's a big piece!). But whatever she lacked in physical attributes, she more than made up for in personality. She was a good sport and was well liked by both boys and girls. Things "happened" to Edie, and whatever they were, she accepted with good grace and sometimes a good laugh at herself.

In our freshman year she developed a boil on her rear end, her *p'i ku*. For several days in class she sat first on one side of her buttocks, and then on the other, twitching miserably from side to side while the rest of us laughed at her discomfort. But soon she appeared with an inflated rubber inner tube and spent the rest of the week sitting on her "doughnut." This was cause for even greater hilarity, especially when she was seen in her rickshaw riding high in her seat suspended by her doughnut. Even weeks after the offending boil had receded, Edie was greeted with, "Hey Edie, how's your *p'i ku*?"

Edie's rickshaw coolie gave cause for more joking. He was a nice looking enough young man but seemed to be afflicted with a chronic case of flatulence. While transporting Edie in the rickshaw, he broke wind frequently and more than just audibly. Edie would pinch her nose with the fingers of one hand while waving away the air in front of her with the other. While the rest of us did not always hear his indiscretions, we always knew when they had occurred because Edie would make a face and her hands would start waving.

The year we put on the play, *Quality Street*, Edie played the part of a neighboring spinster. In one scene she was supposed to leave the stage in a huff over having been excluded from some choice bit of gossip. She stormed dramatically toward the stage door, but unfortunately could not locate it. Without her glasses she could not see the painted outlines of the door in the makeshift set. Her hands ran along the walls as she groped frantically in search of the doorknob. Her search seemed interminable. Just as laughter was beginning to erupt from the audience, she found it and yanked at it, hard. The walls trembled. Edie left the stage.

As I have said, things "happened" to Edie. Once, after a group of us had been rowing on the North Lake at *Pei Hai,* Edie was the last to leave the rowboat. As she was preparing to climb out, her feet still in the boat, but her hands on the pier, the boat started drifting away. The person getting out of the boat before her had inadvertently pushed outwards as he climbed on shore. Even as one of the boys tried to pull the boat in closer at one end, the other end continued to drift outward in a widening arc. The rest of us watched helplessly while Edie's body stretched ever more horizontally until finally she had to jump feet first into the water. Instead of sympathy, we all broke into laughter. Edie was momentarily angry, but soon saw how funny her predicament had been.

Precisely because she was such a good sport, Edie was often the victim of harmless pranks. One time at the beach while she and some of the others were sunning themselves on a large rock, she fell asleep. As the tide came in, the others returned to dry land, leaving Edie asleep on the rock. When she awoke, she found herself surrounded by water. She was furious and for good reason. There had been no danger as she was a strong swimmer, and the tide had not risen that far, but it was a mean trick, one that would not have been forgiven as readily as Edie forgave.

I too was not above taking advantage of Edie's good nature. In one instance at a school play, to fill in the time between acts when the sets were being changed, I was to sing a solo—"Somewhere Over the Rainbow." Not wanting to do it alone, I corralled Edie into joining me. Edie was a good sport and came out on stage with me, but reluctantly. The two of us stood before the curtain. She knew she was not a singer, and though she made a valiant effort, all the audience as well soon knew it. That did not endear me to Mrs. Wang. Nor should it have. Selfish, self-centered, and totally unconcerned with Edie's image, I had had my moment to shine.

Edie's mother didn't like me. I could sense it. Though she always greeted me politely, I always had a vague feeling of not being completely welcome. Neither of us could know that many years later we would become good friends, and that I would not only see her through her last days but play a major role in laying her to rest. Edie's father had died during the years of the Japanese occupation, and she and her mother had moved to Hong Kong where Edie headed up the USIS (United States Information Service) library. I too was in Hong Kong with my husband who was then a political officer with the U.S. Consulate General. I was a non-working housewife with time on my hands and I visited Mrs. Wang frequently when Edie was at work. As an adult I was no longer bothered by Mrs. Wang's bluntness, which I had found quite intimidating when I was in my teens. In fact I now found it refreshing and even admirable that she said exactly what she thought about anything and anyone. This in direct contrast to my mother's credo of "If you can't say anything nice, don't say it at all."

We were sharing a cup of tea in Mrs. Wang's apartment when she told me how she had felt about me when we were all in Peking. "Did you know I disliked you?"

"Well, I never felt that you particularly *liked* me," I said. "I never felt particularly welcome in your house, but I didn't know that you actually *dis*liked me."

"No, I shouldn't have used that word. I didn't really dislike you at all. It was just that every time Edie came home from your house it was always Marguerite this and Marguerite that, or Mrs. Ch'ien this or Mrs. Ch'ien that. I just got so sick of hearing Edie go on and on about something you'd done or rave about your mother's cake or cookies. And then again, I was jealous, on Edie's behalf. You were prettier, and smarter. None of that bothered Edie. There's not a jealous bone in her body. It didn't bother *her* that you got the lead parts in school performances, or that you got better grades, but it bothered me to see my precious daughter so overshadowed by you."

"I can see why you might have *thought* I overshadowed Edie," I admitted. "In some ways I may have had a higher profile as far as a public image was concerned. But Edie was so much better at sports, and she was a much better dancer, and she was popular. Did you know how I envied Edie?"

"You? You envied Edie?" She was surprised. "What could you have envied Edie for?"

"I envied her because she made friends so easily. Everyone liked her. Girls, boys--oh I don't mean in a romantic way--parents, just everyone. People just seemed to be drawn to her. I, on the other hand, had a hard time making new friends, though I didn't discover that until I left home for Shanghai. In fact, during the period we were in Shanghai together, it was always Edie who made the friends and I was the hanger-on. I always felt that *our* friends were really hers, not mine."

"That was another thing." Mrs. Wang added. "When we finally decided to send Edie to Shanghai to study at St. John's, I thought we had finally gotten her away from you."

"And then I went too," I added, laughing.

"Oh yes. You had to follow. I had to resign myself to that. The other thing was, you were always so infernally proper. Your manners were always impeccable and I couldn't really fault you anywhere. I always remember the time I insisted that there should be guest towels in Edie's bathroom. Edie couldn't see why she needed guest towels. She argued that the only people who used her bathroom were her friends, you and Clemy and Shang. 'And they're not really guests,' she said."

"I told her, 'Marguerite will use them.' I was quite sure you would."

"And of course I *did*." I laughed. "I remember, Edie was so annoyed with me. And I couldn't get over why she was so mad. I *was* a guest after all. And what were the towels there for if not to be used?"

"Of course they were to be used. She was mad because you had proved that I was right."

Mrs. Wang died while we were in Hong Kong. During her last days, when the doctors said she could go at any time, Edie and a succession of friends kept a twenty-four hour vigil at Mrs. Wang's bedside. Many an hour I sat in the hospital beside her frail body, listening to the wheeze of her labored breathing. The "any time" dragged into several weeks, but finally she was gone. Edie could not bear the thought of some unknown coolie handling her mother's body. She asked Effie Lim, another childhood friend, and me if we would wash her mother's body. We couldn't refuse.

Effie and I went to the funeral home where we found Mrs. Wang laid out on a makeshift gurney. Her naked body was covered with a white sheet that was more gray than white. The attendant provided us with towels and with soap and hot water in two enamel washbasins. Together, Effie and I washed the shrunken figure. I like to think it was done with love, but for me it was not so. The body before me was not the Mrs. Wang I knew, the one who had become my friend. It was a cadaver, no more no less, a body to be cleaned and prepared for burial as best we could. We washed her feet, her legs, cleaned away the secretions of death. It was not the way I would have chosen to say our last goodbyes.

Chapter 11
First Love

WHEN LILY, MY BIOLOGICAL SISTER in Shanghai, had asked me if I had a boyfriend, I don't know why I said no. Possibly it was an instinctive negative reaction on my part. Her question was intrusive, and I had no wish to share that part of my life with her. In fact I *had* had a boyfriend in Peking. My teenage romance gave me some of the happiest moments of my young life, and also some of the most miserable. It began at the end of my freshman year, when I was fourteen, and ended at the end of my junior year. In between there was what seemed to me a long hiatus of abject misery for me when my boyfriend abandoned me for another girl. Until that time I don't believe there had been an unhappy moment in my life, but suddenly my whole world fell apart. There were no words that marked our breakup. One day he was mine; the next day he was not. He was my first love, and I was as much in love as only a teenage girl can be. I remember vividly the pain and emotional devastation of the first days and weeks after discovering his defection.

The lights in the auditorium were dim. It was the last dance and they were playing "Lights Out, Sweetheart." The music was slow and romantic but it was the words that echoed in my brain. *Lights ou t sweetheart, one more perfect day is through.* It hadn't been perfect for me. Throughout the day I had been dreading it. I was dancing with

Clemy's brother Eddie. He was saying something, I don't know what. His words weren't registering; just sounds with no meaning. My mind was numb; my senses were numb. The dancers around us merged into a kaleidoscopic jumble. My feet moved, but I barely heard the music. I had this sick feeling at the pit of my stomach. All I could think of was Allan and Janet. Even with the lights dimmed I could see them clearly. And when I couldn't see them, I was still seeing them. They were danc-ing cheek-to-cheek, he holding her very close, she looking dreamy with eyes half closed. I couldn't bear to look at them; I couldn't stop looking at them. *We've reached the hour of parting, so kiss me tenderly. And when we part, close your eyes and think of me.* I knew the words so well. But this time the words were not for me. It wasn't me he'd be kissing, or me he'd be thinking of. But I would be thinking of him. Not just that night, but in the days, weeks, and months that followed. Why had he done this? What had gone wrong? He was *my* boyfriend; he *had been* my boyfriend.

All that was over now. Weeks before, during recess, Edie and Clemy had been looking out the window of our classroom and talking in hushed tones. "What on earth are you two whispering about?" I had asked. "What's going on out there?"

They seemed flustered and insisted it was nothing, but I wanted to see for myself. Curious, I walked over to the window and looked out. At first glance I saw nothing unusual. Some children shooting baskets on the basketball court, a few couples walking around the building. But suddenly Allan and Janet came into focus. I was stunned. They weren't holding hands; their actions were innocuous. But at PAS, walking around the building at recess was what the couples who were going steady did. Mostly it was the older students, and mostly it was the American couples. Allan was a junior; Janet a senior I was only a sophomore and had never walked around the building with a boy at re-cess or any other time. When I saw them I felt a tightening in my chest. I wanted to close my eyes to shut out everything. I could feel Edie's and Clemy's eyes on me, feeling sorry for me, wondering how I would react. I looked at them, but no words came out.

Clemy tried to dismiss what we had all seen, "They probably just have something they need to discuss."

But I knew better. Somehow I knew it was more than that.
Edie and Clemy knew it too. At first they tried to console me, but what
could they say? "Why should you care? He's not the only boy around."
But for me he *was* the only boy. The others who hovered around me I
wanted no part of. For weeks after that, Shang, Edie and Clemy continued their efforts to console me. "What's so great about him anyway? I
don't see what you see in him anyway. He's not that good looking. He's
not that smart."

I told myself they were right. He didn't have the slick good
looks of John Shoemaker, the polished manners of Sammy Young, the
brains of Roger Creighton. He wasn't a personality kid like Willie Allston. He was not a leader. He was a good athlete, but in no way a star.
He was a good dancer, but there were others who were better. Why
should I care? But I did. My friends could see me hurting. Soon they
stopped even mentioning his name, or Janet's.

At home I thought a lot about Janet. What did she have that I
did not? I wanted to find fault with her, but other than that she had stolen
my boyfriend, how could I fault her for being what she was? She was
American; tall, almost as tall as Allan, and very fair. She had beautiful
long blonde hair and a lovely figure. Altogether she was an attractive
young woman, whereas I was an immature young girl. What did I have
to offer? Nothing. The inflated self-esteem I had lived with from childhood was suddenly stripped away. I was nothing. I was less than nothing.

In the months that followed Allan dropped out of our group.
My life went on, but movies were less fun; picnics were less fun; and all
the things we'd done before seemed lifeless without him. I could not
bring myself to attend the next school dance, could not bear the thought
of watching them together. At the last minute I complained of feeling
sick and stayed at home, mired in my own misery. At school I avoided
passing Allan in the halls. When our paths did cross I looked the other
way. He did the same. But all things pass. At the end of that school
year, less than four months after Allan had deserted me, Janet graduated.
He took her to the Senior Prom. A few weeks later she was gone.

I first met Allan when I entered the eighth grade at PAS. He
and his family had arrived in Peking from Australia the year before.

They were Australian Chinese. His father had migrated to Australia from Canton in his late teens in search of fame and fortune in the gold fields. Though he found neither, as a successful vegetable farmer supplying fresh foods for the Victoria border area, he was able to bring up five children in comfort. The family's move to Peking after his retirement was made with the intention of reestablishing his children's roots in their native country.

It was not until my freshman year that I started to notice Allan. He had this odd Australian accent that everyone teased him about. I had never heard an Australian accent before and kind of liked it. It made him different. I liked his looks. He wasn't what I thought of as handsome, but he was nice looking, and he was taller than most of the other Chinese boys. There was a shyness in his manner that was somehow appealing. In the winter he often wore a brown sport jacket with kick pleats at the sides that made him look much smarter than the other boys in their sweaters. I don't know at what point we started becoming aware of each other I know that at any gathering, I would find my eyes seeking him out. When our eyes met, which they often did, we would both hastily look away. We were both shy, both inhibited. But somehow we started gravitating toward each other. Allan started coming to the house a lot. He came looking for Luther, but I sensed it was to see me. I hung around them as long as I could without appearing to be interested, but he and Luther would go off somewhere on their bikes leaving me behind. At school games, if neither of us was playing, Allan and I would end up sitting beside each other, our thighs touching, but neither of us acknowledging the search for closeness. At school parties he danced with me often. When he put his cheek tentatively against my forehead, I wanted it to be forever. From then on we danced cheek-to-cheek. And the last dance at every party was reserved for each other. At the movies, though we were always in a group, somehow we would be sitting together, conscious of the warmth of the other's arm, resting on the armrest between us. Soon he was taking my hand in his. All our friends recognized that we had become "steadies."

But even when we were going steady we seldom went out alone. However, within the group it was accepted that Allan and I would pair off. When we did go out alone it was usually to the movies, both of us riding our bicycles to and from. When we went to school dances or to private parties, Allan would pick me up and see me home; me in a rickshaw; he following behind on his bicycle. Once, much to my dismay, he came on his older brother's motorcycle. I had never been on a motorcycle before, and though the thought of riding on the back of one was in itself an exciting adventure, the prospect of doing so in a long billowy evening dress was somewhat daunting. Nevertheless, I hitched my skirt up as best I could to keep the yards of rose-colored net from getting caught in the wheel spokes. With my arms wrapped tightly around his waist we went roaring through the Peking *hut'ungs* leaving clouds of dust behind us. We arrived at the school dance thoroughly windblown and dusty, but I was happier than any girl had a right to be.

Another night, another school dance. Willie Allston, Allan's best friend at the time, was the one to tell me what the evening had in store. "Guess what's going to happen tonight," he said, as if announcing some momentous news. "He's going to kiss you."

At that, I think my heart must actually have skipped a beat but I prodded, "How do *you* know what he's going to do?"

"Because he told me, that's how." Willie said.

Willie and I were dancing when he had dropped this piece of information on me. Riding home in a rickshaw at the end of the evening with both Willie and Allan behind on their bicycles, I grew more and more nervous. The rickshaw pulled off Hatamen Street and rounded the corner into Hsi Tsung Pu Hutung. As we drew nearer to my house, I could feel the thumping in my chest. I had to keep on taking deep breaths to calm myself. I was fifteen, had never been kissed, and wondered if it was really going to happen or if Willie had just been making it all up..

When we reached the house, I stepped out of the rickshaw, slightly shaky with anticipation. The thumping in my chest had stopped, but I found myself holding my breath. Allan got off his bicycle and with a kick of his foot propped it up on its own stand. I had no idea what to expect or what I should do. I reached for the doorbell as I normally would have, and it was only then that he pulled my hand back and turned me around to face him. Overcome with shyness, I looked not at him but at my feet. Then he said something totally unromantic, like "When you take a girl home you're supposed to kiss her goodnight."

Since I did not have the good sense to raise my head, he had to crook his neck to kiss me from the side. But then, blessedly, instinct took over. I lifted my head; he held my face between his hands and kissed me once again. Other than his lips meeting mine and lingering for one brief moment, there was no embrace. My arms remained at my sides. I don't remember if either of us said another word. I do recall suddenly being conscious of the rickshaw coolie's presence, and of Willie Allston, still on his bicycle with one foot on the ground, watching this whole awkward moment. I don't know if it was Allan or I who rang the doorbell, but our houseboy, his eyes heavy with sleep, opened the gate and let me in.

When the gate closed behind me, I walked in a trance through the darkened courtyards to my room. Lying in bed that night my head was full of romantic dreams. I brushed my fingers across my lips, trying to recapture that first kiss, but it was gone. It had not been in the least bit romantic, and in retrospect I could imagine that Willie, watching us, must have had a silly grin on his face. In the weeks and months that followed, though Allan and I seldom went out alone, there were other kisses in other settings. They were sweet, romantic kisses, no longer awkward, but each one equally chaste as the first.

But then there was Janet.

After Janet left Peking, Allan rejoined our group. Sometimes I caught him looking at me, but I pointedly looked away. He started coming to the house again, looking for Luther. At the movies, or at school games, if it looked as if we might be thrown together, I moved so that someone else would be between us. At school parties he danced with me often, but when he leaned his head toward mine, I drew away. I was fiercely proud, and my pride would not let me show that I still cared. I could not let him think that after dropping me, he could simply pick me up again when it pleased him. I could not reach out to him. He would have to reach out to me. Neither of us did a thing.

It was the play that brought us back together. When he and I were cast in the two leading roles of *Quality Street*, we were once again thrown together. At daily rehearsals he was the dashing hero who had deserted me and gone off to the Napoleonic wars. On his return, he realizes I am his true love. He is supposed to look at me with adoration. He must beg me for forgiveness. In the final scene, as hero and heroine confess their love, he kisses me, a quick uncertain peck. Margaret, directing, complains. "Come on, Allan. You can do better than that. Can't you make it look more real? Do it again and hold it just a bit longer." He kisses me again. In the front row of the auditorium someone shouts, "Hey, Allan" and sings out loud and clear, "*Happy days are here again.*"

God was in his world, and in my world all was right again.

For me, it was as if Janet had never been. Throughout our teenage romance I have no recollection whatsoever of what we talked about. About the things we did? School activities? Our friends? Our teachers? Perhaps we talked of the movies we had seen, or the upcoming baseball game, or of what we would do over the weekend. Certainly we did not talk about our feelings. No words of love were ever spoken   and we were more inhibited than most.

A few weeks after the curtain went down on *Quality Street*, we both attended a dance at the home of one of his classmates, Bessie Liang. Between dances, with our fingers interlocked, Allan and I walked along the long covered gallery that ran around the periphery of Bessie's garden. It was a moonlit night, for I remember how bright the garden was, and how, through the fretted borders of the corridor I could clearly see the wisteria vines that twined around the garden trellis. An occasional firefly flitted by. We sat on the long couch at the far end of the garden. Looking across the flowers we could see the dancers through the open windows of the living room. We sat there hand in hand in the semi-darkness, just talking. Of what I can't recall. Perhaps of something funny that had occurred that day; perhaps of the refreshments that had just been served; perhaps of a movie we had just seen, or one we wanted to see. Maybe we just talked about the weather. The only thing I do remember is that he told me then that I was the only one he had ever really cared for. In our entire relationship, it was the only time that either he or I had said a word about our feelings.

Janet faded further into the distance.

At the end of that summer Allan left Peking to attend college in Shanghai. Though we corresponded intermittently, our high school romance came to an end. Back then, in my high school days, there had been no "how-to's" for teenagers on love and romance. On-screen passion was expressed by waves crashing upon the shores or torrential rains punctuated by flashes of lightning. Movie kisses were less than graphic.

Lips were obscured by a cheek, a chin, or the back of a man's head. I knew nothing of parted lips, had never known the kind of kissing that could stir desire, had never felt the kind of touching that could awaken passion. In me, all lay dormant. I was happy and content with the simple love I knew. I looked for nothing more, needed nothing more.

But innocence is not forever.

After Allan there were other boys, other men, each leading me a little further down the path away from innocence. In Shanghai there was Stephen, long and lean with mooning eyes, who gave me my first real kiss. There was Kenneth, smooth, polished, who even through the war years was flush with money. He took me to expensive places for tea and dancing. And there was Philip, the only one who ever called me Maggie. On clear nights we went up to the rooftop of my apartment and sat on the stoop or leaned on the parapet watching the stars. With his arms around me he sang me love songs, or rather, *a* love song, always the same one. *Someday when I'm awfully low, when the world is cold, I will feel a glow just thinking of you, and the way you look tonight.*

Back in Peking there was Kirk, who spoke not a word of English. With him I overnighted twice in our country home in the Western Hills. We were stranded, without intent, and through no fault of our own. It raised many eyebrows and caused some conjecture even among my good friends, but no one really doubted my virtue. Later, in America there were still others. There was fun, romance, and good times, but never once did I even imagine that I was in love with any. I had joy in each relationship while it was in progress; felt no loss when it was over. But in between boyfriends I would find thoughts of Allan resurfacing. I often wondered, "What if? What would it have been like if we had lived out our brief romance?" I fantasized.

It was not until I met Horace, my first husband, and found a deeper enduring love, that I finally put aside those fantasies and all the dreams that went with the teenage love I had once known. But through the years, while those other boyfriends of past years have faded almost into nothingness, that first love, pristine, pure and innocent, remains sweet in memory.

Chapter 12
The Western Hills

FOR OUR FAMILY, summer meant the Western Hills. As soon as school
was out, the family piled into my mother's large luxurious Auburn and
headed for "the Hills." Mother drove and my father sat beside her with
me on his lap. Richard, Lois, and Luther sat in the back, their laps piled
with last-minute items they had forgotten to pack. The cook and amah
had been dispatched earlier by train, he to make sure we had a good meal
waiting for us, and she to make up the beds and to help our resident caretaker prepare the rooms for our arrival.

The Western Hills were only fifteen miles outside the city, but it
sometimes took us more than two hours to make the trip because we had
to make a stop at *T'ien Feng*, the family general store just inside *Hsi
Chih Men*, the main west gate of the city. There Mother ran through the
list of dry foods we needed. The manager always gave me a small bag of
rock sugar that I then sucked on for the rest of the trip. The store be-
longed to the Ch'ien family, and each branch of the family received some
income from it. I am not sure of all the things it stocked but do remember the shallow baskets in which rice, millet, and flour were displayed. I
recall also the rows of large tea canisters on the shelves behind the
counter, as well as the multiple small drawers of medicines and herbs.
Once everything had been loaded into the trunk of the car, we began the

long, dusty drive. The roads were unpaved and the smallest gust of wind sent clouds of dust into the air. We didn't mind. In Peking one was used to dust.

As we approach the village below our house, Tiger's Head, the rock formation at the peak of the hill, is silhouetted against a cloudless blue sky. *Why did they call it Tiger's Head? It always looked more like a lion's head to me.* The villagers stop their chores and wave to us as we drive by. Children are playing with stones in the riverbed nearby. Several donkeys are tethered under the shade trees. My eyes search for my favorite donkey among them but it is not there. The donkeys' handlers are beaming, happy to note the arrival of steady summer customers. The dusty journey behind us, I take a deep breath and feel as if I will burst with joy and anticipation just thinking of the glorious weeks ahead. I want to shout, "We're here; we're here!" Mother zooms up the driveway and parks the car on the landing. I am off my father's lap in an instant and out of the car, anxious to be the first to get up to the house. The double gates are already opened wide awaiting our arrival. I run up the wide center path that leads up to the house but can't resist stopping to check out the two grape arbors. The grape clusters are still hard and green. The apricots too have not yet ripened. I must wait for those. Resigned, I continue to the house and settle myself on the steps, waiting for the others to reach me.

Our Western Hills house was one of the lowest ones on the hill

Western Hills house. I am child at right.

but was still high enough to catch a good breeze. Looking upward from the front gate, the house looked quite imposing, a large stone house with colorful awnings at all the windows. It had originally been planned as a year-round getaway for the family, but though we went there often in the spring and fall, we were never able to use it during the winter months. My parents had envisioned cozy winter evenings by a roaring fire, but unfortunately the roaring fire never materialized. The fireplace never drew properly and was constantly being worked on by masons and assorted workmen. Several times we were assured that the problem had been corrected. The logs would be laid with care--always far to the back of the fireplace--and lit with great expectations. We would watch hopefully as the first curls of smoke seemed to be heading up the chimney, but invariably, as in all the preceding times, clouds of smoke would soon spew forth and leave us coughing and running from the room. The ceiling and walls had to be repainted each time and the stone face of the fireplace scrubbed clean. My parents finally gave up all hope of using the house in the winter months.

Beside the living room was the dining room, which for some strange reason was twice the size of the living room. A large mahogany table, looking quite incongruous in a warm-weather retreat filled with wicker and rattan, sat there in singular splendor. Twelve chairs surrounded the table as if waiting for the convening of a corporate board. In all our years in China, I don't remember eating a single meal in that dining room. A jigsaw puzzle was sometimes spread out on the mahogany table, and occasionally one or the other of us would add a piece or two, but other than that, the dining room was never used. Instead, we always ate on the screened porch that surrounded the house on three sides. The porch was large, but not having been designed for dining, the table at which a dozen or more people were often seated had to be crowded into one corner. It was a struggle to get in and out of our seats at the table, and there was always much squeezing behind chairs and climbing over legs. Sometimes we children crawled under the table to get to our seats. No one minded. No matter how hot it was outside, there was always a cool breeze on that corner of the house, and even if it was pouring rain— which happened rarely—we never retreated to the dining room. Instead, the coolie would let down the rattan blinds (they hung outside the screens), and the light spray that seeped through the blinds, far from disturbing us, was welcomed as an extra coolant in the hot days of summer.

Except for sleeping, we literally lived on the porch. Though the adults went to their bedrooms for their afternoon naps, I always napped on the rattan couch at the far end of the porch. By then the coolie would have completed his afternoon routine of lowering all the rattan blinds that surrounded the porch and have come by several times with his sprinkling can to water the floor. The porous gray tiles soaked up the water and cooled the porch quickly. The strident shrieks of the cicadas filled the summer air, but the never-ending sound bothered me not at all. Sheltered from the hot afternoon sun, I was soon fast asleep.

In the evenings, when the dinner table had been cleared, and there was only the faint sound of dishes being washed in the kitchen at the back of the house, the whole family would pull the porch chairs up to the railing. Resting our feet on the low porch wall, we would sing. Of all my many memories of the Western Hills, those evenings are the ones I cherish most. By then the village below would have grown quiet. No longer was there the sound of children playing. Even the cicadas were silent. Except for an occasional dog's bark, no sounds broke the peaceful silence. As twilight turned to dark, and here and there the glow of fire-flies flickered in the night, we sang. We sang the songs my mother had taught us, old favorites like "Love's Old Sweet Song," "In the Gloam-ing," "There's a Long Long Trail A-winding," and "Beautiful Dreamer." Mother did not have a strong voice, but it was clear and true. Richard had a fine baritone, and he and Daddy were both good at harmonizing. Lois, Luther, and I knew all the words, and we sang along. Sometimes Mother played her mandolin, or Richard played his harmonica. Often he joined us in the melody, but most of the time he wove his notes in and around the tune, creating his own complement to our voices. I marveled at how he could do this, how he knew which notes to play. In the bare hills, sounds travel far, and families who lived both above and below us say they sat in their own gardens or on their own porches each evening waiting for the Ch'ien family concert to begin. Just remembering those long-ago evenings, I can still hear our voices drifting through the hills. *Just a song at twilight, when the lights are low, and the flickering shad-ows, softly come and go...*

When singing was over, it was bedtime for us children. We were always told to go to the bathroom before we went to our rooms up-stairs. The bathroom was around the corner of the porch on the far end of the house, the opposite end from the dining table corner, and was a long way from the upstairs bedrooms. With no electricity, it could be a long, dark walk even with a lighted candle. As a child I remember being afraid to walk down the long porch to the far end of the house after night-fall for fear a fox fairy would appear before me. During the day, Luther and I would often sit on the kitchen stoop behind the house, enthralled by the amah's stories of fox fairies, but when darkness came, I would imagine the foxes emerging from one of the many mounded tombs that dotted the area and changing into human form. I could almost see the beautiful maiden who might accost me. Would she try to lure me into a tomb with her, or would she change back to her fox form before my eyes and dart away into the night? Either prospect was frightening to a small child, and I made sure that I made a last trip to the toilet before the last light of day had faded. If it was after dark that I was reminded to "go," I would always claim that I had already been even if I hadn't. I knew I could always use the chamber pot in the bedroom.

The bathroom actually consisted of two separate rooms. One was no more than a small dark cubicle and held only a toilet. The other—I called it "the fancy bathroom"—contained washbasin, bathtub, and toilet, with modern plumbing fixtures. Both washbasin and tub had hot and cold spigots, and the toilet had a tank with a flushing mechanism. However, at the time there was no electricity *or* running water in the Western Hills and the plumbing fixtures served no useful purpose. They were just for show. All our water came from the well in the village below and was carried to the house by a coolie, two rush buckets on either end of a pole slung over his shoulders, each one holding not more than three or four gallons of water. It was backbreaking labor. The water was stored in large earthenware crocks. There was one in the kitchen, one in the small toilet room, and one in the fancy bathroom. For both washing and for flushing the toilet, we ladled water from the crocks with tin ladles. The rest of us were quite satisfied with this arrangement, but this was not good enough for my mother. She was determined to have a toilet that would flush as it was meant to.

Looking back, I find it hard to understand her obsession with something so inconsequential. It seemed so incongruous to her nature. I have never known another woman who was as good and as kind as she was, or one who cared so deeply about other people. Yet, within her were her own contradictions. Despite her deep concern for the welfare of the poor and downtrodden, she was not above enjoying the fruits of their hard labor and the privileges and benefits that money provided.

To flush her toilet she had a second story built above the bathroom in which was installed a large water tank. By filling the second-story tank, the water could then flow downward into the toilet tank in our bathroom. We could then flush the toilet with a simple push on the handle. What luxury that was! A real flush toilet in a countryside that had no running water! And how many many more trips per day up and down the hillside for the water carrier! At least one trip for each flush of the toilet, whereas two tin ladles from the crock would have done the job! Even I, still a child, felt guilty whenever I flushed.

The enclosed part of the Western Hills property comprised about one and a half acres, although I know we owned land outside the walls as well. Being on a hillside, the land was terraced; six terraces in all, each one fully planted with trees, shrubs, and flowers. From the front gate with its own tiled roof a wide central pathway led upward through each terrace up to the house itself which was located halfway between the fourth and fifth terraces. Narrower service walkways led up each side of the property for workmen and vendors. The one on the right was used routinely by the gardener whose cottage and a vegetable garden were on that side of the second terrace. The various vendors also used the right walkway, as did the villagers who came to my mother's weekly clinics. The walkway on the left served no useful purpose whatsoever except to provide the symmetry that the Chinese find so essential. It was, however, used by the water coolie when watering the trees and plants on the left side. Even the camels that delivered the coal came up the walk on the right.

T'ing tze **at our Western Hills house**

Coal delivery days were exciting ones. The *t'ing tze* at the lower corner of the first terrace commanded an excellent view of the village below, and Luther and I would sit there watching impatiently for the camels' arrival. Even after we had spotted them, it seemed an eternity before they made their way up to the house. But finally they came plodding up the walk, the camel handlers guiding them through the front gate and up the side walkway. They finally came to rest beside the low garden wall behind the house that separated the kitchen from the vegetable garden. Luther and I could hardly wait until the coal had been unloaded and we could climb aboard them and sit between their double humps. Sometimes Luther would get the camel driver to let him ride one of the camels back down to the gate, but just the thought of being that high up in the air, being tilted dangerously forward as the camels descended each flight of terrace stairs, was not for me.

The entire length of the center walkway of the second terrace was covered by a long wisteria arbor, and on each side, at right angles to the wisteria, against the back wall, were the two grape arbors, one of white grapes (the elongated kind that I have never seen in this country), and the other of red. When the wisteria was in bloom, the flowers hung in dense clusters within the arbor, creating a sheltering bower of green leaves and purple blossoms. Our cook routinely gathered some of the blossoms, mixing the petals with honey and sugar to use as a filling for small round Chinese pastries. None of our family developed a taste for the wisteria pastries, but the ones uneaten by the family were welcomed by the servants and were certainly not begrudged by us. For Luther and me, the wisteria arbor was more interesting as a source of sport. We much preferred trying to catch the bumblebees that buzzed around the vine.

Also on that terrace was my father's library and beside it the schoolroom. Even during summer vacation, we had our Chinese lessons. English lessons with Mother were suspended for the summer, but Chinese was still a must--two hours every morning. At the time I gave no thought to where the Chinese tutor came from, but assume my father arranged for him to come from the city. I don't know where he stayed or where he took his meals, only that he appeared each morning to give us our lessons.

The summer when Richard graduated from high school, when I was six, he too was being tutored in Chinese. His tutoring was much more stringent than Luther's and mine. Richard had graduated from high school early, at sixteen, and until that time had had his entire education at PAS, in the English language. Because he was so young, Second Uncle, his birth father, had requested that Richard spend a year in Shanghai with them, his natural family, before going on to Scotland. Too late, my father realized that Second Uncle would be extremely upset that a child of his had not been given a solid Chinese education. Hence, the intense belated tutoring for Richard. I felt so sorry for him. Instead of relaxing and enjoying his vacation with the rest of the family, he was relegated to a small courtyard in the temple below, the same one occupied by my friend Edie's family. There, he and Harvey Liu, a friend whose Chinese was also deemed inadequate by *his* parents, spent their days glued to their Chinese studies under the strict supervision of an iron-willed tutor.

The rest of the family hardly saw Richard at all that summer, but I would often go down to the temple to visit him. I did miss having my big brother around, but I really went to see Harvey, on whom at age six I had a childish crush. I always timed my visits to arrive at lunchtime when I would be guaranteed a good Chinese meal, for the servant who had been hired to wait on the two boys was an excellent cook. Even as a small child I enjoyed Chinese food more than western, and up at the big house we always had western food. It was in that small temple courtyard that I first learned how delicious eggplant could be. The bland mushy vegetable underwent a miraculous metamorphosis in a pungent, garlic-laden sweet and sour sauce.

At the end of the summer, Richard was packed off to Shanghai. As expected, Second Uncle was unhappy that *his* son (Richard was still *his* son even though he had been adopted by my father in the traditional Chinese *kuo chi* arrangement) was deficient in his native language. He compared him unfavorably with his other son Winston who had had a Chinese education.

Richard did not enjoy the year he spent in Shanghai under the watchful eyes of his birth parents. He was keenly aware of their disappointment in him and worked hard at his Chinese studies. But to recoup twelve years of Chinese in a single year was not possible. At the end of that year, he went off to Scotland to the Royal Technical College in Glasgow where he completed a four-year course in mechanical engineering. Throughout those years my father had the Chinese newspaper mailed to him regularly so that Richard would not forget his Chinese. On my parents' one visit to him during those years, my father was not happy to find those papers stacked in a corner of his bedroom, unopened. *Richard, how could you be so stupid, not to get rid of the newspapers before Daddy and Mother arrived?*

The third terrace of the Western Hills property was filled with flowers, along the walkway, along the terrace walls, and in formal beds. The brilliant colors of the portulaca and the zinnias, the masses of nasturtiums, the marguerites, the red salvia, the four-o-clocks, all glowed like neon lights against the dry brown earth. Looking back, it is hard for me to imagine how the gardener kept things growing in the dry heat of summer. Peking was a dry city and the Western Hills were likewise dry. Rainy days were infrequent. Though the distance to the public well was perhaps little more than an eighth of a mile, the last two hundred yards leading to our hillside property were up a steady incline. Despite my mother's concern for the poverty she saw around her, in planning her garden perhaps she had become desensitized to the sight of the coolie plodding from dawn to dusk from well to house and back again.

On that same flowered terrace was a large apricot tree. Every summer when the tree was loaded with fruit, Mother would start her annual jam-making project. She would allow Luther and me each to invite a friend, and the four of us would be assigned to gather the apricots. Each with a basket over an arm, we climbed the spreading branches of the tree. Many of the apricots never reached our baskets, as we ate a great many of those we picked. But there were three more large trees on the last terrace so we had apricots to spare.

In those days I had frequent nosebleeds that seemed to occur more often when we were in the Hills, and were especially bad during apricot season. The blood ran out of my nose like a spigot and couldn't be stopped until I had lain down for at least half an hour with my chin in the air and the amah applying wet towels to my forehead and the back of my neck. She begged my mother not to allow me to eat apricots, claiming that they overheated my system and were the cause of my nosebleeds. Mother didn't place much credence in Chinese theories on the various foods that caused "rising fires" (*shang huo*) in the system but passed the amah's concerns to me nonetheless. I, however, was not about to heed the words of the amah and continued to gorge myself on apricots and to endure the almost daily nosebleeds.

Poor amah! We children paid not the slightest attention to her pleading. Whenever she saw us heading for the large mulberry tree on the top terrace, she would let out a groan and cry out after us, "Please, please don't get them on your clothes!" What wasted words those were!

The spreading branches of the mulberry tree hung over the caretaker's cottage that was located on the kitchen terrace but whose roof was flush with the low wall on the terrace above. It was easily accessible from the wall, and Luther and I would clamber onto it and sit in the shade of the large tree. When the mulberries were ripe and plump, we lay on our backs picking any berries that were within easy reach and staining our hands and clothing with mulberry juice. The amah had to cope with the laundry.

It was also on this flat roof in the shade of the mulberry tree that we worked the sticky glue to catch cicadas. The cook made us this special glue from raw dough that he rinsed and rinsed until all the starch was gone and only a sticky glob remained. We then rolled it into little balls that we stuck on the end of bamboo poles. Armed with these we would track down the cicadas, which were easy to locate by the sound of their buzzing wings. The sticky substance stuck easily to the motionless bodies of the cicadas, and once found, the hapless cicadas were ours. We then released them inside our screened porch, but when confined, the cicadas became inert. They clung to the screen, motionless and soundless until given their freedom. We had no luck with fireflies either; like the cicadas, they refused to perform in confinement.

The last terrace on the property held the tennis court. The court was clay, and in the dry climate of the Hills had to be watered frequently. More work for the water coolie. It also had to be rolled regularly with a large water-filled cylinder about three feet long and two feet in diameter. This was heavy work. The court was separated from a row of apricot trees by a low stone wall. My parents and some of their friends often had afternoon tea under the apricot trees. I remember clearly sitting on the stone wall while the adults sat at a table with tea and cake and cucumber sandwiches spread before them on a white linen tablecloth. Yet I have no picture at all of my parents on the tennis court. Was my mother in the tennis garb that was common then? A longish white skirt? Was my father in white flannel trousers? In my memory I see him only in his Chinese robes. He cannot have played in those. I cannot see either of them at all. Yet I know they both played because Mother used to tell me that my father never liked playing with her because she always beat him.

My parents had originally planned to put a swimming pool on the tennis court level, but this never materialized. *Another indulgence of the filthy rich, to even think of a swimming pool in an area that was without running water.* Years after the construction of the house, when electricity had finally reached the Western Hills, they had a well drilled on the lowest terrace. They always referred to it as an artesian well. Electrically powered pumps at each succeeding terrace were to have pumped water up to the house and farther up to the projected swimming pool. Unfortunately, though there was some water in the well, there was never enough to pump upward. The well ended up serving only as a handy spot--and a very expensive one--for cooling watermelons. The well was not a total loss, however. During the war, when we were surviving only by selling off our possessions one at a time and had reached the point of having little left to sell, we had the pipes dug up and sold for their metal value.

The summers spent at the Western Hills were idyllic times for us children. Many an afternoon, after naptime, we went on donkey rides with our friends. The donkeys all had bells around their halters and when we set off on our donkey expeditions we made a fine tinkling procession. First, down to the foot of our hill via a narrow footpath that had been there long before a wider road was built for Mother's car. Then under the large shade trees leading to the temple below. Under the trees, tiny green worms hung from their own silken cords, and I always urged Luther to lead the way so they would stick to him instead of me. I hated to go first anyway because I could never get the donkeys to obey me. When the coolies yelled "dutt, dutt," the donkeys obediently turned left, and when they cried, "wo-o-h, wo-o-h," they went right, or perhaps it was the other way around, but no matter how hard I yelled or pulled on the reins, my donkey always went straight ahead. I couldn't see how the donkeys could be expected to get their instructions straight. If "dutt" meant left, and "wo-o-oh" meant right, then why did a long drawn out "wo-o-o-h" mean to halt, and why did a sharp smack on the rump, combined with a crisp "dutt woh, dutt woh," make them gallop? I concluded that donkeys were stupid animals.

We always rode past many mounded gravesites, each with its own low double doors, long since sealed. They were not a part of any planned cemetery. They were simply there among the fields, untended, the resting places of unknowns from an unknown past. And then, on through fields of corn into the open countryside. Usually we went

wherever the coolies led us, but sometimes we specified that we go to the spot where the red clay used for pottery and bricks could be found. We would carry an empty bucket, which we filled with the red dirt, and carted it home to mold into clay heads for puppets. Clay figures were sold in the toy stores, but it was fun to make the heads ourselves. The clay had a sticky quality and after mixing it with water, it was a simple matter to press it into the molds that we bought. When partially dried, they came out of the molds easily and then were left in the sun to dry completely. Some were people faces; others of the pig or monkey figures that are such important characters in the legendary Chinese story, *Hsi Yiu Chi,* "Journey to the Western World." Of those that didn't crack apart in the hot sun, we chose the best and painted them in brilliant colors. The amah made them clothing, and the puppets were complete. Most of the time we did nothing with them at all. The fun was in the making.

Many afternoons we went down to the riverbed at the foot of the hill to look for the round chalky stones that were soft enough to draw with. Some were pink; some gray, some brown; and some almost white. With a supply of these we could actually make multicolored drawings. We left many a work of art on the larger rocks of the riverbed for wind and weather to wear away.

Other days, with our bathing suits under our clothes, we headed for the "gully." Looking back, I think of the unspoken dress code we followed in those days. While peasant children of our own age ran about with only their bottoms covered, and tiny tots staggered about completely naked in the summer heat, we of the gentry were always "properly" clothed. Even the boys never shed their shirts until we were actually at the little swimming hole half way up the gully.

The gully started behind the hotel that was in the village at the foot of the hill. A path bordered the gully, but as path and gully climbed uphill, there was an ever-widening distance between the two until at the top of the hill there was about a ten-foot drop from the path to the gully below. At the top the water gushed through and over the rocks in the hillside, its source invisible from the upper end of the path. I have seen and walked in two gorges in my adult life, the Taroko Gorge in Taiwan, one of Taiwan's scenic highlights, and the twelve-mile Samaria Gorge in Crete, but the wonder of both those well-known tourist spots still pales beside the memories of our little gully in the Western Hills. Clear spring water flowed through the gully bed, at some points a tiny rippling stream, at others spilling in small waterfalls through the rocks and boulders. The little pool in which we swam was under a small stone bridge and shaded by large trees bordering the path above. It couldn't have been more than eight feet across, but the water that collected there was deep enough for small bodies to splash about in and even to submerge themselves. The gully was also a favorite evening walk for the adults, but for us children it was for the heat of day.

Other days we climbed to the top of Tiger's Head. Before we started up the hill we often stopped in the vegetable garden behind the kitchen to pick a tomato or some cucumbers to eat when we got to the top. The dry hills had almost no scrub growth except for some small wild jujube bushes (we called them wild dates). Most of the dates were tiny, about the size of a pea, and hardly worth the bother, but some were as large as small green grapes and very sweet--well worth stopping for. The bushes were thorny so we picked with care.

When I think of the Western Hills, I remember it best in my childhood years. Yet it was a part of our lives until we left China in 1945. One of the last times I was there was with Edie. The trip was my present to her on her twenty-first birthday. We decided we would start her year by climbing to Tiger's Head to watch the sun rise. We rose in the dark, but by the time we had collected some rolls from the kitchen and picked some tomatoes and cucumbers from the garden, it had already started to get light. We scrambled up the hill in the semi-darkness, but when we finally reached the top the sun had already risen. Totally out of breath, we sat on one of the stones that made up part of the tiger's head and finally turned to see what remained of the sunrise. I had seen sunrises before, but none to equal this. A great red ball seemed to be floating on top of the lake at the Summer Palace. *That was the first time I was aware that the lake was visible from the top of the hill.* Its twin, paler and slightly rippling, was in the water beneath it. The two seemed to be touching. Totally mesmerized, we watched the two suns as they moved apart. One rose higher and higher, turning from red to orange and then to yellow. Soon it was too bright to look at. The other sank and sank until it seemed to have drowned in the water. It was gone; the water turned to glass. I suddenly felt this indescribable sense of loss. I wanted to cry.

Only one other time in my life have I had this same feeling. It was many many years later when my husband and I were on a scientific expedition with the Earthwatch group to save the leatherback turtle from extinction. Off the beach of St. Croix, in the dark of night, we had watched a giant leatherback lay its more than one hundred eggs at the water's edge; had tagged the turtle while it was resting, and would later move the eggs to a more secure spot. Afterward, exhausted by its efforts, the giant leatherback dragged its thousand-pound body in slow and labored movements across the sand to the water's edge. Then, buoyed by an incoming wave, it slid effortlessly into the blackened sea. Watching that magnificent creature as it left our world and plunged into the darkness of its own, I felt a strange emptiness. It was as if a part of myself had gone with it.

That trip with Edie was one of the last times I was at the Western Hills. Without a car it was a long, arduous trip. First by tram to the railway station in the West City of Peking; then by train to the *Huang Ts'un* Station about two miles from *Pa Ta Ch'u*; and then the last two miles by donkey. When we made the fifteen-mile trip before the war years, before the car had been sold, it was always my mother who drove. Though my father had an official car and driver, Mother always enjoyed driving her own car, the Auburn. It was a dark forest green, and the interior had green leather seats that retained that glorious smell of new leather right up until the time we had to sell it. In the winter the Auburn had its own fur coat. It was not really a fur coat but rather a fur-lined coat. It was of leather, quilted, with the stitching in a diamond pattern, and lined with fur. It had been designed quite ingeniously and was made to snap neatly in place over the entire hood of the car. I am not sure how much good it did in winter temperatures well below freezing, but know that its purpose was to keep the engine from freezing when the car was in the unheated garage.

Mother was so proud of that car, and I suspect she was proud of herself too and of the feeling of independence it gave her. I too was proud of my mother for she was the only woman in Peking who drove a car. I know that she was much admired and even envied by her Chinese women friends, although I'm sure the men wondered why any woman, or any man for that matter, would even *want* to drive herself rather than *be* driven by a chauffeur. I know that the servants and even our chauffeur and the chauffeurs of friends were impressed by what they perceived as *Ch'ien T'ai T'ai*'s courage in manipulating that big car through the streets of Peking.

Courageous she might have been, and certainly independent, but a good driver she was not. I never realized how bad she was until I learned to drive myself many years later in America. Mother managed fine on the flat, but had a terrible time on any kind of incline. At one time people who had homes on the hillside had to walk up the hill. Those who could not walk were taken up in sedan chairs that were suspended between two bamboo poles carried on the shoulders of coolies. I remember following the sedan chairs up the narrow paths. They looked precarious, especially when the path was steep. Our house, being low on the hill, did not require much of a climb, but my parents had a driveway built from the village level up to the house. The driveway was quite steep and narrow and ended at a small landing below the house where a garage was built. There was a sheer drop-off from the landing. Mother had no trouble driving the car up and into the garage, gunning the motor and zooming up the drive with great panache. However, backing out and turning the car around for its downward run was another matter. For me it was a tense and frightening experience. Many times I thought we were going to slide over the hill backwards. Mother would put the car in reverse and step on the gas pedal; the motor would roar. Then she released the clutch; a jerk, and quiet. She repeated this several times. Still, undaunted, she would try again, this time only to bring the rear wheels of the car to the very edge of the landing and to jam on the brakes, hard. Throughout this exercise, the servants would be behind the car yelling "*t'ing, t'ing*" and motioning wildly for her to stop. Once stopped, they would wedge her rear wheels with large stones while she made the shift of gears from reverse to forward. More roaring of the motor; more jerking and stalling. When the car was at last put into motion and its front wheels had reached the opposite edge of the landing, more stones were wedged under her front wheels before she started backward once again. A permanent supply of large stones was placed at each side of the landing for this purpose. No power steering in those days, and the Auburn was a big heavy car. It took four or five forward and backward moves to turn the car around. Finally it was done. All the while I would have my eyes tightly closed.

In those days flat tires were not uncommon, and many times we would be immobilized on the dusty road with one corner of the car at a tilt. We would all get out of the car as Mother began the process of changing the tire. Though she was always able to find some willing peasant to do the physical part of the job, she began the operation herself. If no willing helpers had been available, I am quite sure she would have been capable of doing the whole job herself. I felt my mother could do just about anything. But that was never necessary. By the time she had opened the trunk and taken out the jack, there would have appeared, as if from nowhere, a crowd of peasants and a bevy of barefoot children. They gathered around and stared with unabashed curiosity at this foreign woman who appeared to be in command of not only this grand vehicle but also of its occupants. Having set the jack in place and made the first motions of cranking it up, Mother would then turn to the assembled onlookers and select the most likely looking one to assist her. The man needed no persuasion. He jumped forward, pleased to be the favored one, and eager to be a participant in the unexpected diversion of the day. He would then crank away furiously, lifting the car to a dangerous height. Car jacks in those days left much to be desired, and it seemed to me that one push of a finger could have sent the car crashing down on the poor peasant. Meanwhile, his companions would be jabbering loudly to each other, amazed at the take-charge attitude of the foreign woman, and finding it hard to believe that she was actually speaking Chinese, and intelligible Chinese at that.

Then came the removal of the tire. Mother would again begin the motions of loosening the bolts herself, but her willing helper would immediately take over. When the tire had been removed and the spare put on under her direction, she would show him how to tighten the bolts. When the spare was on securely and the car back down to normal level, a cheer would arise from the assembled onlookers as the chosen helper beamed with pride at his accomplishment.

The whole business of changing the tire must have been the highlight of the day for the local peasants involved. With little contact with the world beyond their own small villages and their own fields, this was high drama for the villagers. They had become accustomed to seeing occasional foreigners on the roads, but a foreign woman, herself driving a big handsome car, was an unusual sight. And the farmer who had done the actual changing of the tire had a story to tell for weeks thereafter, especially when he told of the handsome tip he had received from the foreign woman.

I can't help but smile to myself when I visualize Mother going through the motions of changing a tire. This was the early thirties. She was not the slim-hipped sporty type. No Katherine Hepburn or Lauren Bacall in faded jeans and a man's shirt with casually rolled up sleeves was she. I see her in her usual summer garb for the Western Hills, soft cotton voile dress with smocking at neck and bosom, every inch a gentlewoman.

In later years, during the war when the car had long since been sold, Mother took to riding a bicycle to the local market. I cannot imagine why she went to the market at all, for that was the servant's job. She was well into her sixties then, which in those times made her an elderly woman. Her bicycle riding was even worse than her driving. She had probably been told that once learned, you could never forget how to ride a bicycle. Perhaps she had not learned too well the first time around. After falling off several times and suffering the indignity of having to be picked up by surprised passersby, she gave it up, much to our relief. We were always worried that she would hurt herself, and she surely was charged more for her grocery purchases than the servants would have been. Besides, we thought it a terrible loss of dignity for our mother, and I know it was something of an embarrassment for our three remaining servants.

Chapter 13
The Guesthouse

NINETEEN THIRTY-TWO brought a major change in our lives. By then the government had moved to Nanking. For several years my father had been making frequent trips to the new capital, but now he moved there permanently. Yi Tai Tai, the concubine, and her daughter Mabel were moved to Shanghai where most of my father's family lived. Still very much the responsibility of the Ch'ien family, they moved in with my father's fifth younger sister. Though my father came home for regular visits, from that time on we saw little of him and he was no longer a part of our day-to-day lives. Much of my mother's official social life came to a halt, and though she was still heavily involved with her club work, she felt the need for some other activity. My father suggested that she start a bakery. At that time the only good western bakery in Peking was Karatsis Brothers and the city could have benefited from a second. This did not appeal to my mother.

It was the wife of the American Military Attache who came up with the idea. Colonel and Mrs. Drysdale were close friends, and Mrs. Drysdale had often heard my mother bemoan the fact that visitors to Peking seldom saw the real Peking. "Helen, why don't you start a guesthouse, a real Chinese guesthouse? It would be perfect for you. You've often complained that foreign visitors don't even get to see the inside of a

Chinese home. You could furnish it like a real Chinese home. You could be the hostess, show visitors what life is like in Peking. You're a natural-born hostess and you love people." Mrs. Drysdale grew more enthusiastic with each word. "Do think about it, Helen. It really would be perfect for you."

Mother didn't need to think. She was excited and thrilled by the whole concept. "I don't need to think. It *is* perfect, and it's a brilliant idea." The images started forming in her mind. She could envision even then what she wanted her guesthouse to be.

Mother decided the guesthouse should be located in the East City where most of the foreign community lived. Though there were no defined boundaries to the various areas within Peking, the Forbidden City, in the heart of the city, was a natural dividing point. The area north of it, extending to the northern gates of the city wall, was generally termed the North City, *Pei Ch'eng*. It was primarily a residential area, and it was here that many of the well-to-do Chinese families, including ours, had large homes. The area surrounding the Forbidden City and to the east of it was known as the East City, *Tung Ch'eng*. For some inexplicable reason, the area to the south was never referred to as the South City. There, the two major hotels were located, the Peking Hotel and the Wagons-Lits Hotel. Also some of the western business enterprises as well as the diplomatic missions, which were grouped just within the city walls in an area known as the Legation Quarter. The West City, *Hsi Ch'eng*, was a large sprawling area full of small shops and more modest homes. For us it was only an area we passed through on the way to the Western Hills through the western gates of the city.

Once my mother had decided on the location of the guesthouse, my father lined up several properties for her to look at and she started her search for the house that would be her guesthouse. I was only seven at the time but remember how excited she was when she got home that day.

"It's perfect. Absolutely perfect. Five large courtyards--and the main room is very *very* large--perfect for the living room, with a good-sized room on one end for the dining room, and another on the other end that could be used as a study or library."

"Which one is it?" my father asked.

"It's the one on Hsi Tsung Pu Hutung, No. 29, the one that used to be a prince's palace. It backs onto the Ministry of Foreign Affairs."

My father went to inspect it the next day, gave his approval, and so Mrs. Ch'ien's Guesthouse was born.

Number 29 was indeed a perfect house. Though it didn't have a formal garden, the courtyards themselves, except for the one at the rear, were things of beauty, each one distinctive in its own way. The first of the main courts had a wide raised path running through it, and in the wells on each side were flowering plum trees. Their blooms were the first harbingers of spring, and when the trees were in flower, all who entered the house were welcomed by a profusion of pink blossoms.

The second courtyard was dominated by a large wisteria arbor fully twelve feet high. The vines rose from two ornamental concrete basins each about fifteen feet long that ran lengthwise along the sides of

My father with Luther and me in front of wisteria arbor in second court of guesthouse.

the courtyard. When in bloom the courtyard seemed almost entirely enclosed by purple walls and ceiling.

Most lovely of all was the third courtyard, which I think of always as the mimosa court. Unlike most courtyards, most of which had rooms facing onto them, this one was bordered by four bare walls, its bareness unbroken by either rooms opening onto it or by covered walkways passing through it. Like the first court, a wide raised path ran down its center, and in the deep wells on either side mimosa trees raised their feathery branches. When the mimosa were in flower, that courtyard was a breathtaking sight, the blossoms filling the entire court with pale pink froth that spilled over the walls and rooftops. Yet the courtyard served no useful purpose. Except for the mimosa trees, there was nothing in it. It seemed that its sole reason for being was to bring a moment of beauty to all who passed through it.

His anger seemed to be subsiding. After Mother's first attempts to explain that his unexpected early arrival had caught us off guard, she had not gone further in putting the blame for the cold room on him. I think, however, that he knew the fault had been more his than ours, and also that he had become conscious of the boorish way he was behaving. In any case, he relented and agreed to stay on. That evening, returning to a room that was warm and comfortable, he came to our living room and apologized to Mother for his behavior. During the next week he was a frequent visitor to our modest living/dining room and shared many pleasant evenings with the family. When he learned that Luther was in America, he volunteered to become Luther's financial sponsor. Another guest had become a friend.

The first year after America entered the war we had to limit our spending in many ways, but so did all our friends. Our income was drastically reduced. Funds no longer came regularly from my father, and our family of five lived on the rent from the rooms and on the sale of our belongings. We were fortunate in that we had more material possessions to sell than most people. However, as the number of saleable items dwindled, Mother was becoming increasingly worried about how to keep our family fed and clothed.

The car had already been sold. It was one of the first things to go. Then the furniture, including those of the Beautyrest mattresses that were not being used. *Mother had been so proud of them.* Then went decorative ornaments, silver, dishes, even blankets and linens-- everything that was not an absolute necessity. The buyers came to the house and went through our belongings, picking and choosing those items they knew would bring the greatest return. They did handle the ornaments and dishes with care, but camelhair blankets, appliqued bedspreads, elaborately embroidered linens, all were just stuffed into large sacks as if they were no more than old rags. Wads of paper money were then thrust unceremoniously into Mother's hands. We stood by helplessly.

Of all the sales made, the most painful to watch was the sale of the silver. All silver items were bought by weight alone; no consideration whatsoever given by buyers for beautiful design or fine workmanship. I never saw my mother cry, but she was close to it as she watched her favorite silver bowl, her rose bowl she called it, being weighed for sale. It was no more than ten inches in diameter, but it was heavy. It was richly embossed with four panels, each representing one of four seasons: peonies for spring, roses for summer, chrysanthemums for fall, and bamboo for winter. Mother called it her rose bowl, not because of the design, but because in better times she often had it filled with roses. One by one the silver merchant placed silver dishes, candelabras, serving bowls and platters on the brass pan that hung on one end of his bamboo weighing rod, balancing them with metal weights on the other end. As he placed the treasured rose bowl on the pan, I could almost physically feel my mother's pain. "Oh, Mother, does it have to go?" I asked. And her reply, "Yes, Marguerite, it has to go." I looked on helplessly as the cherished bowl was tossed casually on top of the other silver items in the large basket. With the clattering sound of metal on metal, I saw my mother close her eyes. Almost imperceptibly, she winced. A stack of almost worthless paper money was thrust upon her--a few more weeks of food for our family.

At the beginning of 1943, surprisingly, a wealthy Chinese man from Shanghai, offered to buy our North City House. Mother was reluctant to sell the home we all loved, but saw no other way of raising money. The house for all practical purposes was already lost to us since we had no way of getting it away from the Japanese military. The prospective buyer, Mr. Li, had high-level official Japanese contacts and was in a position to reclaim the house if he were the owner. He was one of the despicable group we labeled as Japanese collaborators. Mother sold the house, for a pittance. To the best of my recollection it was about the equivalent of U.S. $6000. The sale did not include the small rear courtyard that had once held Richard's suite and the storerooms. Mr. Li had wanted very much to have it included in the sale and I recall meeting him at the property to discuss the matter. I was barely eighteen at the time, and I am not sure why my mother gave me this responsibility, but I think she felt that I could be more hardheaded in business matters than she. She did not turn to Lois. Mr. Li declared the small piece of property was worthless and that it should be included in the sale price. "What do you want it for? It's a useless piece of property," he insisted.

"If it's so useless, then surely you shouldn't want it," I rebutted. In the end it was I who won the battle of words. The courtyard was not included in the sale. We kept the property and let our old family retainer, Liu Yeh, occupy it. In retrospect, if we had not sold the house, we could have reclaimed it at the end of the war, assuming American victory. But at that time we had no idea what the future held, and survival was foremost in Mother's mind.

The proceeds were received in cash. It was paid in Chinese dollars, and with daily currency devaluation, it could have become worthless in weeks. Other Americans, their own remittances no longer coming through from the U.S., were also having difficulty making ends meet. With the exception of what we needed to keep ourselves going, Mother lent the entire amount to American friends who in return gave her promissory notes for the then equivalent amounts in U.S. dollars. After the war, when we arrived in the U.S., it was the repayment of these loans that financed our new life.

Chapter 15
American Exodus

IN JUNE 1942, through the auspices of the International Red Cross, many of the Americans in Peking, including all diplomatic personnel, were repatriated on the Gripsholm, a Swedish ship chartered by the United States. In March 1943 those Americans who remained were sent to an internment camp in Wei-hsien in Shantung province. Their homes and all their belongings were left behind. They were allowed to take only what they could carry. Those were sad and painful days for all of us who had been part of the small westernized community in Peking. Those who were leaving were stoic, not knowing what the future held for them.

At the last church service before the American departure, there were few dry eyes in the congregation. Our regular pastor presided for the last time, and as he thanked each of the departees for their past services to the church, handkerchiefs appeared and tears and sniffles became audible. Mr. Grimes directed the choir for the last time, and the music we produced was sadly ragged with voices catching and unable to continue. After the service, I left the platform hurriedly, trying to make a quick exit before the tears I had been struggling to hold back could be held back no longer. Mr. Grimes caught me as I passed by. Taking my hands between his, he said, "Marguerite, I don't know when I will see you again. Take my love and hold it tight." The crush I had had on him had come and gone, but now it returned, full force. I don't know how I managed to stay dry-eyed as I said what I thought was a last goodbye to this man I had been so enamored of for so many years. I did not know then that the next day, the last day before the American departure, Mother would ask him for a final lunch at our house. During lunch he said to Mother, "Keep an eye on this model daughter of yours. She's become so serious, I worry about her. Don't let her glue herself to her books." Later, saying his goodbyes, he patted the two children, Derek and Jeannie, on their heads; then told Lois how much he had enjoyed knowing her. To Mother he said, "Mrs. Ch'ien, I've treasured your friendship more than you'll ever know." And last to me. He took my face between his hands, and saying simply, "Goodbye, dear Marguerite," he kissed me gently on the forehead. I dissolved.

That afternoon Edie, Clemy, Shang, and I made the rounds of our American friends. Through tears shed and tears held back we said our goodbyes. Some gave us gifts of things once prized that they could not take with them. Miss Moore had three PAS cups that she asked us to keep for the school. She entrusted to me the "scholarship cup," to Edie the "Henry Hussey Sports Cup," and to Shang another cup whose name I can't recall. *They were left behind in China. I have no idea where those cups are today.* The next morning the Americans all assembled at the American Embassy. We watched them walking from the embassy to the train station, herded into a line like convicts. All had red tags sewn on the front of their clothes. Miss Moore got slightly out of line and was pushed back roughly by the soldiers who flanked the procession. Weeks before, many had made makeshift carts--they called them their "Cheerful Sams"--to carry their luggage, but now all were carrying their own bags, had apparently not been allowed to use the carts. As they passed the spot where we had stationed ourselves, we waved our goodbyes. With both arms weighted down by their baggage, they could only smile in return. Then we rushed to Hatamen gate where their train would be passing in hopes of waving just one more time. Many others were gathered there. When the train went by, it was going so fast we couldn't see or recognize any faces. Three carloads of waving white handkerchiefs and the Americans were gone. We didn't know when, or if, we would ever see them again.

The following week, the British followed the Americans, and Peking was left with little foreign presence. Mother was exempted from concentration camp because she had minor Chinese children. This was supposedly an act of compassion on the part of the Japanese, but during the next two and a half years I often thought she would have been better off had she gone. It was not until the war was over, and we had been reunited with many of our friends who had been interned at Wei Hsien, that we learned how short their internment had been. Through the International Red Cross, they had been released and repatriated to the United States only seven months after their internment. Had Mother gone with them, she too would have been repatriated and spared the hardships she endured in Peking during the final two years of the war.

Many a night the Japanese gendarmes would bang on the door and take her down to the gendarmerie for questioning. There they would keep her for hours, hammering her with questions about my father's whereabouts, about her own family, and about Luther and Richard. These interrogations happened again and again, sometimes during the day, and sometimes at three or four in the morning. Several times they took me with her and questioned us separately. They were quite easy on me, assuming I suppose that I knew nothing of use to them. However, one time they had me sitting just outside the room where they were questioning Mother. Through the frosted glass partition I could hear them yelling questions at her repeatedly. "Where is your husband? What is his job? Is he working for the Americans? What are his responsibilities? Why is your son in America? What is he doing there?" I don't know what they expected to find out with this line of questioning or what they suspected. Through the glass partition I could see only the outline of their figures as they thrust their faces into hers and shook their fists threateningly at her. However, they always stopped short of striking her. Though the Japanese never physically hurt Mother, they treated her roughly, pushing, shoving, and prodding her if she moved too slowly or was slow in answering their questions. The physical abuse, however, was nothing compared to the emotional anguish she suffered at their hands. At the end of the war, after VJ day, she weighed only eight-six pounds. Her normal weight for her five-foot-three inch frame had been one hundred and thirty-five.

One time the gendarmes came to the back door instead of the front. They banged repeatedly and shouted for someone to open the door. The servants slept in the front of the house in a small room next to the kitchen and could not hear. Finally, when the persistent pounding and shouting did not stop, Mr. Kami got up and went to the door himself in his dressing gown, ready to put a stop to this unreasonable behavior. He unbarred the gate, but before he could say a word, the gendarmes had pushed him aside roughly and demanded to see my mother. Despite Mr. Kami's protests, as usual they took her with them to the gendarmerie. Mr. Kami was furious. He recounted his experience to us with some indignation the following morning and put in an immediate complaint to the gendarmerie headquarters. We hoped that this would bring a stop to their continual harassment, but we were not to be so fortunate. Their visits did not stop.

As the war wore on, rationing became more stringent daily and the quality of rationed foodstuffs deteriorated. Rice, already augmented with chaff to increase its bulk, now contained small stones to increase its weight as well. I recall Shang May's little sister sitting on the steps of their house laboriously picking stones from the rice. Her face was always streaked with dried tears because picking the stones was her punishment for any kind of misbehavior. Flour rations, more important to northern Chinese than rice, were reduced and hard corn kernels substituted, the kind used for animal feed. Mother soaked the corn and then ground it coarsely in the meat grinder. The porridge that she made from it was good. We also started eating *wo t'ou*, an unleavened cornbread that in better days had been only for the very poor. It was hard and dry, but sliced very thin, and toasted, it was palatable. Our diet changed considerably and we ate Chinese food almost exclusively as it required less meat than western food. Meat was not rationed but was expensive. We normally bought four ounces for the day's fare, but as our money dwindled, often we bought only two ounces; this for a family of five.

We no longer had a cook, but Hsueh, our houseboy, in addition to his other duties, took over the Chinese cooking. We ate a lot of vegetables, and with a few shreds of meat they could be quite tasty. Chinese nappa cabbage was a staple, as was tofu in its many forms. We bought the cabbage more than a hundred pounds at a time. It hung outside under the kitchen eaves, fifteen to twenty heads strung together. It was a versatile vegetable. Cut vertically in thin strips and stir-fried quickly it was crisp and sweet; in larger pieces and smothered gently in its own juice it became a totally different vegetable. With some threads of green-pea vermicelli it was a good ingredient for soup too. With a bit of this added and a bit of something else, our cabbage soup became quite good. Potatoes, not commonly used in Chinese food, became a larger part of our diet. Hsueh cut them into matchstick-like pieces and sautéed them quickly so that they were still crisp. They became almost like a radish in consistency. With soy sauce added, and a dash of vinegar and some crushed Ssuchuan peppercorns, they were delicious. Sweet and sour radishes were a special treat. When fried in deep fat and then bathed in a pungent sauce, they tasted as good as spareribs had in better days. We had them rarely because of the large amount of oil required for deep-frying. Eggplant, which I had learned to love, had to be cut out of our diet completely, again because of the large amount of oil required.

During this period we would occasionally receive a letter from Luther. His letters from America came through several layers of intermediaries. First to my father in the interior; then to *T'ien Feng*, the Ch'ien family store in the West City; and finally to us via *T'ien Feng*'s manager. He always brought the letters to us in person. In his letters Luther advised us more than once to start a victory garden. In a house where the courtyards were completely paved with brick, the idea was ludicrous. Besides, it was not vegetables we were short of. It was rice, and flour, and meat, and oil. We were fortunate to have Mr. Kami's rations.

Mr. Kami had become a friend, and I believe he thought of himself as something of a protector even though he had not been able to stop the gendarmes from their frequent interrogations of my mother. Once, when I was out later than usual—it was about ten o'clock—I found both Mother and Mr. Kami in the front courtyard waiting up for me. He was in his pajamas and dressing gown but had refused to retire until he knew I was home safely. It was almost as if he considered himself part of the family. *He had less faith in the Japanese soldiers on the streets than we had.*

Several times he asked the whole family out to dinner, including Jeannie and Derek, and though it was a joy to be treated to a real meal, I was always so worried that we would be seen fraternizing with a Japanese, that some of the pleasure of the meal was lost. Mr. Kami knew of our financial difficulties and he arranged for Mother to give English lessons to a Mr. Suzuki, a young Japanese officer from the Japanese Embassy. When Mother, for one reason or another, was unable to take him for his scheduled lesson, I substituted as teacher. In addition to the small amount of money Mr. Suzuki paid for his lessons, he also gave us a bag of flour per month, appreciated far more than the cash. But more important than either his tuition payments or the bag of flour was the help he gave us in another way. At about this time, our financial situation was the worst it had ever been. We had been told that the iron pipes from the totally useless artesian well in the Western Hills could be converted to cash, but had no way of getting the pipes to the city. It was Mr. Suzuki who himself volunteered a truck. We were grateful for his help.

A few days later, sandwiched between two uniformed Japanese soldiers, I found myself in the front seat of a Japanese army truck. As the truck lurched through the dusty Peking streets, I shrank myself into the smallest bundle I could to avoid coming into contact with either one. The two soldiers talked across me, sometimes laughing uproariously. I wondered if I was the cause of their amusement, a young Chinese girl, obviously nervous. I was eighteen at the time and wishing fervently that someone else could have carried out this exercise. The soldiers had arrived at the house only minutes before and had stood politely by while Mother gave me some last words of reassurance before I boarded the truck. She was nervous about letting me do this chore, but as an American, an enemy national, she was not allowed to leave the city.

She tried to be positive though I could sense her misgivings. "Don't worry, Marguerite," she said. "You'll be all right. Mr. Suzuki assured me that the soldiers wouldn't give you any problems." Hsueh, our houseboy, shook his head. He was more worried than Mother and was not happy at all that Mother was allowing me to go alone with the two Japanese soldiers. As for me, I was nervous and scared, but scared for all the wrong reasons. I should have been worried that they might harm me in some way. But at that time I had not yet been exposed to the post-war reports of Japanese atrocities. The thought of rape never entered my mind. No, my major concern was that I might be seen by someone I knew who might then wonder what I was doing in a Japanese truck. *It would have been worse than being seen with Mr. Kami.* They might think our family was collaborating with the Japanese, an absolutely unforgivable sin.

The trip to the Western Hills with the two soldiers was uneventful. Their behavior was exemplary. When we arrived at our house, the pipes had already been dug up by coolies and were just waiting to be loaded onto the truck. The coolies took care of this with dispatch and it was then back to the city to unload the pipes in a large yard filled with all manner of scrap metal and to receive payment from the man in charge. Mother and Hsueh were happy that I arrived home safely and none the worse for the trip. I have no recollection of how much we netted from the sale of the pipes, but know that we needed the money to add to our shrinking resources. When Mr. Suzuki was transferred back to Japan he presented Mother and me each with a beautiful silk kimono. I still have mine today. Enemy or not, he was a nice man, and both Mother and I genuinely liked him.

In addition to Mr. Suzuki, Mother had already started teaching English again to a number of other students. She hadn't done this since we were children, but now we needed the added income. I too started teaching and had nine high school seniors from Yu Ying Boys School as students. English classes at all the Chinese schools had been eliminated and replaced by Japanese, which became the compulsory foreign language. Still, there were many students who wanted to continue with English. My students were a joy to teach, bright and eager to learn, so eager that they were willing to come to me at six in the morning before school. They worked hard, and they improved rapidly. I took them in groups of three in my bedroom. I wonder now why I didn't use the living room, which would not have been in use at that hour. My room was not large and I sat on the edge of my bed, with them on straight chairs around me. I know it tickled them to have me for a teacher instead of my mother. I was only a few years older than they and was known to some of their friends. *I am quite sure these friends were given a detailed description of my bedroom.* It was while I was teaching these boys that I first became aware of the rumblings of the Communist movement. Before that, in my narrow insulated world I had not even been aware of what was going on in the rest of China. These boys even then were concerned, not about the Japanese, who they were confident would be defeated, but about the Communist threat.

Though both Mother and I had some income from our teaching, economies were still necessary on every front, including clothing. From the guesthouse we still had curtains that had not been sold, most of them of heavy cotton damask. They made fine dress material. I made several dresses from the different curtains and bedspreads in the house. Mother also clothed a little beggar boy in the same damask. Though in normal times she would not have tolerated a beggar near our gates, she took pity on this homeless child who was so often huddled nearby in the *hut'ung*.. He appeared about ten or eleven years old. He was frail, and Mother was sure he was sick. She put him in a rickshaw and took him to the doctor who diagnosed him as having tuberculosis. She did not have the heart to drive him away. During the day, he sat on the narrow sidewalk of our *hut'ung*, on the shady side during the often over one-hundred-degree heat, and on the sunny side during the bitter cold of winter. He was wrapped in old blankets and quilts that we and others had cast off. At night he slept in the alcove of our recessed front gate, but always vacated before the gates were opened in the morning. Hsueh gave him any left-over food that was in the house. I don't know who else might have fed him also. I don't remember how long he stayed in our *hut'ung*, perhaps a year, maybe more, but suddenly and miraculously he was well. Mother made him new clothing from our green damask curtains. They matched my favorite dress. He was so proud. Whenever he saw me in a rickshaw wearing my damask dress, he would run along beside me for a distance, yanking at his own clothing, then pointing to mine. He was showing the world around that his clothing matched mine.

Curtains were not the only things that could be converted to clothing. Embroidered tablecloths made attractive blouses. Blankets made fine coats and jackets. I had a handsome ski-style outfit made of a camel's hair blanket. The jacket had a hounds tooth vest-like front and dressed in it I felt at the height of style.

If new material was expensive, leather was even more so. Lois's amah, Wu Nai Nai, taught me to make Chinese cloth soles, and it was a great challenge to design my own summer sandals. The soles cost nothing to make—nothing, that is, except time and labor. They consisted of nothing more than old scraps of cloth held together with a thin paste made from flour and water. First we spread the paste on a board. Over that we laid scraps of fabric, large or small pieces, whatever was available. When this was totally dry, another layer of paste and then more fabric. After four or five layers, we had a sheet that resembled a thin piece of cardboard. From this we used scissors to cut out many outlines of the sole. The next step was to cut narrow strips of white cloth on the bias. We wrapped the bias strips, again with paste, around each cut-out sole. Then came the hard part. We stacked together six or seven soles, each already bound with white bias tape. These we held together with a few large basted stitches before applying ourselves to the finer stitching that was required. We had to use an awl to bore through all thicknesses of the soles. Each stitch required boring a new hole before the thick hemp string could be pulled through. The stitching was done round and round in concentric circles working from the outside in. It was slow and laborious work.

The next step was to design the shoe itself, parallel straps--criss-crossed, or whatever other design I could think of. I assembled the tops on the sewing machine and then took tops and soles to the shoe store for final assembly. I was as pleased with my homemade cloth-soled sandals as I had been in the past with new leather shoes. Wu Nai Nai and I together made sandals for Lois too, which she showed off proudly to her friends. I couldn't help being annoyed, however, when she took credit for these creations on which she had not sewn a stitch herself.

Once we had given up the big guesthouse at Number 29, we were reduced to only three servants, our houseboy Hsueh, a coolie, Pai, and Lois's baby amah, Wu Nai Nai. Wu Nai Nai took care of Lois's rooms and did the laundering of our personal clothing, but Hsueh and Pai did everything else. That included cleaning all the other rooms and courtyards, keeping the coal fires in each room going in the winter, doing the laundry for the guest rooms, doing the shopping and most of the cooking, work that in the past would have been done by at least five or six if not more. I don't know how they managed. But they too were well aware that there was a war on. They were devoted to Mother, and I know that either of them would have borne the entire burden alone if she had but asked. I don't know what our family would have done without Hsueh. In addition to the physical labor within the house, waiting on us, the cleaning, and much of the cooking, he also did the shopping, paid the various vendors, kept the accounts, and did myriad other chores. And yet, he was a servant. Mother had been to his home to care for his children when they were sick. *She* had met his family. *She* cared about Hsueh, and she cared about Pai. But the rest of us, Lois and I? We did not know Hsueh's wife, his mother, or his children. I didn't know how many he had, or how old they were. Hsueh was a servant. He was there to serve; we to *be* served. *Heartless, thoughtless, selfish children of privilege!*

Chapter 16
Shanghai

IN THE FALL OF 1943 I left Peking to attend St. John's University in Shanghai. St. John's was founded by the American Episcopal Church, and though its American teachers had been sent to the internment camp in Wei Hsien, classes were still taught in English. Edie had already made the move a few months earlier, but much as I wanted to join her, I felt I could not leave my mother. Before Edie left, she, Shang, Clemy, and I went for a last farewell get-together at one of our favorite spots on top of the city wall. We each drank in turn from a single glass of grape wine, and in vowing our eternal friendship, each of us placed on her finger one of the four silver rings with a chain design that we had especially ordered from a local jeweler as symbols of that friendship. Finally, we smashed the glass at our feet amid much giggling. But despite the giggling, we parted solemnly. We had been so close; none of us wanted to face the thought of separation.

Soon after Edie's departure, Clemy too left Peking to join her brother in the interior. Many of our friends had already gone. Clemy was one of the last to leave. Though Shang remained, with our American friends gone, as well as most of our closer Chinese friends, I felt very much alone. I made new friends at Fu Jen but none as close as the ones I had lost. I was not unhappy at Fu Jen, but I was not looking forward to beginning another school year there.

Barely a month after Clemy had left, Fu P'ing Chang, a friend of my brother Richard's, came to visit from Shanghai. Fu P'ing was some ten years older than I and took a brotherly interest in my progress. When he spoke of the advantages of continuing my education at an English-language college such as St. John's, I let myself be persuaded all too readily that Shanghai was the best place for me. I knew that Mother would miss me terribly--her relationship with Lois was in a constant state of deterioration, and she had become more and more dependent on me--but the opportunity to get away from Peking was irresistible. All my noble thoughts of remaining for my mother's sake were forgotten. I rationalized and told myself that it would be an opportunity for me to get to know my father's side of the family. And Mother, ever deferring to me, agreed. In a matter of days I was on my way. When Fu P'ing returned home to Shanghai, I went with him. I was thrilled to be going to the big city.

For about a month I stayed with Fu P'ing and his widowed mother in their home. My room was on the stair landing between the ground floor and second floor. It had originally been used as a storeroom and so was filled with boxes and trunks; but still there was room for a bed, a small desk, and a dresser. It was quite comfortable and I had no complaints. Fu P'ing's mother was a sweet woman whom I addressed as Chang *Po Mu* (Auntie Chang), and I became very fond of her. However, Fu P'ing, for all his good intentions, soon became a difficult presence for me. Having persuaded my mother to let me make the move to Shanghai, he no doubt felt some responsibility for my welfare. Consequently, he intruded into every aspect of my new life. He had comments and guidance on the courses I selected at school, how I went about my homework, which relatives I should see and how often, and of course how I should handle all my social contacts, both old friends and new.

I cannot remember if Fu P'ing was working or what his working hours were, but it seemed to me he was ever present in the house when I was home. He hovered over me constantly with his questions and advice. Even in the evenings when I was in my room trying to do my homework, I could not get away from of him. Sometimes he stood behind me, looking over my shoulder at what I was writing. Other times he

sat on the edge of my bed, observing that I had misspelled a word or that
I had omitted something he deemed important in an outline. He played
with my hair, twiddling it between his fingers; sometimes he stroked my
hair. I wanted to scream, "Leave me alone! Leave me alone!"

It was a welcome relief when my parents decided that during my
stay in Shanghai I should live with relatives rather than continue to impose on family friends. Fourth Uncle and Aunt, my biological parents,
wanted and expected me to stay with them, but my mother objected. I
think she was concerned that I might become too attached to my natural
family. In the end my parents decided that I should stay with Second
Uncle and Aunt who lived in an apartment in the French Concession.
Their unmarried daughter Helen lived with them, and also a grandson
and granddaughter, children of their son Winston, who, like so many
others, had gone to the interior. I believe Helen was happy to have me
staying with them, as I was something of a diversion in what seemed to
me her rather dull life. Helen was eight years older than I. She was a
pretty girl, modest and unassuming in an old-fashioned way. She had
been engaged to her cousin David for years, but I had the distinct impression that he was stalling on a wedding date. The match had been arranged by the two sets of parents. He was a thoroughly modern man-
about-town who moved in a swinging social set--i.e, in the days before
"swinging" had sexual implications--and Helen did not fit the model of a
modern girl. I don't recall his visiting often, or taking her out. Neither
did Helen seem to have any close female friends. She spent a great deal
of time at her Chinese brush painting, for which she had considerable
talent. We got on well, but never became very close. She took a great
interest in my friends and activities, and it seemed to me that she got a
vicarious pleasure from hearing of my experiences at St. John's University.

The two little children, Tung Tung and Soo Erh, were well behaved and quite likable, but my memories of them are not of their sweet
dispositions, but of the strong smell that exuded from their every pore
during the winter months. Second Aunt, long before the western phar-
maceutical firms had started pushing the medical merits of garlic, insisted
that each of them chew a whole clove of garlic every morning to ward off
winter colds. We always knew when they were approaching. The perva-

sive odor was all around them. Fortunately, the same preventive meas-
ures were not required of me or the other adults of the household.

When I joined the household, Second Uncle was already retired
and was home throughout the day. He was a distinguished-looking man
and I thought better looking than my father, but had a stern unbending
demeanor. I had been somewhat apprehensive about staying with him
and Second Aunt because I remembered that Richard had not been happy
during the year he was with them. They had clearly expressed their unhappiness with Richard's non-Chinese upbringing and I did not want to
incur the same displeasure. Consequently, I did my best to mind my
Chinese manners. I never failed to stand when either of them entered the
room, never preceded them through a door, never touched a morsel of
food before they did, and never failed to greet my seniors promptly by
speaking their names and deferential titles. If they did find me lacking,
they didn't voice their criticism. The difference between Richard and me
was that he was their biological son whose non-Chinese upbringing was
of greater concern than whatever failings I exhibited. They were good to
me, and I have no complaints about their treatment. However, it did
bother me that they were so singularly uncommunicative. They spent
most of their time in their bedroom, which was large and contained a
couch and easy chair in addition to the normal bedroom furnishings. The
only time I really saw them was during meals, and even then they spoke
little. The two little ones, in an age when children were to be seen and
not heard, kept their mouths politely shut. Helen too was quiet. I took
my cue from her and spoke when spoken to but seldom initiated conversations. Meals were dreary affairs. No spontaneous conversation whatsoever. A few perfunctory questions from Second Aunt or Uncle on the
events of the day. Nothing more. We sat; we ate; we retired to our
rooms. Second Uncle must have been a fast eater--or perhaps he didn't
eat as much--because he was always finished before the rest of us. Then,
in what I learned was Shanghai fashion, he would point at each of us in
turn with his chopsticks, saying at the same time, *"Man Yung, man yung"*
(Eat slowly). He would then leave the table, leaving the rest of us to fin-
ish our meal without him.

Second Aunt was an unappealing woman. She always wore a
short Chinese mandarin-style jacket over loose trousers and appeared
ungainly and dumpy. Though she was not fat, her girth in the middle

regions was large and gave her a pear-shaped look. She seldom wore her false teeth, which certainly did not help her appearance, and her speech was consequently marred by a slight lisp. However, other habits were more disturbing. It was on my first day in their household that I heard the loud unmistakable sound of someone breaking wind. I know I had a smirk on my face as I looked toward the children. I assumed it was one of them and expected a giggle of embarrassment accompanied by an adult reprimand of some sort. Much to my surprise there was no sign that anyone else had even heard. I realized with some shock that it was not the children, but Second Aunt, who had committed the indiscretion. I soon found that this was to be a quite regular occurrence. Throughout the year and a half that I remained in Shanghai I grew accustomed to hearing Second Aunt moving about the apartment discharging her flatulence at will with little concern about the effect it had on others. I don't remember ever passing this on to my mother. She would have been shocked. *A lady is someone who at all times and in all places is mindful of the feelings of others.* Apparently Second Aunt had not been brought up with my mother's favorite rule of behavior--or maybe she couldn't help it!

I usually had my breakfast alone, the two little children leaving the apartment for school ahead of me. Second Uncle and Aunt and Helen got up much later. My first impressions were that the family was very stingy with their food. Breakfast was always *p'ao fan*, leftover scorched rice scraped from the bottom of the previous night's rice pot with boiling water poured over it. With the *p'ao fan* the amah usually gave me some salted peanuts or salted pickles. Only a few weeks into my stay, I discovered that a basket of other more tasty-looking foods was suspended by a wire from the kitchen ceiling. I concluded that Second Aunt begrudged me this extra food and had instructed the amah to keep these out of sight. With some chagrin I later learned that the contents of the basket were dishes for our dinner and were suspended that way at night against the mice, not me. Also, that *p'ao fan* was not an effort at frugality but was the standard breakfast fare for Shanghai Chinese.

With only three bedrooms in the apartment, Second Uncle and Aunt did not really have room for me. I was put in a tiny room that they used for storage and was once again surrounded by boxes and trunks stacked to the ceiling. The room, however, was bright and airy, and its window looked down on the bustling activity at the rear of the building. I could see the delivery carts and the food vendors who came every morning; and I watched with fascination as baskets of cabbages, onions, whole chickens, and all manner of household items rode up and down the walls of the apartment building. The servants, who were not allowed to use the building's single elevator, had rigged up simple pulleys to lift their morning purchases to their apartments.

Small as it was, my room was pleasant, and I was happy to have the privacy of a room to myself. There was space for a single bed against one wall. A small dresser was pushed up against the boxes on one side of the room, and a folding table against the trunks on the other side. The table served both as my desk and my bedside table. It was a tight squeeze. The bed was like the ones our servants used at home, the mattress consisting of a thin quilted pad that lay on a wooden frame with a woven straw matting stretched over it. Though it was not as soft as the ones at home, I soon got used to it.

I was quite comfortable in that tiny room, my only complaint being that the windows were not screened and I was being bitten every night by mosquitoes. No one else was bothered. I would scratch throughout the night, but in the morning the welts would be gone. Second Aunt was sympathetic and had the amah provide me with incense coils that I burned beside my bed at night. It didn't help. What I couldn't understand was that I was being bitten on parts of me that were under the bedclothes. Then, one night while reading in bed, I actually felt a bite on my leg. I threw back the covers and saw to my horror a small black bug scurry out of sight. I spent the rest of that night on the living room couch. The next morning we took the whole bed up to the roof of the apartment building, headboard, footboard, and mattress frame. The amah set each of the four legs in a basin of water. She seemed to know exactly what to do and had obviously done it before. She then poured boiling water over every inch of the bed. The bedbugs swarmed out of the wood, and the water in each basin was covered with little black wiggling dots. My skin crawled at the sight of these creatures--my bedfellows. Only recently I learned from a friend of his experience with bedbugs while in Chungking. He too was being bitten by bedbugs and   advised to put a dirty sweaty shirt in bed before he got into it. The bedbugs would then converge on the shirt instead of him. Smart idea but unfortunately I learned of it too late. Besides, I had serious doubts that the bedbugs would be deceived throughout the entire night.

At the time I moved to Shanghai, all my father's family except his oldest sister lived in Shanghai. His second brother, his fourth brother (my biological father), his second sister, his fifth sister, and the son of his deceased oldest brother, all were in Shanghai with their families. Yi Tai Tai also was by then moved to Shanghai and once again became a part of my life. She was at that time living with Mabel and her husband in a very fine apartment. They were the only ones among the relatives who were affluent enough to be in an apartment that still had hot running water, and many weekends I went there to have a bath.

I liked Mabel's husband, John Chen. He was some twenty years older than Mabel, a highly successful broker, and was considered a good catch for Mabel. Yi Tai Tai was pleased with the match, as she had every right to be. In earlier days a man of his status would have been reluctant to marry a concubine's daughter, but by then we were moving into modern times. Mabel was pretty, smart, and college-educated--she had graduated from St. John's University--and not to be dismissed as marriage material because she was the daughter of a concubine. It was while Yi Tai Tai was living with them that she became skilled in playing the stock market, which was highly volatile at the time. She had been totally illiterate, had had no formal education, but she had learned to read and write, and she was smart, very smart. She did well in her investments and was better off in the war years than our other relatives.

Family by family, I met all of my father's relatives. During the eighteen months I was in Shanghai, I came to know them all and was frequently invited to their homes. Some I liked better than others, but all were nice to me and welcomed me warmly. Strangely--but perhaps not so strangely--the ones with whom I developed the least rapport were Fourth Uncle and Aunt and their family. Though they made a great fuss over me, reminding me again and again that I was their child by birth, I never felt really comfortable with them. In retrospect I wonder if I distanced myself from them emotionally because of subconscious fears that they would try to lay some claim to me. I dutifully visited them on many weekends, but did not become close to my biological family. How strange and moving it was for me, forty years later, when I met brother Ling Ling again in Hong Kong to see the tears flow freely down his cheeks. I still felt no sisterly attachment to him, but to him, though long-separated, I was sister still.

It was on one of my earliest visits to Fourth Uncle and Fourth Aunt that she drew me aside and said in an undertone, "Huan Huan, come into my bedroom for a moment. There is something special I want to tell you." Her tone was so very secretive, I couldn't imagine what she had on her mind or why it couldn't be said in front of the others. Little did I realize that she was about to tell me something that I must keep secret for the next twenty-six years.

I followed her into the bedroom--I had never been in it before--and stood, waiting expectantly. "Huan Huan, first you must promise me that you won't ever tell your mother what I am going to tell you," she said. "Do you promise?"

I was even more perplexed. Without having any idea of what I was promising, I promised. Her next words: "You know that you are my child. But I want you to know that Luther is not. I did not give birth to Luther."

At first I couldn't grasp what she was saying. Luther was not her child? From as early as I could remember both Luther and I had been given to understand that Luther and I were born of the same mother and father. Richard was really my cousin; Lois was an adoption from outside the family and not related by blood, but Luther and I were true brother and sister, both born to Fourth Aunt. Now Fourth Aunt was telling me that Luther was not hers. That meant he was not my brother, not my real brother. Then who were his parents, and what was his relationship to the rest of us?

Fourth Aunt answered my question before I had a chance to ask. "Luther is your father's own child. *T'a shih ni pa pa wai mien yiang ti. .* He is your father's child from an outside relationship. It was your father who asked me to pretend that Luther was mine." She cautioned me once again not to tell my mother the truth under any circumstances. "Remember, you promised," she repeated again.

I don't know if Fourth Aunt realized the impact her words had on me. All I could think of at that moment was that Luther was not my brother, but later that evening, in the quiet of my own room, the full import of what she had said came home to me. It meant that Daddy had not been faithful to Mother. It meant that Fourth Uncle and Aunt, by claiming Luther was their child, had deceived my mother and our Peking branch of the Ch'ien family. I was shaken. I wanted to talk to someone, but who? I certainly couldn't tell Luther. Lois? She couldn't keep anything to herself. Richard? No. It would only further weaken his relationship with my father, which had never been good. A friend? Edie? No, not even Edie. This was a family affair. And so, I kept it to myself. And as far as our family in Peking and all our friends were concerned, it remained a secret for over twenty years. Mother never knew. Nor did Richard or Lois. Luther himself learned of his parentage long after my mother's death. Looking back, I often wonder why I didn't ask Fourth Aunt more about the circumstances that surrounded Luther's adoption. But then, it wasn't my place to ask. Who was I, a girl of eighteen, to be questioning her? But today I wonder. Other than lying to my mother, had Fourth Aunt taken a more active part in the deception? Had Luther been taken to her as an infant so that she could personally deliver him to my mother in Peking as she had me? And too late, though my mother had told me many times the story of my own adoption, and had also told me of how Lois had been adopted, I had never thought to ask her the details of Richard's *kuo chi* adoption into our branch of the family, or Luther's.

     In the days after I learned that Luther was not my "real" brother, I examined my feelings about our changed relationship. It made no difference. Blood was not thicker than water. He was the same brother he had always been and I felt as close to him as I had always felt. However, questions about my father that I had ignored in the past floated to the surface. I remembered Lois telling me a long time ago that Mr. Liu, a family friend, had once told her quite calmly that Mother was only my father's concubine and that his *cheng t'ai t'ai*, his proper wife, lived in Tientsin. At the time the very idea seemed so ridiculous that I had dismissed it without a second thought. Throughout my early childhood I had known only love and warmth within our home; I could not conceive of my father having any other wife elsewhere during those years. But what of the years after 1932, when he had lived away from home and returned only sporadically? Perhaps he had had his women on the side, but there was no question in my mind that Mother was wife, not concubine. For a few days the thought of my father's infidelity bothered me, but then I put the whole matter out of my mind. It did not resurface until some thirty years later.

Despite the warm welcome I received from my father's side of the family, I never learned to like Shanghai. Though I had initially been excited about living in a big cosmopolitan city, the reality differed from my expectations. Apartment living, with people above and below and on either side, compared so unfavorably with the privacy of the courtyards in Peking. I hated having to listen to the sounds that came from neighboring apartments, people shouting, mahjong tiles clicking, even the sounds of cooking, the chop-chop-chopping of the cleaver, or the loud sizzle of food being plunged into hot oil. I was incredulous that in this modern metropolis the wastewater from kitchen sinks and washbasins ran down exterior pipes to open gutters at the base of the buildings. Soapsuds, bits and pieces of kitchen refuse, were all plainly visible as they floated through the gutters. The streets of the French Concession where our apartment was located were tree-lined and quiet and had some lovely, gracious European-style homes, but the downtown streets were crammed with people pushing and jostling each other in their haste to get to who knows where.

I didn't like the climate either. I was not there during the hot, humid summer months, but the winter months were cold. Not the dry crisp cold of Peking, but a bitter, penetrating, damp chill. Due to the fuel shortage, neither our apartment, which had originally been centrally heated, nor the classrooms at St. John's had any heat. Shanghai's winter temperature seldom reached the freezing point, but was often in the forties. With no heat at all, one is chilled to the bone. I slept in my flannel pajamas and a woolen dressing gown and wool socks. To school I wore a woolen undershirt and wool slacks under a quilted Chinese gown. Over that, a fur-lined overcoat. It was difficult taking notes in class while wearing woolen gloves. Many of us got chilblains. They were often no worse than sore purple spots on the hands or feet, but often they swelled with inflammation and became filled with pus. I was lucky that mine were never bad enough to break. Edie was not so fortunate. As usual, she was the one to whom things "happened." If anyone's chilblains were to break, it would be hers. Several times her chilblains did break, and she then had to endure the pain of raw, ulcerated flesh that was slow to heal.

With no fuel for heating, there was also no fuel for the hot water boilers of the apartment building. Our only hot water was either boiled on the kitchen stove or "bought." The amah always had a water kettle filled with hot water in the bathroom to wash our faces with in the morning. It was not like having hot water from the tap, but with a little from the kettle added to the cold, at least we didn't have to wash in icy water. Bathing was another thing. Once a week we would indulge in "buying" hot water. The amah would be sent off to summon a coolie, who would bring the water up to the fifth floor in two five-gallon gasoline cans at a time. He carried the square cans on either end of a shoulder pole. I don't know where or how the water was heated. For me it was enough that it was available, for a price of course. Each member of the household got one can. The five gallons barely covered the bottom of the tub.

The building's single elevator was too small to hold a bicycle. Since bicycles, or anything else could not be left in the downstairs hall for fear of theft, I kept mine in the entry hall of our apartment. Any time I went out I had to carry my bicycle down four flights of stairs. Not so difficult when I didn't have school books to carry, but with a basket full of books on the handlebars it was not easy. Going back up the stairs was worse.

For me, language was an added problem. I hated not understanding what people were saying. I spoke only Mandarin, and though all my relatives spoke Mandarin to me, it was only natural that they should revert to Shanghai dialect much of the time. The two dialects are very different and I was often totally out of touch with ongoing conversations. It made me feel stupid and I did not enjoy feeling stupid. Yet I never made the effort to learn Shanghai dialect. Mandarin is the national language of China, and in my arrogance I thought others should be speaking Mandarin, my language, instead of me speaking theirs. In later years I learned to speak Cantonese quite passably but still cannot speak Shanghai dialect, or understand it.

But what I disliked most about Shanghai were the people. I found them too smooth, too sophisticated, too everything that I was not. While scorning what I perceived as their superficiality, I was also envious of their smart appearance and self-assured style. By that time the Chinese *ch'i p'ao* had metamorphosed from a straight-cut garment to a form-fitting sheath that showed off the trim figures of the Shanghai girls to perfection. I was intimidated by their elegance--no blue cotton cover-alls for them--and never stopped feeling gauche and out of place among them. Edie and I were jealously critical of their apparent vanity and over-emphasis on appearance. We also thought their habit of walking with hands linked looked totally ridiculous for those of the same sex, but nonetheless took to copying them, giggling all the while.

Given the discomfort I felt among the local Shanghai students, I found most of my new friends among those from North China or among the overseas Chinese from Southeast Asia, who, like Edie and me, had come to Shanghai to study. The language common to all of us was English.

Edie was quick to make new friends. They became mine as well, and we were soon actively involved in a new circle. Chief among these new friends was Rosie Ting. Rosie and her sister Lucy lived alone in a comfortable apartment. It was rather unusual in that day and age for two young Chinese girls to be given that amount of independence, but their father was single, and his business-- he owned a soft drink factory in South East Asia--did not permit him to live permanently in Shanghai. Edie and I spent a great deal of time in that apartment, often staying over the weekend. Rosie and Lucy normally shared the apartment's double bed, but when Edie and I stayed over, Lucy was relegated to the couch. The bed was not wide enough for three, so Edie, Rosie, and I slept horizontally across the bed with three chairs pushed up against its side to hold our feet.

Among our new friends was a wealthy family whose origins had originally been in Tientsin. Now, one branch of the family, the Chens, had made their home in Shanghai in a large imposing castle-like mansion in the center of town. Their cousins, Robert and Clarence Tsai, whose home was still in Tientsin, had joined them in Shanghai for the years they would be attending St. John's. The house was always humming with activity. Five members of the family played musical instruments, and they had their own five-piece combo. Their music room was the hub for their frequent jam sessions. At several of the smaller nightspots that we frequented, late in the evening when the crowd had thinned out, the boys would take over the bandstand and I would have a chance to sing with the mike.

Despite the fact that I did not like the city of Shanghai, I had some good times there. And despite the fact that the city was under Japanese occupation, it sometimes seemed to me that the people of Shanghai were unaware that there was a war on at all. The shops on Nanking Road and Yu Yuan Road were full of merchandise, and the streets pulsated with activity. Obviously not everyone had been impoverished by war. Throngs of eager shoppers filled the streets and the big department stores like Sinceres, Wing Ons, and the Sun Company. Though I had no money to buy, I nonetheless enjoyed an occasional visit to one of them, riding the escalators--things I had only heard of but never seen--and wandering through the aisles with their row on rows of glass cases. Peking had nothing to parallel these large commercial establishments. The closest thing to a department store in Peking was the British Whiteaway Laidlaws, which though labeled a department store, occupied only one floor whose total space was not a quarter of a single floor of Wing Ons. In Shanghai, the big, imposing bank buildings along the famous waterfront Bund were doing a thriving business, and the neon-lit downtown streets were alive with activity. The city's nightspots continued to thrive, as did its numerous gambling sports. Those with money continued to crowd the racetrack, the Hai-a-lai stadiums, and the dog-racing tracks. The movie halls were still packed, but now Hollywood movies gave way to Chinese movies. Chinese stage plays too became popular. Dance halls and nightclubs were as busy as they had always been. The only difference was that now American popular music was replaced by the new Chinese dance music, jazz with an oriental flavor.

Ballroom dancing had always been a popular recreation in Shanghai, and during the time I was there tea dances were a big thing. The Paramount was the largest and most popular, but the choicest nightspot in all Shanghai was the Mandarin Room. Small, exclusive, and very, very expensive, it was a place everyone knew about but few could afford. In my wildest dreams I never expected to have the chance to go there, but before I left Shanghai I was there twice, both times at the invitation of a sophisticated man many years my senior.

When I think of my brief acquaintance with Chang Hsiao Lung, it often surprises me that Second Uncle and Aunt did not ask more questions about my contact with him. I do recall telling them of my first meeting with his wife, but beyond that, they did not question me at all

and did not raise any objections. In some ways I think they were somewhat intimidated by this niece who seemed so independent, so indocile,
so little like their own daughter. While I was in their care I often spent
nights away from the apartment, and my polite requests for permission
were more along the lines of informing them of my plans than asking for
their permission.

Edie and I had returned to Peking for the summer after our first
year at St. John's. At the end of the summer we returned to Shanghai by
air, and it was on that return trip that we met Mrs. Chang. The flight was
miserable. It was hot, the fans were not working well, and what air pressure control there was was not working efficiently. There was a lot of
turbulence, and the woman across the aisle was looking green. She was
searching frantically for the airsick bag that should have been in the seat
pocket in front of her but was having no luck. I said to Edie, "Oh-oh, I
think she's going to be sick." I rummaged around for my own airsick
bag, but Edie found hers first. "Quick, give her this one," she said. Fortunately, we were just in time. When the woman recovered from her
upheaval, she was perspiring heavily so we asked the stewardess for a
wet towel. As she mopped her face, from across the aisle I fanned her
with the fan I always carried. When she had recovered somewhat, she
thanked us profusely and introduced herself. On learning that we were
not being met by anyone at the airport and would be taking pedicabs
home, she insisted that she take us home in her car. The car was very
plush, and as the uniformed chauffeur snapped to attention and opened
the door for us, once again for all too short a period we knew the luxury
of past better days.

Less than a week after our meeting on the plane, I received an
unexpected phone call from Mrs. Chang. She invited both Edie and me
to dinner that weekend at Hsin Ya, one of Shanghai's best-known restaurants. It seemed we had made a new friend. She said, "I'll send the car
for you."

The chauffeur knocked at the door of our apartment at the appointed time, and as I collected my coat and purse, little Tung Tung was
peering out the window to catch a glimpse of the car. I heard him say in
awe, "Wow, it's got a Number 2 license plate!" and Helen's much- impressed comment, "They must really be important people."

After picking up Edie, we proceeded to the restaurant. There we were met by Mrs. Chang, her husband, and one other couple whose names I don't recall. The meal was elegant, and after several years of frugal fare, it was all I could do to keep from making a pig of myself. But the high point of the evening came afterward. We were to go on to the Mandarin Club! *Wait till I tell my friends where I've been. Wait till I tell Helen. Wait till I tell the world. I've been to the Mandarin Club! Joy, joy, joy!*

It met all my expectations. Small, intimate, dimly lit, luxurious. There was no orchestra; the music was provided by a single organ that dominated the room. The music was so different from a dance orchestra; it was unique and wonderful. The manager fawned over our host. The waiters hovered over him. The service was superb. Chang Hsiao Lung was very proper. He danced with his wife; he danced with me. He danced with Edie; and he danced with me. He danced with the extra woman, and he danced with me many more times. In the ladies' room Edie said to me, "I think he's quite taken with you."

"But he's so old," I said. I had no idea how old he was, but guessed in his early fifties. "He's a great dancer, though," I added. Edie agreed.

He was not particularly good looking, but he was smooth, urbane, sophisticated, and obviously important. I was well aware that he liked me and was flattered at having captured his attention. *Foolish girl!*

A week later he called. They--presumably he and his wife-- would like to take us out to dinner again. Another good meal; another elegant nightclub. Where would it be this time? I relayed the invitation to Edie. We were thrilled. This time Chang Hsiao Lung himself was waiting for me in the car. His wife was nowhere to be seen. "Where is Mrs. Chang? Will she be meeting us?" I asked.

"No, I'm sorry she was not feeling well. She asks to be excused."

I wasn't in the least perturbed. She was a nice woman, but difficult to talk to. I wondered if the evening would include dancing again. That would be more fun than just conversation. We went on to pick up Edie and were joined at the restaurant by another man--no wife--a partner for Edie. Another good meal and on to the Mandarin Club again. It was a lovely evening and I basked in the luxury of the elegant surroundings, the unsurpassable music, and the unaccustomed attentions of an older man.

The next time he called I wondered if his wife would be present. I say that I wondered, but I suppose I really knew she would not. I accepted the invitation anyway. There was something deliciously intoxicating about being singled out by an older sophisticated man. And I told myself I would not be alone with him. Edie would be with me. Chang Hsiao Lung was again waiting in the car alone. Again he made apologies for his wife. She had been called to the bedside of her sister who was seriously ill. Again we picked up Edie, and again a partner--the same one--was waiting for us at the restaurant. This time it was the ballroom of the prestigious Park Hotel and western food instead of Chinese. We had barely begun our meal when another party was ushered to the table next to ours. I was surprised to see that Professor Han, our Chinese teacher from St. John's, was among the group. We exchanged greetings and he seemed even more surprised to see Edie and me. The Park Hotel was not a place normally frequented by college students. But how lucky it was for us that our paths crossed that evening! After dinner, when Edie and I returned from the ladies' room, our table was empty. Professor Han was looking anxiously in our direction, and no sooner had we sat down than he came rushing over to talk to us.

He had a very concerned look on his face. "I know it is not my business, but when your partners left the table I overheard them say that they were going to the front desk to *k'ai fang chien*. I think you girls should know what you're in for."

I looked at him, perplexed. "*K'ai fang chien?*"

"Don't you know what that means?" he asked. "It means they are going to reserve rooms. It means they expect more from you than just dancing."

Edie and I looked at each other in dismay. We knew what he meant, but surely he must be wrong. Surely no one could think we were *that* kind of girls.

"I can't believe you are so naive," he continued. "You foolish young girls don't know the ways of people in Shanghai. Do you have any idea who you are with? I don't recognize the other man, but Chang Hsiao Lung is the Chinese advisor to the occupation government. He's a collaborator, important, and powerful. What you do is your business, but

I advise you girls to steer clear of him." With that he returned to his table, shaking his head with a worried look on his face.

I was stunned. What to do? We had to get out of this. "Think of some excuse, Edie," I said. But Edie was speechless; she was just as stunned as I. I groped frantically for a way to get out of the situation. "I'll say we have homework, that we have a test tomorrow. No, that won't do. If we had a test we wouldn't have come out tonight. I'll say I don't feel well. I'll say that I must have been allergic to the shrimp cocktail." It was a poor excuse, but we could think of no other. I had wanted to be an actress. "Well, act." I told myself. When the men returned I put on the sickest expression I could muster. Leaning forward, I clutched my stomach as if in pain. It must have been convincing. Minutes later we were being driven home, unscathed by our outing.

Looking back, I cannot imagine what I had been thinking. Among family and friends I had always been the sane sensible one, always the voice of reason while others went off on wild tangents. But in this instance I had gone totally off track, had been lured by the trappings of money, by the flattery to my ego, by the promise of good times in fancy surroundings. Worse, it had not bothered me a bit that Chang Hsiao Lung was a married man and that it was his wife who had been so nice to us. When he called again, I declined, telling him I had to attend a family gathering. He called once more and once more I politely declined because of an exam the next day. My reckless escapade was over, and I had come back to my senses. I never told my mother. And I never told Lois. She would have been delighted to let Mother know that her goody-good, model child was not really so good after all.

By the end of 1944, American planes began flying over the industrial areas on the outskirts of Shanghai. It was cause for exhilaration but also frightening. When we heard the bombing, Second Aunt would herd the family into the inner hall of the apartment to avoid the possibility of flying glass. Japanese propaganda was spreading the word that American planes were indiscriminately bombing the residential areas of Shanghai. My mother in Peking was concerned enough that she wanted me out of the area. Edie's mother too wanted her home, as did the family of our Tientsin friends. This time we took the train. Five of us, Robert and Clarence Tsai, Edie and I, and another friend left Shanghai in the middle of a total blackout. The train was jammed with people and lug-

gage. Bundles blocked the aisles. Even the toilet cubicles were filled
with bundles and baskets that held the doors permanently open. Among
the five of us we managed to grab three seats. Throughout the trip we
took turns standing or trying to create makeshift seating on other people's
bundles.   Uniformed Japanese soldiers occupied many of the seats.
Some had spread themselves into more than one seat with their own belongings. No one dared to question them. During the long journey, in
one of my standing periods, I was surprised when one of the Japanese
soldiers offered me his seat. In an effort to distract myself from the misery of standing, I had been humming "China Nights," a Japanese tune
that had become particularly popular with the Japanese during the war.
The soldier looked at me with approval, I suppose because I was humming a Japanese song. Then he actually rose, pointed to his seat, and
saying a single word, "*tsoh!*" indicated that I should sit. Exhausted as I
was, I did not want to accept this favor from a Japanese soldier. And I
certainly did not want to sit among them. I shook my head and turned
away. He shrugged and sat down again. What did he care? He had
made the gesture. It didn't matter to him that this young Chinese girl had
spurned his offer.

Midway in the stretch between Shanghai and Nanking, the train
sounded warning signals that an air raid was about to take place. An
announcement over the loudspeaker informed us that we should leave the
train and take cover. With the throng of others I headed for the surrounding cornfields. The planes roared overhead and were gone in minutes
without incident. Hidden by the corn stalks, I was glad to have a chance
to relieve myself in the cleanliness of nature. Before that, the only way
to use the toilet on board was to climb over the many bundles that held
the door open, and to have someone hold up a coat as a makeshift screen.
Edie has no recollection of this incident. Yet it is vivid in my mind.
Sometimes I wonder if I only dreamed it.

The train stopped over in Nanking where the boys found us a
small local inn near the train station where we could spend the night. A
small concrete building with two floors, it looked decent enough, but
inside it was dismal. We were given two adjoining rooms. The bedding,
one quilt for each bed, looked as if it had never been washed. Edie and I-
-I particularly because of my past experience with bedbugs--were afraid
they might be vermin-filled. What I wouldn't have given for the cool

white sheets I had found fault with as a child! The boys lent us their padded winter Chinese gowns to use for covers. I don't know what they used. The toilets were so filthy we couldn't bring ourselves to use them. We used the spittoon instead. Every sound could be heard through the thin walls of wooden board, and Edie and I joined in a loud chorus of "Roll Out the Barrel" in an effort to mask the resounding noise of urine hitting the tin spittoon. In later years we had some good laughs over the ordeals of that night. The rest of our trip was uneventful. As the train drew nearer to Peking, its final destination, the crowd of people had thinned out and all of us were able to get seats. The three boys left us at Tientsin, and Edie and I proceeded home in relative comfort. It was January 1945.

Chapter 17
War's End

BY THE TIME I RETURNED home, the family situation in Peking had grown worse. Money received from the sale of our North City house had long since been spent. Funds from my father came even less frequently than before. Flour, rice, and oil rations had been cut further, and the meager four ounces of meat per day that we had finally adjusted to was reduced permanently to two. Added to our problems of survival was my mother's discovery of large debts incurred by my father. The knowledge came to her only piecemeal, as one by one old friends approached her to ask very tentatively if she could possibly repay something toward the amounts my father had borrowed. If they had not been as much in need of funds as we were, I doubt that they would ever have asked. My father had never hesitated to help his friends when they were in need, and had received the same generosity from them. He had borrowed without a qualm, without a thought to how the debts would be repaid. He had never told my mother. Now she was staggered by the size of his debts. With her rigid standards of right and wrong, she felt obligated to make whatever repayments she could. Whenever funds were received from my father, or there was extra rental income from a transient guest, a small part of it went toward paying off my father's debts. The full amounts were never repaid. Apart from the added strain to our financial state, my mother now had the added mental burden of wondering how much of that debt had been her doing. *Had even the guesthouse been started on borrowed funds? Had the extensive renovations, the antique furnishings, the Beautyrest mattresses been paid for with borrowed money?*

But more disturbing to me than our dwindling funds and the knowledge of unpaid debts were the frayed tempers within the household. Lois and Mother squabbled constantly. Each flared up at the other with little provocation, and I, who had always gotten along so well with Mother, was caught in the middle of their quarrels. Mother, burdened with the extra support of Lois and Derek, looked for some measure of gratitude. Lois was instead defensive about her own position. She felt herself to be a victim of circumstances; Mother felt that she had brought the circumstances upon herself. I felt sorry for Lois, but when I defended her, it resulted in my quarrelling with Mother. When I tried to make Lois see things from Mother's standpoint, it ended in a quarrel with Lois. Each thought that I took the side of the other. All our tempers were strained to the breaking point, and Mother's in particular. I could see signs that she was reaching the end of her rope the day I watched in dismay as she slapped little Jeannie in the face simply because she would not stop crying. She was filled with remorse after that incident, could not believe it of herself. And I could hardly believe it of my mother. Through the difficult times she had held us all together, never showing any signs of weakness. Now I could see the first signs of disintegration. That night, I knelt beside my bed and prayed. To the God whose existence I had questioned, I prayed. *Please God, if there really is a you, if you are really there, please, please, make it stop.*

In pre-war years, though our world was pretty much bounded by Peking's city walls, we had had newspapers and radio to keep us informed of the major events in the world. We had also had the newsreels that preceded most American movies. But under the Japanese occupation neither the local newspapers, English or Chinese, or the local radio stations carried any war news that the Japanese did not control. We were completely cut off from the outside world except for our short-wave radio. It was hidden in the false bottom of an antique wooden cabinet where we stored linens. The radio was covered by a stack of tablecloths and napkins. The reception was poor, but once in a while we would get a glimmer of how the war was progressing, and by the end of 1944 we

knew that the tide was turning. Despite the fact that the Japanese gendarmes had been in and out of the house, they never made more than a
cursory inspection of the premises. The radio was never discovered. It
brought us our first news of the Japanese surrender. It must have been a
day of great jubilation, but I have no recollection of victory celebrations
or of dancing in the streets or of greeting friends with hugs and shouts of
joy. It was over. The war was over. Our country had been at war for
eight long years, since 1937; yet we had survived, our bodies and minds
intact. We had faced some hardships, had endured some mental and
emotional anguish, but we had not been physically harmed. We had not
been victims of the atrocities at the hands of the Japanese that occurred
elsewhere in China as they marched southward. We had little idea then
how lucky we had been.

In the weeks immediately after VJ day, American troops started
trickling into Peking. Some OSS (Office of Strategic Services, the pre-
cursor of the CIA) officers were among the first to arrive. Once again
there were parties and dancing and dating. Whereas in the past it had
meant a total loss of reputation for a Chinese girl to be fraternizing with
an American Marine, it now became a social coup to be invited out by an
American officer. The Americans were now the conquering heroes, and
besides, these were officers, not enlisted men. It was acceptable. Lois
and I double-dated often. She was happy again and fun to be with. We
had a good time together. I felt closer to her than I ever had in the past.
During those brief months Lois became friend as well as sister.

For me, going out with an American was something new. Despite having an American mother and having attended an American high
school, I had never dated an American or been out anywhere with an
American boy alone. The Americans came in with money. They wanted
to see Peking. On different occasions, several asked me to go with them
sightseeing and to Chinese restaurants. After years of deprivation, it was
a joy to share a sumptuous restaurant meal, sometimes a whole Peking
duck, with just one other person. An American officer took me one evening to a local nightclub. I had never been to a "public" nightspot in Peking except to the highly respectable and high-class Peking Hotel ballroom. I was horrified. This was not an elegant, luxurious nightclub like
those in Shanghai. Here the tiny tables were packed together so tightly
that one's legs were literally brushing the legs of the people at the next

table. There was hardly room to move. The room was filled with smoke; the music loud. I was sure that some of the women there were bar girls or even prostitutes. I sat in stony silence throughout most of the evening, upset at having been brought to such a place. I don't know what my American date must have thought of me. How was he to know that in my narrow world, nice girls of the higher classes didn't frequent such places?

Within the first week or two after VJ day, the American flyers who had been part of then Colonel Jimmy Doolittle's raid on Tokyo— America's first strike against Japan on Japan's home turf—were brought into Peking. They had been shot down over occupied Chinese territory, captured by the Japanese, and imprisoned in Shanghai's notorious Bridge House. There they had been tortured, starved, and subjected to untold sadism on the part of the guards. Some had died while in captivity. Those who survived were brought to Peking. The sixth floor of the Peking Hotel was converted into a hospital ward, and the eight or ten members of the Doolittle group were hospitalized there for recuperation. All were emaciated; some still able to walk, but barely. A few were totally bedridden. During the next few weeks, many of the English-speaking community visited them frequently. Lois, Edie, and I were among them. A few weeks after they had returned home to America, much to my surprise, and to Lois's, I received a letter from one of them wanting to keep in touch. Lois said, "*You* got a letter from George Barr?" She couldn't get over that. Even I was surprised. She was the one who attracted men, the one with the sex appeal, not I. Why had George wanted to keep in touch with me and not Lois? But George and I began a correspondence. Before the war, in civilian life, he had been a high school basketball coach. Now he had returned to a coaching job in New York. When I came to America and visited New York, he and his mother gave me a royal welcome. I kept in touch with both of them for several years after that.

It seemed the war was barely over when all Americans still in Peking were advised by the International Red Cross that a U.S. naval ship was available to evacuate all American nationals who wished to return to America. The ship would leave in twenty-four hours. Mother did not hesitate. She had struggled through almost four years of misery and extreme hardship. Those years had been hard on her. She was ready to go. Jeannie, only seven at the time, as a minor child of an American, was eligible to accompany Mother as a dependent. I had been scheduled to attend Smith College in the fall of 1942, but the war had intervened. Mother hoped that they would still accept me. She requested permission of the Red Cross to take me also and was told that though I could go on the ship, they could give no assurance that I would not be turned back by the U.S. immigration authorities in San Francisco. We took that chance.

Lois was twenty-six, no longer a minor, no longer qualifying as a dependent of my mother, and was not eligible for passage on an evacuation ship for American nationals. She and her son Derek could not join us. At the time, I am not sure what Mother's intentions were for her future. It was my impression that she would stay in the U.S. for a year or two and then return to China. But at that moment, all she wanted was to leave. None of us had any idea of the upheaval the Communist takeover was to bring or that we would not be returning to our home in Peking. Together with other Americans who were returning home, Mother, Jeannie, and I left Peking by train for Tientsin to board the American Navy ship.

All our friends were at the station to see us off. While we stood on the station platform, another train came through full of American soldiers. As it pulled to a stop, the soldiers leaned out the window calling out to a group of us Chinese girls, "You speaky English?" One of us, I don't remember who, responded, "Yes, we speaky English. You speaky Chinese?" And added, "Yes, we speak English." They knew we were joking and were amazed and visibly happy to hear us respond in their language. Leaning farther out the window, they shouted to friends in the cars behind, "Hey, they speak English! These gals speak English!" They started hurling questions at us, laughing uproariously at some joke. I didn't get what one of them was saying. "Say that again. I guess I'm not very quick on the uptake," I said. That sent them into more peals of laughter. "Did you hear what she said? She's not very quick on the uptake!" They were still laughing when their train pulled out of the station, and still amazed that they had not only discovered Chinese girls who spoke English, but ones who were familiar with American colloquialisms.

Soon after that, our train arrived and we were ready to board. I shed no tears. The excitement of life ahead drowned out any sadness about what I was leaving behind. Some of the American officers who had taken me out were also at the station to see us off. Earlier, mindful of the difference in our cultures, one, a young lieutenant whom I had been out with twice, had asked me very formally if I would allow him to kiss me goodbye at the station. I told him it would not be proper. He was a gentleman and took me at my word. We shook hands solemnly and I thanked him for having been so nice to me. Another, however, unfazed by possible cultural restraints, swept me up in his arms and planted a long ardent kiss on my surprised lips. The young lieutenant looked on.

The train took us to the Tientsin port of Ta Ku where we boarded the U.S.S. Lavaca, a Navy attack transport. We did not know that my father was on his way from the Interior to rejoin us. He arrived in Peking the day after we left. We had not seen him for eight years, since that day in 1937 when our family vacation in Tientsin had been interrupted by the outbreak of the Sino-Japanese war, eight long years ago. It was to be another two years before we were to see him again.

When my father arrived in Peking, we were gone. He had missed us by one day. He had never fully accepted Lois as a daughter of the Ch'ien family, but now she was the only one to whom he returned. My mother and I did not see him until he came to America to attend my graduation from college in the summer of 1947, a full ten years since we had last been together. By then the itinerant life my mother had led for almost a year, visiting for a few months with one of her siblings and a few months with another, had come to a halt. She had settled in a large three-story house in Cambridge near the Harvard campus, and with no other source of income, was renting rooms to students. After thirty-three years in China, experiencing first a life of luxury and then difficult times, her life had come full circle, back to a rooming house in Cambridge.

My father arrived in Cambridge in the spring of 1947 with no means of support. Mother's only income was from the rents she received from the ground floor apartment of the house and from the four rooms on the third floor. She had bought the Cambridge house with money from the sale of her mother's cottage in Peabody, the one she and my father had bought for her parents years before, years when she had plenty and her parents little. She also had the money owed to her by fellow Americans to whom she had lent the proceeds from the sale of our North City house in Peking. When we arrived in San Francisco aboard the U.S. evacuation ship, Dr. William Pettus, former head of the College of Chinese Studies in Peking, had come on board to greet us with check in hand. He had taken it upon himself to collect on those loans on my mother's behalf.

Most of what my mother had went into the purchase of the Cambridge house. The remainder she used to supplement her rents. She lived frugally. She cleaned the five students' rooms, made their beds daily, washed their ten sheets and their towels every week, and our own. These were the days of wringer washers and before dryers existed. The sheets had to be carried from the basement up to the back yard for drying on the outdoor lines. I don't know how many times she climbed from basement to yard level and the three flights from basement to third floor.

I was away at college most of the time, but when I returned for vacations or weekends it pained me to see how hard she worked. Fortunately, Luther was not dependent on her. He had graduated from Harvard, joined the Navy during the war, and was continuing his studies at MIT under the GI Bill. Though I was on a full tuition scholarship at Smith, Mother still had to pay for my room and board. Most of the professors announced at the beginning of the school term whether they permitted knitting in their classes and I took advantage of those who did. I earned my own spending money by knitting sweaters and argyle socks. A steady customer for argyles was Mr. Crane of Crane Plumbing. I'm sure he never knew the name of the college student who supplied the socks. I assume he gave them as gifts to friends since he could not possibly have worn the many pairs that he bought from me. The sales arrangements were made by a Chinese-American divorcee from Hawaii who was personal assistant to Ripley of "Ripley's Believe It or Not." She had once been one of Mother's "guests" at the guesthouse and like so many other former guests had become a fast friend.

Gladys Li Hi was a flamboyant, go-getting type of woman the likes of which I had never known. I don't believe Mother had ever known anyone like her either. Her conversation was sprinkled with four letter words like "fart," "shit," and worse. Words like "Hell!" " Goddamn!" and "Jesus Christ!" poured liberally from her mouth. I had always thought of Mother as something of a prude, and she certainly would not have allowed words like those to be used in our house, but in

Gladys's case, both the language and the speaker were excused. Mother liked her. I liked her too. I was paid a ridiculous $12 per pair for argyle socks, big money in those days, and I could imagine Gladys negotiating a price, saying to the hapless Mr. Crane, "Come on, you old fart. You can do better than that."

I don't believe Gladys knew any Chinese at all, but she had parlayed her Chineseness into a high art form. With her hair always done up like a Manchu princess, piled high and filled with ornaments, she evoked images of Carmen Miranda, Chinese style. And she was every bit as exuberant. Her apartment was papered in squares of gold Chinese tea-paper, and there was almost nothing in her apartment that hadn't been converted from some kind of Chinese artifact. An antique opium couch served as a double bed, porcelain figurines were made into lamp bases, abacuses made into bookends, bronze sacrificial wine vessels used as pencil holders, lacquered wedding boxes served as coffee tables, ornate mandarin robes as wall hangings. There seemed no end to the Chinese artifacts that had been converted to practical use. And always the fragrance of Chinese incense wafted through the dimly lit apartment adding to the oriental mystique.

My father stayed with us only a few months, totally dependent on my mother. Life was not easy for her, but neither were the few months he spent in America easy for him. He had few friends in the immediate area, and without funds he could not travel as often as he would have liked to visit those in New York and elsewhere. Most of his friends were well off, and I'm sure my father felt keenly the difference between his financial situation and theirs. With my mother working as hard as she did, there was no way he could avoid doing many of the menial chores of the household such as sweeping the steps and raking the leaves. Most demeaning of all was hauling the garbage cans out to the street. He didn't complain, but his resigned expression and the set of his shoulders told of his discouragement more eloquently than words. At the end of the summer he returned to China, supposedly to settle his affairs. I think he was glad to leave behind the household chores. We did not see him again for another ten years.

During those ten years, China was experiencing the upheaval of the Communist revolution. My father, after a brief stay with Lois in Peking, returned to Shanghai where he stayed with his fifth sister and her

family.   He was fortunate in that he no longer held a position of promi-
nence. He was not singled out for persecution or public denunciation for
having been a capitalist. The Communist government welcomed foreign
exchange and we were able to send him money, which gave him a few of
the small luxuries he no longer had. He made regular petitions for an exit
permit to leave China, but each time the petitions were denied. We had
given up hope of ever seeing him again when quite unexpectedly, in the
summer of 1957, he again reentered our lives.

By then I was married, and my husband, Horace Eng, had just
been assigned to the U. S. Consulate General in Hong Kong. At the time
the State Department was still reluctant to assign Chinese-Americans to
their country of origin. My husband was one of the few who had been
posted there up to that time. We had barely arrived there with our three
children and were staying with Horace's sister while waiting for our
apartment to be ready, when I was contacted by Mr. Huang, an old friend
of my father's. It came as a complete surprise when he told me that my
father was already in Macau. After years of having his requests for an
exit permit routinely denied, the Communist government had suddenly
had a change of heart. I was overjoyed at the news but disturbed when I
heard Mr. Huang say that he was going to try to smuggle my father into
Hong Kong.

At that time, the island was being swamped with refugees flee-
ing from China. I knew that immigration rules were stringent, but the
thought of my father boarding some small fishing boat or sampan and
climbing onto an unmanned shore undercover of darkness was unthinkable to me. "There has to be another way," I insisted.

"No, there isn't any other way," Mr. Huang maintained. "That's
the only way we can get him in."

Neither he nor I had any idea at the time that Horace's brother-
in-law would be able to arrange legal entry. Y. K. Kan, the husband of
Horace's oldest sister, was a prominent Hong Kong lawyer and a member
of Hong Kong's Urban Council. He was later to be knighted by Queen
Elizabeth and to become *Sir* Y.K. With him vouching for my father, my
father was given legal entry within days.

As the passengers swarmed off the ferry, I strained my eyes
searching for the father I remembered. *Why had I expected to see him as
he had been years ago?* My conscious mind knew that he must have

aged and that years of deprivation during the Communist years would have left their mark, but for some totally irrational reason, I was still picturing him in the long silk robes of my childhood. When he finally appeared, I was dismayed. It was not only that he had aged, but he looked so much like the coolies in our Peking household had once looked. He was wearing a short jacket and pants of the roughest dark cotton. I ached for him, for what he had once been, for the life he had once known, and for what he was that day. I thought of the comfortable life I was leading, the silks I wore, the sumptuous banquets I attended, while his life had gone steadily downhill.

The U.S Consulate arranged for a visa immediately, and a week later he was on his way to join my mother in New Jersey. I did not see him again until 1959 when we went home on leave from Hong Kong. I saw him again in 1961 and 1964, each time for only a few weeks while we were on home leave. By the time I came home to stay, in 1969, he was dead. I had had a full-time father only till the age of seven; from seven to twelve I had had a part-time father; from twelve years old on I had seen him only four times, and each time for only a few weeks or days.

Whenever I had been with him in my adult life, I could not help being drawn to him. He was so very likable. To the Chinese he was what could be described as a *ta hao lao*, a jovial, good-natured fellow, and that he was. He had a round, benign *fu ch'i* face, a good fortune face. Friends and family spoke of him as "a wonderful old man." He looked like a person who had had a happy life, and to a great extent he had. But his final years? As was the case with my mother, in his last years he had little. In his letters to me after my mother's death, he was so humbly grateful for the small amounts I sent him. I was embarrassed by his gratitude, that this once important man felt the need to be grateful. He lived with my brother Luther and had for spending money only what Luther and I contributed. He supplemented this with some translating work and occasionally sold a painting or two. When he was reunited with my mother in 1957, after twenty years apart (with the exception of the few months in 1947), they did not get on well. Each complained about the other. Luther bore the brunt of their mutual dissatisfaction. They had grown too far apart. Yet, when she died at the end of 1964, he lived for only a few months. It was as if without her to chide and bicker with, there was nothing to hold him. I never knew his age, but guessed him to have been in his late seventies. His *fu ch'i* face, with its promise of good fortune, had come through for him in his early life, but had failed him in his declining years. Yet, in death, fate was good to him. His death was an easy one, as the Chinese say, a *hsiao shang*, "a happy tragedy," dizziness, a slight chest pain, and death before the ambulance reached the hospital. I was sorry to see him go, the father whom as an adult I had barely known, whom I wish I had known better.

Chapter 18
Lois

UNTIL JEANNIE WAS ADOPTED, Lois was the only one of us children who had not been born into some branch of the Ch'ien family. As far back as I can remember I knew that all of us were adopted. I don't know when I was told that Richard was really a Ch'ien cousin, or that Lois was adopted from outside the family. Where each of them came from was immaterial to me; they were my brothers and sister, a part of my family. I never noted any differences in the way we were treated by our parents. It was years later, from my mother, that I learned of my father's early rejection of Lois. And it wasn't until well after much unhappiness had occurred in Lois's life that I started wondering if the way her personality and her life evolved was due at least partially to that rejection, or if she was simply "fated" to be unhappy.

Lois had what the Chinese call a *k'u ming* face. Literally translated as a "bitter fate" face, it is a term used by both laymen and fortune-tellers that presages unhappiness. Among the wide spectrum of facial types, the Chinese are quick to label one type, at one end of the spectrum, a *fu ch'i* (good fortune) face, and the one at the other end, a *k'u ming* one. Most faces do not readily fall into either category and lie between the two. But occasionally a face will be instantly pegged by the Chinese as *fu ch'i,* another as *k'u ming.* My father had a *fu ch'i* face, as did Luther. Mine was not noticeably one or the other. But Lois's face was *k'u ming.*

Among my friends, the other person who had a *k'u ming* face was my best friend Shang May. She was pert, pretty, and sparkling with personality, but there was something in her face that gave her a "bitter fate" look. The exact features of either facial type have never been spelled out for me, but most Chinese can instantly recognize a distinctly *fu ch'i* face or a *k'u ming* one. I have always thought of a "good fortune" face as one that is somewhat Buddha-like, with smooth, rounded, expansive features, and always with great, long ear lobes. I have never been able to pin down any distinct features on a "bitter fate" look. One would have thought it might have a pinched look, possibly with a downward droop of eyes or mouth, but not so, and especially not in Lois's case. She was Cantonese, and her eyes were set much deeper than the eyes of most northern Chinese. She had high cheekbones, slightly hollowed, and a wide, generous mouth; an attractive face but one that nonetheless the Chinese did not hesitate to give a negative label.

I recall an instance during the war. Lois had been married only a few months and had stopped by for the afternoon. It was a warm summer afternoon and Mother, Lois, and I were sitting in the front courtyard when we heard the click-click-clicking of the small bamboo sticks of the fortuneteller. The sound could be heard easily from within the courtyard in spite of the high walls between street and court. Though the Chinese are a very superstitious people, our family, being unChinese in so many ways, did not put much credence in their predictions. We regarded fortune telling as merely an amusing diversion, and occasionally on social occasions my mother would have a fortuneteller come in to read the fortunes of her guests. Though there are many ways in which a Chinese fortuneteller reads the future, most use the *suan pa tze,* the "eight characters" method, which, much like the reading of one's horoscope by an astrologer, is based on the time of birth: the year, month, day, and hour. Many, if not blind--as so many Chinese fortunetellers are--combine the eight-characters method with a study of the face.

That afternoon it was Lois's idea to get our fortunes told. We had been thumbing through some old magazines and had nothing better to do so thought it would be fun to have our fortunes told. We sent Hsueh out to get him.

As Hsueh moved toward the door I called out, "Don't get him unless he's blind."

But Lois thought differently. She yelled after Hsueh, "Never mind if he's blind or not. Get him anyway." And to me, "What difference does it make if he's blind or not?"

"Of course it makes a difference. The sighted ones can base their predictions on what they see of us," I said. "You know, they can see how old we are, what we're wearing, what kind of a house we live in and all that."

Lois disagreed. "What does it matter anyway? We don't really take what they say seriously. It's just for fun, and besides, I bet some of the blind ones aren't really blind anyway. They just pretend to be."

Hsueh went out to get him. When the fortuneteller appeared it was obvious that he was sighted, not blind. We asked him what method he used, and as we had thought, he confirmed that he used the eight characters method combined with *k'an hsiang*, a study of the face.

Mother decided she would be first. After being told the pertinent details of Mother's birth, the fortuneteller foretold a glowing future and a long life. I was next, and for me too he predicted good things. I would have a happy marriage and three children. All would be successful in life. I would never be in want. I would do much travelling. I thought, "What a wasted exercise. He's just giving us the standard spiel, telling us all these good things so we'll pay him generously."

But then it was Lois's turn. As in Mother's case and mine, Lois had given the fortuneteller the required specifics of her birth, but in her case he scrutinized her face with much greater care. She had been waiting impatiently and was eager to hear what he had to say about her future. His predictions came all too soon. He foretold a dire fate for Lois. For her there was to be no life of joy, but instead much unhappiness ahead. He predicted that her marriage would be a failure. She was born in the year of the lamb; her husband in the year of the tiger. The dominant element in her horoscope was fire; in his, water. The two were incompatible.

Lois's eyes were already brimming over with tears, but the fortuneteller continued. I couldn't believe the things he was saying. I wanted to tell him to stop, but he went on relentlessly. "You will have two male children, both of whom will die young. They will be a disappointment." Lois had been married only a few months. She was pregnant. By this time she was convulsed in tears. The fortuneteller was not blind. *Couldn't he see the pain he was causing?* But still, he continued. "You will be unhappy in old age." He offered not a glimmer of future happiness to assuage her pain. Hsueh, passing through the courtyard, on seeing the scene before him, had stopped midway in his household chores. He was as amazed at what he was hearing as Mother and I were. Fortunetellers did not predict ill for their customers. Why had this one spoken so freely? Mother beckoned to Hsueh to get the fortuneteller out of the house quickly and out of Lois's sight. Hsueh hustled him to the gate. He must have paid him off.

Lois was sobbing uncontrollably.

Mother tried to console her. "Lois, you know we don't ever take these fortune tellers seriously," she said. "He was probably just trying to make himself more credible by throwing in some bad things as well as good."

"But all the bad things were about *my* future, and none about yours," Lois wailed. "Why did he say that just *my* life would be unhappy?"

I couldn't blame her for wondering, but tried to minimize the damage. "By the time he got to you he probably realized he'd been overdoing the good fortunes for Mother and me. If you'd been before me he probably would have given *you* a good fortune and me a bad one. Besides, Lois, you said yourself that we didn't take these fortune tellers seriously."

Lois's tears gradually subsided, but both Mother and I knew that she was badly shaken and that the fortuneteller's words would linger long in her memory. As her life progressed, his words must have come back to her often, as they did to me. Her later life played out much as the fortuneteller had predicted; it was as if his predictions and her *k'u ming* face had dictated the direction of her life.

Lois had not been found in a refugee camp or left to die on some street corner. She was born in a hospital. Hospitals were not for the very poor, so her family could not have been destitute. Yet, because she was born a girl, she was unwanted by both parents who had been hoping for a boy. My mother was in Tientsin, visiting an old friend in the hospital, when she heard of the unwanted child from one of the nurses. Mother already had Richard, who was then four years old, but for several years she had been yearning for a girl. Without prior consultation with my father, Mother took the baby back to Peking. I don't know if my father was upset or angry at this rash action. The child was already in his house; he did not insist on her being given up. However, he did not re-gard Lois as a member of his family and my mother told me that to the servants he would sometimes refer to Lois as *ya t'o*, an old term for slave girl or servant girl. Lois learned many years later that her name was not even entered in the Ch'ien family records. She could not have been unaware of my father's rejection, but not being recorded in the family records must have made her even more painfully aware of what she must already have felt, her non-status within the Ch'ien family. Lois's adop-tion did not have an auspicious beginning, and in the ensuing years many things went wrong for her.

Even as a small child I was conscious of Lois's imperious man-ner with the servants. I suspect that her lack of standing with my father might have been reflected in the servants' attitude toward her, and that she in turn had to *demand* their services in a high-handed manner. They served her, but grudgingly. My American cousin, the one who had once declared that my mother had married for money, in her usual acerbic manner remembered Lois as "a nasty little thing." In a letter from Helen, my Shanghai cousin, she tells of a summer she spent with our family in the Western Hills. "Your sister did bad to me. She kicked me with her feet." Mother was very fond of Helen and it is probable that Lois felt herself being further displaced by this usurper. No, Lois did not have a sweet disposition. Given the unfortunate circumstances of her childhood it was understandable, but the fact remains that she was a difficult child.

To make matters worse, as a child her complexion was very dark. In North China, where a fair complexion is admired and a dark skin abhorred, she was considered ugly. The Chinese have a saying, "*Huang mao ya t'o shih pa pien.*" Loosely translated, it means that a girl-child in her lifetime goes through eighteen changes. I have never heard or read of when these changes take place, but the saying merely means that a pretty girl-child can turn into an ugly woman, and that an ugly child can become beautiful. In Lois's case, each change was for the better. She became an attractive teenager and later, in the opinion of many, a beautiful woman.

She was, however, in many ways a disappointment to my mother. She was a mediocre student and despite much urging, refused to participate in extra-curricular school activities. She did not join the Brownies or the Girl Scouts. She avoided sports of any kind and was not on any of the school teams. At home she took no interest in girl-things like sewing or knitting. She did, however, love to sing, but unfortunately, in a family that loved music, she could not carry a tune. During family singing sessions she would sing out at the top of her lungs and I remember Mother saying again and again, "Please Lois, not quite so loud."

She was, however, an excellent ballroom dancer. She was small, just over five feet, and had a lovely figure, long-legged and graceful. It was a source of great pride to her that during her years at PAS she was the only girl, who while still in junior high, was invited by two boys, both three or four years older than herself, to both the high school junior and senior proms. These were among her few happy memories. Lois was also proud of her appeal to the opposite sex, and even Luther recognized that she exuded sex appeal. She was popular with both the boys at school and later with the younger male guests at the guesthouse. This was a source of some friction between Lois and my mother. When she was still a young teen, Mother walked into her bedroom to find her and her then current boyfriend on her bed, locked in an amorous embrace. I recall Mother's tirade against Lois, Lois's defiance, and Philip's *swearing* that they had been "only kissing." Courtyard houses provided much personal privacy, and it was difficult for Mother to oversee Lois's behavior. Philip was forbidden from the house for months but eventually readmitted after much pleading and many promises to behave. At the guesthouse the servants saw more than my mother, and they disapproved strongly of what they regarded as Lois's over-familiarity with the guests. Their disapproval was only thinly disguised, and they had little use for Lois. As in her childhood, the servants took her orders but grudgingly.

When Lois graduated from high school she was not interested in college, but at Mother's insistence that she learn some skill with which she could support herself if the need arose, she agreed to go to secretarial school in Tientsin, a three-hour train ride from Peking. There she met and fell in love with a Chinese-American businessman. When she became pregnant soon after, she and Ben were hastily married in a civil ceremony in Tientsin.   My parents knew nothing of this until after the fact.   By then my father was no longer in Peking, but my mother arranged a "proper" wedding conducted by our minister.   In the conservative missionary-oriented society of that period, a civil ceremony was not considered acceptable.   The wedding was held at our North City home.   It was small and attended by only family and a few close friends, but it lent a degree of respectability to the marriage.   Lois was eighteen.   She wore white satin and carried calla lilies.   My brother Richard was best man.   I was her maid of honor and only attendant.   At twelve years old, I was totally unaware of the undercurrents surrounding this home wedding and knew only the excitement of being part of the ceremony and wearing my first long dress.   It was of the palest green tulle and lovely.

Six months later the child was born, declared to be "premature." The child, a boy, lived only a month.   Lois and Ben occupied a single-courtyard house.   Their bedroom was on one side of the court; the baby had been, not in a room beside theirs, but on the other side of the court. It was not within hearing distance.   Lois was young.   She had not had the good sense to keep the baby near her.   The baby had seemed to be in good health.   It had not been sick.   Its death may have been an unavoidable crib death, one that today would have been called sudden infant death syndrome, but Lois had not only the loss of her child to endure but the guilt that must have accompanied it.

Immediately, Lois became pregnant for the second time.   Again she had a boy whom she named after her husband Ben: Benedict Roderick Chen.   They called him Derek.   But then, unknown to Lois, Ben was already involved with another woman.   He wanted a divorce. While Lois was still in the hospital Ben had moved the other woman into their house.   On leaving the hospital, Lois had no alternative but to come home to the family, her life a shambles.   She was still desperately in love with Ben.   She could not understand where or how she had failed.   They were divorced as soon as possible thereafter and Lois was left to bring up Derek alone.   No provisions were made for alimony or child support.   It is possible there might have been a small financial settlement, for when Lois returned to the family I believe she had some money of her own.

Understandably Lois cried a lot and found solace in cradling her baby Derek.   She rocked him back and forth, saying again and again, "Poor baby, poor baby, you have no father."   And as he reached the age of two and then of four and then of six, she still hugged him to her, repeating her sorrowful litany, "Poor baby, poor baby, you're without a father." That picture remains with me still, of Lois rocking, rocking, rocking, and repeating endlessly the sad refrain. But as the years passed, her self-pity and pity for her child, instead of diminishing, only increased.

It was hard for Mother to take. Her problems were greater than Lois's. She had to keep food on the table for us all. By then she had resumed her teaching to add to the family income. I too had begun teaching for the extra income. Lois spent most of her time reading romantic novels and old movie magazines left over from the pre-war years, at the same time eating watermelon seeds, a pound at a sitting. Her left front tooth had a permanent groove in it from cracking those melon seeds. In warm weather, she sat in the courtyard sunning her beautifully shaped bare legs to a rich, tawny brown. Even among Chinese, suntanned skin had become popular, and the dark complexion of her childhood, no longer a liability, had become an asset. Her hands were long and graceful and she used her hours in the sun manicuring her fingernails and toenails. A friend of Mother's, noting what a beautiful job of manicuring Lois did, offered her a job as a mani-

Lois

curist in her beauty shop. The pay was minimal, but both Lois and Mother were pleased that Lois would have something to occupy her time and at the same time might contribute a little toward the family's maintenance. Unfortunately, the job was short-lived. Lois was so nervous that she cut the finger of her first customer while trimming her cuticles. Much embarrassment for my mother's friend, and more tears from Lois.

During the six years that Lois lived with us after her divorce, she and I got on well, but her relationship with my mother steadily deteriorated. When she first came home, knowing the heartache Lois was suffering, Mother was unstinting in sympathy and moral support. But as our financial situation worsened and Mother's concerns turned more and more toward maintaining our livelihood, her sympathy for Lois, who seemed mired in her own misery, turned to irritation. Again and again they would exchange sharp words. I felt sorry for them both--for Lois, continually sorry for herself and resenting her situation of dependence; for Mother, for being saddled at an already stressful time with what she perceived as an ungrateful daughter.

Compounding the already stressful situation was Mother's disapproval of Lois's relationship with men. Before going to Tientsin to secretarial school, Lois had been having a heated romance with an American guest at the guesthouse. Mother suspected that he, and not Lois's husband, might have been the father of Lois's first child. The baby had looked to Mother more Caucasian than Chinese. She questioned Lois, but Lois indignantly denied it. Mother also suspected that Lois's friendship with one of the permanent guests who shared the rear courtyard with her and little Derek was more than just friendly. The one, however, who caused the most friction between Mother and Lois was an American businessman, more than twice Lois's age, probably in his fifties. William Palmer was a Peking resident, a representative of a large American company. He was single, a bachelor, and known for throwing lavish parties. Lois was not included in his cocktail parties or his dinner parties, but he invited her to his home frequently for dinner. He always sent his car for her and also had her driven home late in the evening. Mother objected strongly to Lois's seeing him.

"Why does he always have you to dinner alone?" Mother would ask.

And Lois's defiant reply: "He likes me."

"If he likes you so much, why doesn't he include you in his parties with his other friends?"

"Because he enjoys talking to me alone. That's why." Lois would start getting defensive.

"And are you sure that's all you do? Talk?" Mother pressed on.

"No, that's *not* all we do. We have a lovely dinner, with food like we never have at home anymore, and wine, and dessert, and chocolates. Sometimes we have champagne." The sarcasm would have crept into Lois's voice by now, and Mother would stop her questioning and end with resignation. "Lois, I can't stop you, but you must know how it looks to other people."

"Other people don't have to know, and it's none of their business anyway," she insisted.

"That's where you're wrong. They *do* know. The servants know, and they talk," Mother insisted.

"And I don't care what the servants know, or what they think. What I do is none of their business." Lois would go off in a huff. And that would be the end of that until the next time. Then the same argument would repeat itself.

Lois was young and attractive, and being divorced had not diminished her sex appeal. One of our transient guests, a young Chinese-American businessman, became enamored of her. Another romance began. I said to Lois one day, "I wish you'd marry Herman. He's such a nice guy." On further reflection I added, "On the other hand, I guess he's not very exciting. He's kind of a homebody. If you married him, you probably wouldn't be faithful."

Lois's face darkened and there was real anger in her voice when she spoke. "And just what do you mean by *that*? Who do you think *you* are to make a judgment like that about me?"

I was totally taken aback. "What are you getting so mad about? What did I say? I didn't say anything."

"You know what you said," she insisted.

Mother had heard our exchange and tried to placate her. "Lois, don't get so upset. She didn't know what she was saying."

"Of course she knew what she was saying. What kind of person does she think I am?" And to me: "What *did* you mean when you said I wouldn't be faithful?"

I was still perplexed. "I meant you'd probably get tired of him. And you probably would. I don't know what you're getting all excited about."

"Oh, never mind." She turned away in disgust.

My innocence was real, but unbelievable to Lois. At my age, then fourteen, Lois had known it all. Looking back, I sometimes wondered where she had learned it. From her girlfriends? Or perhaps from her boyfriends. But I wondered too if the godfather whom she adored had played a role in that part of her education.

Walter Drexel and his wife were Lois's godparents. They were longtime residents of Peking and were close friends of my parents, almost like family. They spent a great deal of time with us, often sharing family get-togethers and Christmases and going with us on family outings. They had no children of their own, and Uncle Walter lavished his attention on us, particularly on Lois. And she, largely ignored by my father, found a father figure in him. I too loved Uncle Walter. It was fun having him around.

I remember how cold it was that morning when we all piled into Mother's car. She was taking the Drexels and three guests from the guesthouse out to the visit the Temple of the Sleeping Buddha. "No, you don't get to come with us this time, Marguerite. There isn't room." Mother had said.

"But I don't take up much space, Mother. Please, I want to go," I begged. "Please, please."

Uncle Walter interceded. "Oh come on, Helen. There's plenty of room. She can sit on my lap." Mother gave in.

Happily, I hopped into the car and onto Uncle Walter's lap. I was snug and comfortable with his arms around me and the fur blanket pulled up under my chin.. The trip went quickly. But it was cold walking around the temple, and when we got back into the car for our return journey, I was shivering.

As I got back onto Uncle Walter's lap he said, "We'll have you warmed up in no time." He pulled me up close and I snuggled happily against him as he pulled the blanket up under my arms. He rubbed my arms and then my legs, and I was soon cozy and warm, but his hands didn't stop. I felt them moving up under my skirt, and then between my legs. I could feel his fingers on my skin. They crept under my panties.

I couldn't have been more than five or six. No psychologist had told me the difference between good touching and bad touching. No one had held up a doll and pointed out the parts of the body that were private. I *knew* which parts were private. I *knew* which parts were not to be touched. I *knew* this was bad touching. I squirmed. Uncle Walter said, "Don't be so wiggly." I squirmed some more. Mother, in front in the driver's seat, reprimanded, "Keep still, Marguerite, or we'll leave you home next time."

I never told my mother of that incident. Back then, child abuse was not an open topic. Children had not been told that "bad touching" should be reported to an adult. I kept it to myself, but I no longer thought Uncle Walter was fun to have around. I avoided him.

For me this had been a single incident. It never happened again. I don't believe I was psychologically damaged. But for Lois, I cannot help wondering. Was Uncle Walter a much-needed father figure? Or was he something else? I came upon them once in the library, the western library, the same one where my sex education had begun with my discovery of *Lady Chatterley's Lover*. Lois was on Uncle Walter's lap but got off hastily when I entered. She was probably then around fourteen, or maybe fifteen. I was a child; I hadn't thought anything of it at the time. Children often sat on the laps of adults, but Lois had not been that young a child, and it was the guilty looks on their faces that I remembered later. It was not until recent years when the media had started focusing on child abuse that I started wondering. Lois had worshipped Uncle Walter.

When Mother, Jeannie, and I left Peking, Richard was in Scotland. Luther had already left China for college in America. Lois and Derek were the only ones remaining in Peking. Lois had been dependent on my mother for the past six years, and apart from the brief period of her marriage, she had never been totally independent of the family. Now she had to assume full responsibility for herself and Derek. When American forces arrived in Peking after VJ day, Lois had no trouble getting a secretarial job with the American Executive Headquarters. She enjoyed her work and her contact with the Americans. Financially she had no problems; she had the same house rentals that had supported the whole family in addition to her secretarial salary. And once again she had an active social life. For several years life was good.

But with the Communist takeover in 1948, and the departure of the Americans, Lois's income reverted to the rents she received from the house. Though the Communists did her no physical harm, they plagued her frequently with questions about her relatives in America. It was during this period that a deep-seated resentment started to build up in Lois that grew and festered. Part of it was directed against Mother, but most was directed against me. Mother had deserted her, left her to cope alone with the Communist regime. No matter that Mother had had no control over who had or had not been eligible for transport on the American evacuation ship. And no matter that Mother had had no presentiment of the turmoil into which China was to be thrown. It was Mother's fault that Lois had been left behind. As for me, why had I been the favored one? That I had been scheduled for college in America was not good enough reason for my being taken to America. I had been favored; she had not.

And so, Lois, with the ever increasing sense that she had been voluntarily deserted, coped alone, while we in America led our separate lives. Mother again was wrapped up in just making ends meet. I was wrapped up in myself and my own problems of adjustment. We did not write as often as we should have. Lois felt more and more alone. For years I begged forgiveness for my negligence. But I was not to be forgiven. Lois could not forgive; nor could she forget.

In 1951, an American doctor, Dr. Ledbetter, was leaving China to return home. Lois's son Derek, then twelve, had been giving Lois problems. He was in Chinese school where the students' minds were being filled with Communist doctrine. She wanted to get him away. Dr. Ledbetter offered to take Derek out of China and deliver him to my mother in Cambridge. Mother was seventy-two at the time, physically spent from the demands of the rooming house. I dreaded her being saddled with another responsibility. In a long letter to Lois I wrote, "Lois, please don't ask this of Mother. I know she will not be able to say no to you, but I beg of you to spare her. She is seventy-two years old. Yes, I know her real age, and I know you do too. Do you have any idea what life is like for her?" I described at length the hard life Mother led, the steep climbs up three flights of stairs, the sheer physical labor involved in taking care of the five roomers, doing their laundry, cleaning their rooms. "All this just to make ends meet," I wrote. "Do you have any idea how exhausted it leaves her? Please, Lois. In China she was there for you when you needed her, but please, please don't ask her now to take on Derek as well."

There was no answer from Lois. Weeks later, Dr. Ledbetter delivered Derek to our door. My effort to stop his coming was one more count on which I was not to be forgiven. In later years, every time Lois and I were together, no matter what the subject of conversation, Lois always managed to remind me how we had left her to suffer alone in China, each time ending in a flood of tears. The first time my husband met her, we were on home leave and staying with Luther. Lois was there too on a visit, and Horace was exposed to her many bouts of weeping. Not wanting to be a witness to her tears and never-ending recriminations, he stayed out of her way. She couldn't help noticing, and in a letter to me she complained, "Every time I entered the room, he left." She was not used to being avoided by men. Years earlier, when I had written to tell her of my marriage, she had said to Edie, "I bet I could take him away from her." Now he had not even given her a chance to get acquainted, much less to charm him..

At all of our meetings Lois was the accuser and I the accused. I had no defense. I had let her down, had not written when I should have, had not cared enough. Each time I was contrite, admitted our negligence, admitted *my* negligence, and asked her to forgive, begged her to forgive, but it was not enough. But how often must I beg for forgiveness? And how often were my pleadings to be rejected? I remember the one occasion shortly after my husband's death—he died at the age of fifty-six just before my forty-fourth birthday-- when I retaliated, lashed out at her full force. I don't recall how it started, only how it ended. I had done my usual apologizing, asking her to forgive, had been rejected once again. I was sick of it. I ended up screaming at her, yelling. "I'm sick of hearing your accusations. I'm sick of your complaints of how you suffered. I've said I'm sorry. I *am* sorry, but how often do I have to say it? I've asked you to forgive me--a million times I've asked you. I know you had troubles, but how often do we have to hear about them? We've listened to them for twenty years, no, thirty. Have you ever thought that other people have troubles too? You're not the only one. Your son Derek has troubles. Mother had troubles. It may be hard for you to believe, but even I have troubles."

Lois looked stunned. She was speechless. I couldn't stop myself. "How often do I have to ask for your forgiveness? How often do I have to *beg* for forgiveness? I've spent most of my adult life telling you how sorry I am. I'm not going to spend the rest of it apologizing to you. I don't give a damn any more. If you can't forgive, you can go to hell. Go to hell for all I care! Just go to hell!"

Lois was shocked at my outburst. I am still shocked that it happened, that I had been so totally out of control. I'm not sure, however, that I am sorry. Lois spoke so often of the loving sisterly relationships she saw in other families, but I wonder if she ever really wanted that of me. From me I believe she wanted and needed something else, a justification for her resentment. Sometimes I don't blame her for resenting me. To her it always seemed that I was the favored one, and admittedly I *was*, but it was not I who curried the favor, and I resented being made to feel guilty. I remember how angry she was with me when she found that Aunt Irene had given me some old family photographs that she had wanted and asked for. Aunt Irene had said no, she was saving them for me. Lois had been visiting in America when Uncle John was ill and on his deathbed. During that time, Lois had stayed with them for several months helping Aunt Irene to care for Uncle John. Yet Aunt Irene had saved the photos for *me*, for me who had not lifted a finger. I had done nothing for her or Uncle John, but the cherished pictures were for me.

Lois had demanded of me, "Why do *you* get everything?" I didn't have a reply. I had not asked for the pictures; had not even known they existed, but as was the case in so many other instances, I was the favored one.

In 1953, Lois married Robert Simenon, a Frenchman who was studying Chinese in Peking at the time. Together they left China to make their home in Paris. He later became a prominent Sinologist well known in academic circles both in Europe and the U.S. The two seemed devoted to each other and at last it seemed Lois's life would be happy. But not so. Robert was a full professor at the Sorbonne. As head of the Department of Chinese Language and Literature, he received a good salary by French standards, but because of the high cost of housing in Paris, they lived in a tiny, rent-controlled, sixth floor walk-up apartment. Despite Robert's lavish professions of love, calling Lois his *hsiao pao pei*, his little precious one, at every turn, he had a weakness for other women that could hardly have escaped Lois's notice. On one of his many visits to America, a longtime friend, single and female, offered to put him up, only to have him appear in her bedroom stark naked in the middle of the night. She ordered him out immediately and put an end to any false expectations he might have had.

Apart from his interest in other women, he had some other aberrant traits. While visiting my brother Luther in New Jersey, the cleaning woman complained that Robert had exposed himself to her. On another occasion he was picked up by the local police when he was found jogging naked in the woods around Luther's house. I don't know if Lois was ever told of these incidents.

Once married to Lois, nothing would do for Robert than that his new son--whom he never legally adopted--should be brought up a Frenchman. After two years in the U.S. learning his abc's from scratch-- Mother had worked hard with Derek and finally brought him up to his own grade level--Derek was to become a Frenchman. At age fourteen, not speaking a word of French, he joined Lois and Robert in Paris and was put into French school. He could not keep up, could not cope, and was miserably unhappy. His parents switched him to the American school where he had wanted to be, but by then he was again behind in English. Both Lois and Robert then acknowledged defeat. They sent him to Luther, who in a fit of generosity had offered to take him. Derek was then sixteen. In the small town in New Jersey the neighbors complained of his reckless driving. He borrowed money from the gas station that he didn't repay. It wasn't long before Luther had had his fill. He kicked him out. The family of Derek's best friend took him in. He spent his adult years working successively as a gas station mechanic and a construction worker. Though Lois herself was without a college education, being from a well-to-do family and being married to a professor, she was ashamed of Derek and his wife. She was ashamed that a son of hers, in her words, had descended to "a lower class." Derek's language had deteriorated. He drank heavily, and as a result his marriage ended in divorce. One of his two children, a son, proved to be "slow."

Instead of sympathy and concern for Derek and his wife, Lois's sorrow was for herself. Why had fate given *her* a "retarded" grandson? She regarded all Derek's misfortunes as extensions of her own fate. Her relations with him and her daughter-in-law were superficial. In a letter to me she described herself as "a grandmother in name only--an old Chinese woman who sends a little money at Christmas." She was only forty-six at that writing but had already cast herself as old and unloved. But perhaps she felt older than her years. She had developed breast cancer, one more in a series of misfortunes. She did not lose her breast, but the cobalt treatments took their toll. She tired easily and lost the full use of her arm for almost two years.

As Lois's woes piled up one on another, her resentment of me increased. In many ways I could understand her feelings. From the time of my adoption, though I was oblivious to the differences in our lives, Lois must have been acutely aware of those differences. She endured my father's indifference, my mother's frequent reprimands; I received approval at every turn. With a six-year difference in age, our school lives never overlapped. She was in American high school while I was in Chinese grammar school. When I entered PAS, she had already graduated. Yet comparisons were inevitable. All the expectations my mother had had of Lois, expectations unfulfilled, were met in me. I was a good student, sang in the glee club and choir; was on the softball and basketball teams; I knit; I sewed; I did all the things dear to my mother's heart. And I was oh so good! I was not disobedient. I was not rebellious. I was not insolent. For me there was no incentive to be bad. *My children today say I must have been obnoxious, and I know that too much goodness in another can be hard to take.* I know now that I was a trial to Lois.

In a letter written to me years ago, she expresses more clearly than I can how she viewed our lives: "You know, Marguerite, how I picture the difference in the events in our lives. That you gave birth to your son on Mother's birthday, and she was buried on my son's birthday. You were married on Luther's birthday, and that was the day I entered the hospital with no hope of having another child." Always, she associated my life with happiness, hers with hardship and misery.

Her words were all too true. Except for the short-term defection of my high school boyfriend, not a trace of unhappiness had entered my life until the death of my first husband. At that point, if I had been destitute and unable to cope, if for once Lois could have told herself that she had more in life than I, she might have forgiven me my past good fortune. But grief-stricken as I was with the loss of my much-loved husband and the end of a wonderfully happy marriage, I fared better than most widows. I found work easily, and my friends did not drop me from their social lives. I was not a neglected widow. My three children, then twelve, fourteen, and sixteen, did not become delinquents. Together we worked hard on our suburban home. The children, brought up abroad with servants, had never wielded a hammer, banged a nail, or used a shovel, but they put up shelves, planted shrubs. I made curtains, planted flowers. We were proud of what we had accomplished. When Lois came to visit, she saw our pride in the home we had made. She didn't see the extent of my loss or my children's loss. And why should she have? I had lost a husband, but so had she. And she had had much less than I when Ben left her so many years ago. Once again she saw only the trappings of an idyllic lifestyle that I seemed to have and she did not.

Lois died in 1978 of heart failure. She was fifty-nine. Until her death she climbed six flights of stairs with groceries and loads of wash done at the commercial laundry. She never forgave me for being party to leaving her behind in China after the war. She never forgave me for trying to dissuade her from sending Derek to Mother. But most of all, she never forgave me for having everything that she did not.

Chapter 19
Relationships

AS IN MY CASE, Luther had always been told that he was my "real" brother; we were both the children of my father's younger brother, our Fourth Uncle. Though I had learned that Luther was my father's child when I was only twenty, Luther knew nothing of his true parentage until many years later. It was 1969, and I had returned from Taipei after the death of my husband. I had bought a house in Vienna, Virginia, and Luther was helping me sort out some things in the basement, boxes that had been in storage and never opened in our nine years overseas. We had been talking of my parents--then both deceased--and the problems they had had living together after so many years of separation.

"They were always complaining about each other," Luther said. "I got so that I just closed my ears and tuned them out so that I wouldn't have to hear them."

"I know," I added. "Each time I was home, Mother would complain to me too. She said Daddy insisted on having this enormous bowl of ice cream every night that they could ill afford. And she complained about how he expected to be waited on all the time, especially about his making a mess in the bathroom and not cleaning up after himself.

Luther said, "Oh, yes, I heard about that too. Daddy was so irritated that Mother wanted him to urinate sitting down on the toilet because she said he sprayed all over the place when standing. But Daddy complained just as much as Mother. He had a never-ending string of complaints about her. I asked him once why he had married her. He said that it was because he thought a foreign wife would keep him in line better than a Chinese wife."

"What did he mean by 'keep him in line'?" I asked.

"Well, according to him, he was something of a playboy in his younger days and he knew it was time for him to settle down."

"And he thought Mother could control him? That's certainly an interesting reason for marrying someone," I observed. "But when we were small I thought they were pretty happy together. I don't remember any fights or arguments. And you have to admit they gave us a good childhood."

Luther agreed but fell silent for a few moments. We went on with our sorting. I was setting aside the things to be thrown out. Luther was looking through them to see if any should be salvaged. I had my back to him when out of the blue I heard the question: "Marguerite, would you feel any differently toward me if I were not your real brother?"

For an instant I caught my breath. In that moment I knew that he knew. All those years, twenty-six to be exact, I had kept my father's secret. Apart from the initial shock of knowing that Luther was the product of an illicit affair of my father's, it had had no bearing on my life or on Luther's. My father was still *our* father. Luther and I were still brother and sister.

But now Luther knew what I had known for all my adult years, that he was not my real brother, not the son of Fourth Uncle and Aunt. I knew it must have been my father who had told him. Where else, or how else could he have learned of it? But I wanted to know precisely what my father had said. "What do you mean? Not my real brother?"

Luther then explained that a few weeks before my father's death, he had told him that Luther was his own natural child. With Mother gone--she had died three months earlier--the not so secret "secret" of his infidelity no longer had to be kept from Luther. Perhaps my father thought his confession would bring them closer as father and son. Or perhaps he sensed his own mortality. My father died in 1965, but now it was 1969. Luther had not divulged to me his newfound knowledge of himself for four years.

At this point I was so relieved that the secret I had carried so long was at last known to him that I confessed I had known for over twenty years. Though I was able to reassure him about my feelings about him as a brother, my having known for so long brought home to him the fact that others in the family had also known. He asked me how I had learned, and I told him of my conversation with Fourth Aunt twenty-six years earlier in Shanghai when she had told me that Luther was not her child and made me promise never to tell Mother. I could see that Luther was shaken by the information. I think what hurt him more than discovering the altered circumstances of his birth was the knowledge that others too had not only known of the deception but conspired to keep it from him. He did not ask if I knew anything of his real mother. I volunteered nothing.

It was more than ten years later that Luther raised the subject of his mother. When he had asked my father about his mother's identity, my father had replied, "It's in the past. There's no need for you to know." Luther had accepted that. Now Luther was asking me if I knew who his mother was. I can't remember how the subject came up. I know only that it was the furthest thing from my mind, another thing learned and long pushed into the back of my mind. But for a fraction of a second I must have hesitated. That brief hesitation said it all. "You know, don't you?" he insisted. "You know."

He was right. I did know. The story of Luther's parentage had come to me in two parts: the identity of his father from Fourth Aunt's own lips when I was in Shanghai in 1943 as a student; the identity of his mother, eighteen years later when I was living in Taiwan. The year was 1961.

My husband had been assigned to Taiwan where we lived with our three children until his death in 1969. We were barely settled in our new home when I received a letter from my father telling me that I had a sister in Taipei and that I should soon expect a call from her. This came as a complete surprise to me, as until that time I had known of only two sisters from my birth family. I had met Lily, my youngest sister, at age eighteen when I was attending St. John's in Shanghai. My oldest sister Eva, though responsible for, and present at my adoption, I had not met until I was twenty-four or five when she and her family immigrated to America. And now, in Taiwan, at age thirty-four, I was to find a third sister. Thus, the sisters from my biological family, whom as a young girl I had thought of as no more than cousins, had each come back into my adult life as sisters. In the years that followed, we four sisters, related by blood, but brought up apart, met together a total of four times, once in the early sixties, and again in 1977, 1983, and 1985.

My father's letter said only that this sister was a blood sister from my birth family. No other explanation. I couldn't help thinking

**Four biological sisters 1983. *Left to right*:
Lily, Kao Kao, me and Eva.:**

how strange our family was. If this new sibling was a blood sister, that meant she was also the daughter of Fourth Aunt and Uncle. Where had she been all these years? Had they given her away too in a *kuo chi* adoption? And what was her name?

A few days later, our amah announced a caller, a Mrs. Li. Without being told, I knew it must be my new sister. When I entered the living room, she was standing with her back to me. She was looking at one of the paintings on the wall, examining the inscription and hadn't heard me come in. For me it was an awkward moment and I was at a loss as to how to greet her. If she had been an ordinary visitor, I would simply have spoken her name, *"Li T'ai T'ai,"* but she was not an ordinary guest. A sister could have been greeted by name, or as Second Sister, Third Sister, or whatever sister she was, but I didn't know her name, and didn't even know if she was older or younger than I. I stood, speechless for a moment, and finally, I coughed.

When Kao Kao turned around, I saw an attractive woman who looked about my own age. She was not as pretty as Eva, or Lily, but she had a pleasant, friendly face. She didn't call me Huan Huan, the name my birth family used, or Jung Huan, the Chinese name my father had given me. Instead, with a strong Chinese accent, she called me by my English name. Through the next nine years that we lived in Taipai, she and her husband continued to use my English name, though their three children called me Huan Yi (Maternal Aunt Huan).

Kao Kao could sense my discomfort at this our first meeting and quickly dispelled my feelings of awkwardness. She introduced herself and launched immediately into an explanation of our relationship. She was my blood sister, six years older than I (the same age as Lois) and born of the same parents. She too had been adopted, in the traditional *kuo chi* arrangement. However, in her case, it was her mother, her adoptive mother, who had been from the Ch'ien family. She was the daughter of my grandfather's brother (and thus a Ch'ien), and had married into the Chiang family. Though Kao Kao, had become a Chiang, she was still a member of a family carrying the Ch'ien bloodline.

During the next eight years that we lived in Taipei, despite the differences in our upbringing (she had had no exposure at all to western culture), Kao Kao and I became good friends. It was from her that I learned more about the makeup of the Ch'ien family than either my mother or father had told me. I had always known that my father had two living brothers, Second Uncle and Fourth Uncle (my biological father). It was from Kao Kao that I learned that Fourth Uncle, like me, had been adopted *out* of his birth family, out of my grandfather's line. But whereas I had been adopted back *into* my grandfather's line, Kao Kao had been adopted farther away from it.

All this new information about the way the children in our family had been passed about, from brother to brother, from cousin to cousin, was at first hard to absorb. I was determined to get it all down on paper. I pumped Kao Kao for more, and it was while we were discussing our family relationships that Kao Kao told me the identity of Luther's mother. *Luther's mother was my grandfather's concubine, Yi Tai Tai.* I am not

sure where she got this information and I never asked her, but I was under the impression that it was a known fact. Somehow it didn't surprise
me. What did surprise me was her informing me that Daddy had fathered
not only Luther, but also Yi Tai Tai's daughter Mabel, who, since she
was presumably my grandfather's child, I had always thought of as my
aunt.

As a child I had given no thought to Yi Tai Tai's presence in our
household. She had simply been there. Now a new picture took shape:
the many meals at Yi Tai Tai's house, Mother's migraine headaches, her
often disparaging comments about Yi Tai Tai, particularly her claim that
Mabel could not have been fathered by my grandfather because he was
severely paralyzed at the time of Mabel's conception. Mother was quite
sure that Yi Tai Tai had been having an affair with my cousin, Chao
Yuan, the son of my father's oldest brother, and that Chao Yuan was
Mabel's real father.

Kao Kao seemed to know so much more about our family than
Eva. But perhaps it only seemed so because I had never questioned Eva
about the family, only about my own adoption. Kao Kao and her husband had also been in the interior with my father during the war years.
Kao Kao's husband was much older than Kao Kao and the two had mixed
freely with my father's circle of friends. She said that many of these
friends joked with him about his past life in Peking. One would say,
"What a great setup you had! An American wife and a Chinese concubine!" And another would add, "And living in the same compound too."
Never mind that the concubine was his father's. She was spoken of as
his. And another friend would add, "Or is it a Chinese wife and an
American concubine?" And my father, neither admitting nor denying,
would simply nod his head and smile enigmatically.

Listening to Kao Kao speak of my father, I remembered what
Lois had told me years before during the war, that a Chinese friend had
spoken quite casually of Mother being my father's concubine. I had
seemed so ridiculous that I had instantly rejected it at the time and put it
out of my mind. It still seemed preposterous, but now I couldn't help
wondering how widespread the perception was among my father's Chinese friends that Mother *was* his American concubine.

Chart of Ch'ien Family Relationships

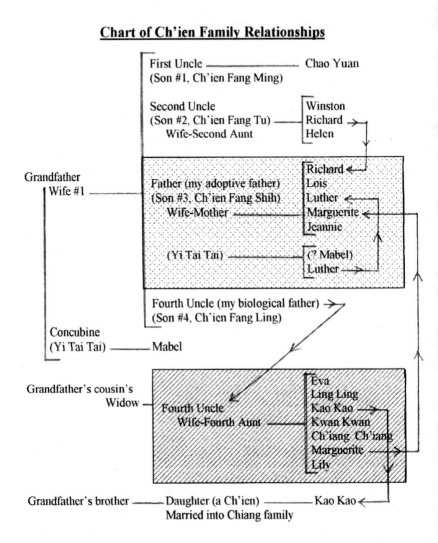

First Uncle ——————————— Chao Yuan
(Son #1, Ch'ien Fang Ming)

Second Uncle
(Son #2, Ch'ien Fang Tu) ——— Winston
    Wife-Second Aunt   Richard →
                   Helen

Grandfather
  Wife #1 ——————— Father (my adoptive father)   Richard ←
                   (Son #3, Ch'ien Fang Shih)   Lois
                       Wife-Mother ——— Luther ←
                                 Marguerite ←
                                 Jeannie

         (Yi Tai Tai) ——————— (? Mabel)
                                 Luther →

        Fourth Uncle (my biological father) →
        (Son #4, Ch'ien Fang Ling)

Concubine
  (Yi Tai Tai) ——————— Mabel

Grandfather's cousin's
        Widow —— Fourth Uncle   Eva
                                Ling Ling
                                Kao Kao →
                 Wife-Fourth Aunt ——— Kwan Kwan
                                Ch'iang Ch'iang
                                Marguerite →
                                Lily

Grandfather's brother ——— Daughter (a Ch'ien) ——— Kao Kao ←
          Married into Chiang family

Note: The above chart includes only those family members who are major characters in my story. Others, some briefly mentioned, have been omitted to avoid confusion. The arrows point from person's biological origin to adoptive position within the family.

    My Adoptive Family   My Biological Family

When Luther asked me about his mother, I repeated what my father had told him. It was in the past and best forgotten. It seemed to me that if my father had wanted him to know, he would have told him. But Luther pressed me. "Marguerite, if you know, it's your duty to tell me. I have a right to know who my mother is." I was in a quandary. Should I tell him? He already knew that I knew. Did he have the right to know? I consulted Eva. Eva too had a hard time making a decision but finally decided, "I suppose he does have a right to know." She also thought that since Luther had lost me as a blood-related sister, he might be pleased to know he had gained a sister in Mabel. In the end I told Luther all that I had learned through the years.

On learning that Yi Tai Tai was his mother, Luther became sober and reflective but did not seem surprised. "I used to wonder if my mother might have been a prostitute," he mused, "But I suspected it just might have been Yi Tai Tai." Having accepted Yi Tai Tai as his mother, he had no trouble accepting that Mabel too had been fathered by Daddy. Like Luther, Mabel bore a striking resemblance to my father, and she and Luther looked much alike. Though I could not tell how disturbed he was about discovering that Yi Tai Tai was his mother, he was clearly excited to find that Mabel was his blood sister. He had always been fond of her and was eager to share his newly learned information with her.

Mabel was at that time in China living under the Communist regime, but when she came to America for a visit in 1985, Luther told her that he too was Yi Tai Tai's child and eagerly told her of their relationship. Mabel accepted readily the fact that she and Luther shared the same mother. She admitted to vague recollections of her mother going away for several months and leaving her in the care of the servants at about the time of Luther's birth. However, she flatly rejected Luther's claim that she too was my father's daughter and not the daughter of our grandfather. She was indignant to be thought of as the product of an illicit relationship. Also, if Mabel had acknowledged Daddy as her father, she would then be of our generation, our sister rather than our aunt. To the Chinese, a person's generational placement within a family is not to be taken lightly, and I suspect that Mabel was not inclined to accept readily this demotion to a lower generation.

When I was at Ming Ming Primary School, a cousin of my friend Edie was constantly objecting to Edie's addressing him by his first name instead of his proper title, Ssu Shu (Fourth Paternal Uncle). He was quite serious about this.   His father and Edie's grandfather were brothers, which made him of the senior generation.   It all seemed so ludicrous.   He was in fact two years younger than Edie, and she adamantly refused to call him by anything other than his first name. In those days I completely sympathized with Edie. We were fourth graders. Why should she have to address an eight-year-old child as uncle? Yet in later years, when I became better acquainted with the Chinese side of my family, nothing seemed more natural than that Eva's sons, and Kao Kao's children, should call me Huan Yi (Maternal Aunt Huan).   This even though the oldest of my nephews is only two years younger than I. Even today, in his seventies, he continues to address me as aunt. By Chinese custom, addressing me in any other way would not occur to him, and I confess I would be shocked if he were to call me Marguerite.

Mabel died last year, to the end aunt, never sister.

Today, Luther says he was not in the least disturbed to learn of his parentage. "I always suspected I was Daddy's son," he says now, "especially because I look so much like him."   Their resemblance became more pronounced as Luther grew older. Not only their facial features, but the set of their shoulders, their gait. Now, thirty-three years since he learned the truth, Luther seems to have forgotten his earlier words of recrimination against Daddy. Then he had spoken bitterly of how he felt that Daddy and the family had deceived him.

It was true that Luther had been deceived. But by claiming Luther was his brother's son, my father was able to adopt him honorably--in the time-honored Chinese tradition of a *kuo chi* adoption from within the family. Had my father not devised this deception, Luther would have been the unclaimed son of my grandfather's concubine, conceived well after my grandfather's death. Yes, Luther had been deceived, but what a remarkable and satisfactory deception it was! No hint of scandal had touched the family. Luther carried no stigma of illicit birth. The family had resolved its own problems, had taken care of its own.

So many years have passed since my father's death, and my few remaining cousins and friends who knew him still speak of him as a "wonderful old man." Yet, I cannot help but be aware of the unhappiness he caused for every member of my family except me. Today I don't know if Luther is still smarting from the discovery of his origins. He has had a successful career, was respected by colleagues, and loved by friends and family. That should be enough for any man, but I suspect, that because he is Chinese, he still feels deeply the loss of identity that came with the discovery that he was not who he thought he was. I say to him, "This is America; we're in the twentieth century. People don't care or judge you by your parentage. What does it matter now?"

He says, "It matters to me."

Lois is gone now. With so many other problems between us, we never talked about her relationship with my father, but I often wonder if her life would have evolved differently if my father had accepted her as a member of the family. Certainly the servants would then have accorded her the deference due her as a daughter of the house. And if Lois had known a father's love as a child, would she have been less susceptible to the blandishments of her beloved godfather, and would she have been less inclined to seek the love of other men? I may be playing at amateur psychology, but it is difficult not to wonder. I know that even in her teen-age years she cried easily. As a child I couldn't understand those tears. Coming out of a movie that I found not at all sad, her eyes would be red and swollen. I kept thinking how ridiculous it was, to be crying over nothing. "What are you crying for, Lois? It wasn't even a sad movie." But she had known unhappiness; I had not.

And Richard. Though he was not literally my father's "firstborn," he was by adoption the Number One Son, and as such would normally have been coddled, spoiled, and loved. Yet there were problems between him and my father of which I was unaware. I knew only from my mother in later years that my father had constantly found fault with Richard, had refused to finance him further once Richard had departed for Scotland, had in effect cut him off. It was Mother who sent Richard the money to fund his education until he became self-supporting. It is only in recent years that I learned from Richard's widow that their marriage of some thirty years was never consummated. She confessed that he was impotent, but I wonder now if it is possible that there were signs of latent homosexuality. Perhaps my father saw this and found it reason enough to cut him off. Whatever the reason, I know that neither Richard nor my father had much use for the other, and I suspect that this relationship played a large part in Richard's decision to make his home in

England, away from the rest of the family. For my part, I have only fond memories of my big brother.

As for Mother, my father provided her with many years of luxury, but also gave her the burden of raising his family for many years alone. I suspect too that he must have given her many unhappy hours. Though I cannot believe that he was actively carrying on an affair with Yi Tai Tai during my childhood years in the North City house, surely the many hours he spent in Yi Tai Tai's house and the many meals shared with her must have been painful for my mother. To make matters worse, he took Luther and me with him, so she was deserted not by one, but by three. As a child I was blissfully unaware of the hurt she must have suffered, but looking back on those years, it is hard for me to dismiss my father's callous behavior. *Yet, I liked him. I could not help it. Even realizing the pain he had caused, I liked him.* Did I love him? As a daughter loves her father, as a daughter *should* love her father? I don't know.

As for Yi Tai Tai, did he hurt even her? On Mabel's visit to America in 1985, she complained that he and Second Uncle had squandered the family fortunes, thus depriving her mother of her "entitlements." None of those remaining in the family can tell me what those entitlements were. From friends whose grandparents had once had concubines in the family I gather that entitlements varied according to individual circumstances and were governed by family tradition, not by law. Mabel also spoke bitterly of how much better my mother's lot had been than her mother's. To me she complained, "Your mother got everything. Mine got nothing." At the time, this statement came as a surprise to me, as it seemed to me, that having been a concubine and not a legal wife, surely Yi Tai Tai should not have expected the same or been entitled to the same. Or perhaps there had been some measure of truth in the jokes my father's friends had once made of his "Chinese wife and American concubine." Had he given Yi Tai Tai some legal status, or some expectation of legal status? We will never know.

What I do know is that Yi Tai Tai had a profound influence on my life. If her house had not been a part of the family compound I wonder how much exposure I would have had to things Chinese. Luther and I were in and out of her house so much. It was there that we ate Chu Shih Fu's Chinese cooking, his green-onion cakes and his thin vegetable crepes. It was in her living room that we banged on the brass tray and watched our toy opera figures twirl around. It was there that I watched the quilts being assembled. And at Chinese New Year, though we had many of the trappings of the new year in our westernized part of the compound, it was in Yi Tai Tai's house that we received most of our red envelopes, each containing two silver dollars.

Looking back, I cannot help wondering what Yi Tai Tai was like as a young woman and what her life was like. She had been a pretty servant girl, probably doing menial chores. She had captured the attention of my grandfather, and later of my father, and also of my oldest cousin Chao Yuen. Three generations of males in the Ch'ien family had been enamoured of her. No mean accomplishment. And what were her charms? Had she been a seductive young thing deliberately setting out to tantalize? Had she sent out signals under veiled eyes? Or had she been a passive victim, trying earnestly to ward off their attentions? And once selected as concubine, how had she behaved with the servants who had once been her equals or more? Was she disliked by those whom she had risen above? Did she flaunt her newly exalted status? I suspect she did. I know that my mother had no use for her from the start.

And which of the three men had fathered Mabel? My grandfather, my father, or my cousin. My grandfather was paralyzed at the time of Mabel's conception, but we now know that paralysis is not necessarily a hindrance to conception. Kao Kao had told me that Mabel was my father's child, but I never knew where she got that information. I accepted it simply because she told it to me as fact, not conjecture or rumor. Luther accepted it because of Mabel's strong resemblance to my father and to himself. But what of my cousin Chao Yuen? Had he also been her lover as my mother had suspected? According to my cousin Helen, *her* mother, Second Aunt, had also been quite sure that ChaoYuen was the father. Had others thought so too? And if Chao Yuen had really been Mabel's father, then, fathered by my cousin, but ostensibly by my grandfather, could she have said, like the words of the old song, "I am my own grandma?"

Though a Chinese family by tradition was supposed to be responsible for the support of a concubine and her children, I have not been able to find out how this responsibility was allocated within the Ch'ien family, or how much support was given. I don't know how

Mabel's education was financed but assume it was by the family. Helen believes that Yi Tai Tai received a share of the income from the family store in Peking. I assume that while Yi Tai Tai lived in Peking in our family compound that her expenses were covered by my father. But after that? If the family did not provide her support, it is no wonder that she was pleased to have found for Mabel a husband who would provide for both Mabel and herself.

Within our family, Yi Tai Tai was the only one of my parents' generation who improved her lot steadily through the years. The others had had their day, but in the end their lives had deteriorated. Yi Tai Tai had started as no more than a *ya t'o*, a servant girl, but her origins had not held her back. She died in 1945, of cancer, never having had to face the deprivations the other relatives endured under the Communist regime. She would have been pleased to know that one of her grandsons, Mabel's oldest child, became a millionaire businessman in Hong Kong.

Chapter 20
Return to China

MY PERSONAL CONTACT with the Chinese side of the family came to a halt when I left Shanghai in January 1945. When the war ended soon after that, I left for America with Mother and Jeannie aboard the American Navy attack transport. Only two or three days into our journey across the Pacific, Jeannie, age seven, decided she would speak only English. When Mother or I spoke to her in Chinese, she brushed us aside with a frown, "Don't talk that way. Nobody talks that way here." China was behind her; a new world lay ahead.

And for me as well, a new life lay ahead. College, a job, marriage, children, tours abroad. All followed in quick succession. America was good to me. Life was full. Then my husband's death, a new career for myself, the raising of three children, remarriage, the start of a business enterprise, and finally, retirement. Now I play tennis three times a week; plant, replant, and over plant the small garden of our townhouse. I knit and sew for my grandchildren, visit family and friends. My husband and I travel. On scientific research expeditions we have been to St. Croix, walking ten miles of soft sand along the beach each night to save the leatherback turtle; to the Galapagos and Grenada to study wildlife; to Papua New Guinea to learn about insects. So-called "adventure trips" have taken us in a land rover to the Imilchil Bridal Fair in the Moroccan

High Atlas and to the Pushkar camel fair in India. We've hiked the twelve-mile Samaria Gorge in Crete, watched the once-every-seven-year passion play in Oberammergau, cruised up the coast of Norway, and explored the cave dwellings of Cappadocia. We've kayaked in the waters of Alaska, walked among the penguins in the Antarctic, and watched the whales frolicking in their own habitat. I can't name all the places we've been and sights we've seen, but not until five years ago had I returned to the China I had left fifty years before. One by one my friends, both Chinese and American, made the trip, some to rave about the wonders of China, others to deplore the loss of what used to be. I was reluctant to go, and afraid. I had beautiful memories of a Peking I loved. I was afraid those memories would be superseded by what I found in the new Beijing. But as this memoir took shape, and as events, long forgotten, reemerged in memory, I found myself longing to return, to see once more the home of my childhood. I was delighted that two of my children and their spouses wanted to join us. One grandchild would join us too. I made plans for the trip. I would see the new Beijing, but my children would also see through my eyes the old Peking I had once known and loved.

We arrived in Peking in the early days of fall in 1995. Though we had originally scheduled our trip for May, I was glad to be missing the dust storms that plague Peking in the spring. Despite my eager anticipation, I had had misgivings about the trip. Luther and several friends had warned me that we would not see the Peking that I had known. Childhood schoolmates had told me not to expect to find our old homes. If I did find them, they said they would be dilapidated and unrecognizable. One friend had located her home and had found it occupied by thirteen families. Others, still in Peking and who had never left, told me that the East City was changed beyond recognition, that the courtyards of traditional courtyard houses were fast disappearing as families built inward into the courtyards and consumed the entire courtyard space. They said, however, that many of the larger homes in the North City had been taken over by high-level government cadres and were still intact. I was hopeful that our house might be among them. I also hoped to find our summer home in the Western Hills. Lois's French husband Robert, visiting China in the seventies, had been told that the house was then being used as a VIP hostel. My friend Shang May thought the house might still be there, but its many terraces probably filled with other buildings. I was determined to look for them all.

We had been advised by our travel agent to contract for pre-set meals with our tour, but all of us were resolute about eating on our own in Peking, all agreeing that part of the joy of travelling was in searching out foods and places to eat. Local Peking friends advised us to eat in the larger restaurants, or if we insisted on eating at the smaller places, to carry our own bowls and chopsticks as they did. They warned us about the lack of adequate sanitation, as without hot water, the dishwashing often consisted of a mere rinsing in cold. I had been told we should not be surprised if friends and relatives asked if they could come to our hotel room to have a bath, a rare treat. My daughter Kathy was shocked when I told her that few of my friends had hot water in their homes. "How do they take a bath?" she asked. "They boil water on the stove," I told her. Kathy found it hard to believe that these friends had once shared the affluent lifestyle of my childhood.

We planned our trip so that my husband John and I would arrive in Peking two days ahead of the others, to give us oldsters time to recover from jetlag and flight-fatigue before starting on a busy sightseeing schedule at the pace of the younger generation. It was already dark but not so dark that we could not see the heavy traffic on the highway on our one-hour drive from airport to city. But we had been warned and were mentally prepared. What we were not prepared for was the opulence of the four-star hotel to which we were delivered. We had been told of the hotel's many amenities: sauna, exercise rooms, swimming pool, and numerous restaurants and bars; but the four-piece string ensemble in full dress performing in the lobby and the soprano soloist in evening gown were beyond our expectations. The musicians and the singer were good. Attendants in brocade jackets and long slim skirts slit high up the thigh served refreshments. Still, there was a contrived air about the whole display. We were impressed and amused at the same time. I could not help thinking of Mrs. Ch'ien's Guesthouse and comparing its simple dignity with the studied elegance of this grand establishment.

We were given the key to our room and were left to find it for ourselves. I looked nervously for our luggage; it was to be brought up separately. We found the room without difficulty but found ourselves standing in the room's doorway in complete darkness. We groped blindly along the walls for the light switches, none of which seemed to work. In the dark we could not even find the telephone to call the front desk. Seasoned travelers that we thought we were, we had not learned that the lights were activated by putting the room key into a slot just inside the door. Back down to the receptionist desk to explain our plight and admit our ignorance. Peking had progressed further into the modern world than we had.

Finally, we examined our room. Nicely furnished and spacious enough for a comfortable seating area, but no more luxurious than many medium-priced U.S. motels. It had a complicated lighting system that could be controlled from a panel on the bedside table. A friend who had made the trip to China before us had spoken of the many buttons and knobs that had confronted her, some of which did not work. She said that on one button were the words, "Don't bother." At the time I assumed she meant this sign had been posted by some frustrated hotel guest, but found that the words in English, "No bother" were actually printed on one of the buttons. It was not until our third day that we noticed a small light in the hall outside our door that said in Chinese, "Do not disturb." We tried the "No bother" button by our bed, and wonder of wonders, the "Do not disturb" light outside our door flashed a blinking red.

Our bathroom was sumptuous--all marble and chrome, with a dazzling display of toiletries. Again I thought of my mother's guesthouse, this time of the modest bathrooms attached to each room. There had been no lotions or hair conditioners in fancy containers, only immaculate cleanliness, hot and cold running water, and flush toilets, of course. Here, despite the polished marble and glistening chrome, we caught the faint but unmistakable smell of urine.

On our first morning we set about familiarizing ourselves with the area around the hotel. The street we were on, Wangfujing, retained its old Chinese name, but no longer carried its old western name of Morrison Street. It had once been the central business district for many western companies. As we walked along the sidewalk we were startled by some plaster falling from a deteriorating portico of a building that faced the street. I was surprised to see that it was the old Salvation Army building where my grandfather's portrait had hung so long ago at the head of the stairs. We did not try to go in. We walked down the street that paralleled Wangfujing. It had once been Hatamen Street, our "Main

Street," but its name had been changed. I missed the triple-arched *p'ai lous* under which we had ridden our bicycles daily to school. They had been removed years ago, an obstruction to traffic. The road was unrecognizable. Fifty years before, the only building above two stories had been the shoe store and factory, Glasses Pang's. Now, it and the many little one-story shops and stalls were gone, and in their place a multitude of shops, restaurants, and theatres, all apparently thriving. Gone too was the Eastern Peace Market. We would not be eating at the favorite restaurant of my high school days. I would not be showing my family the store where Luther and I had bought our opera headgear or the stall that sold the spiced grasshoppers my friends and I had eyed so often but lacked the nerve to try. But I had been told already that the market had been torn down.

What we did find were the old *hut'ungs* where so many of us had once lived. True, there were many tall buildings where once there had been none, but the gray walls that fronted the streets remained, and the *hut'ungs* retained some of their former character. In searching for the old Peking American School building, we came across a bicycle-drawn cart surrounded by people apparently enjoying a morning breakfast. The owner was busily cooking on a large griddle. His entire "kitchen" sat atop the cart, and his customers stood around him. We stopped to watch and inevitably to join the others at breakfast. Our "chef" ladled some batter onto the grill and spread it out to make a ten-inch crepe. Over that he cracked one egg, or two (U.S. $.20 with one egg, $.25 with two), which he stirred and spread to the edges. Then a sprinkling of chopped scallions, followed by a spreading of soybean paste, hot sauce (optional), and another sprinkling of black sesame seeds. A crisp rectangular fried cruller was placed in the center and the edges of the crepe folded over it into a neat package. The whole thing, so hot we could barely handle it, was delivered to our hands in coarse brown paper. We shared one between the two of us but could not resist ordering a second. All thoughts of elaborate western breakfasts in the hotel dining room were put aside. Breakfast in the streets was for us. What a study in contrasts! Black-tie musicians playing Strauss waltzes on the evening of arrival; breakfast the next morning standing in a Beijing *hut'ung*.

When my children arrived two days later, we insisted on their first breakfast in China being on us. They demurred. "Why should you pay?" they said. "We'll go Dutch." But we insisted, "We've found a wonderful restaurant and have gotten to know the owner." We were still arguing over who would pay when we arrived at our "restaurant." They laughed, were fascinated by the whole operation and thrilled with their breakfast. The meal was a huge success! By then we did know the owner well and also some of his morning regulars. They all wanted to know where we were from and marveled that after fifty years I could still speak Chinese. We returned to his cart for breakfast two more times during our stay.

Serious sightseeing began after breakfast, but first we had to visit the old PAS school building where I had spent so many happy years. It was now being used as a training institute for local Chinese employees of foreign embassies. The former playground and sports areas had been filled in with more buildings, but the school building itself had been well maintained and was in remarkably good condition. It was now covered with ivy whereas it had been bare of growth during my school years. I remembered how big it had appeared to me when I first moved there from the tiny Ming Ming Grade School. Now it looked so small. The head of the institute was extremely cordial and ushered us through the building. There was little change. The only noteworthy difference was in the girls' bathroom. Of the three former toilet cubicles, two had been converted to "squatters." My children were more impressed with our breakfast cart than with the school.

Through the head of the institute we rented a van and driver whom we were told to address as Wang *Hsien Sheng* (Mr. Wang). In the old days a driver would not have accorded the "Mr." title. During the next few days we covered most of the major historical sights: the Great Wall of course, the Ming Tombs, the Forbidden City, the Temple of Heaven, Coal Hill, and the Winter and Summer Palaces, all beautifully refurbished for the flourishing tourist trade. With the exception of the Ming Tombs, all were jammed with people and the approaches filled with tour busses. At the ticket booths, charges for *nei pin* (native Chinese) were half or less than charges for tourists and *wai pin* (overseas Chinese). The first few days I routinely bought the higher priced tickets for all seven of us, but soon decided that I should be entitled to the reduced price of a native Chinese. After all, I was a native Chinese even though I was now living abroad. Soon I was paying the native price for

myself *and* my two children. My daughter Kathy couldn't resist trying
out her Chinese at the ticket counter and was elated when, using her almost forgotten Chinese (learned as a child when we were stationed in
Taiwan), she asked for seven *nei pin* tickets and was charged the "native"
price. Her accent and pronunciation had passed muster. My son Bean
poured cold water on our money-pinching achievement. "I don't see why
you two get such a kick out of pretending you're native. After all, we *are*
tourists, so why shouldn't we pay the tourist price?"

All the tourist sites were filled with vendors, though with few
exceptions they stayed within their booths and allocated areas and were
not objectionable. Every effort had been made to make the vending areas
attractive, and the pavilions or covered walkways that housed them were
built in the same architectural style as existing buildings so that new and
old were uniform. All the restoration work was admirable. But, unrea-
sonably I know, I missed the weathered colors of the past where faded
reds had blended gently with muted greens, the colors undisturbing to the
eye. Now the newness of the paint, the reds too red, the greens too green,
bordered on garishness. Still, I was glad to see that these historic spots
were being well maintained, for I remembered the often crumbled walls
of the past, the missing tiles, the flaking paint, and the broken and frequently missing figures on the roofs of buildings.

As a child I had been to the Great Wall only once with some
guests from the guesthouse. Then its wonder had been lost on me. Now
I admired its magnificence, but it held no particular memories. At the
Ming Tombs I remembered the large stone animals that lined the walk,
now labeled grandiosely The Sacred Way. Years before it had had no
name at all. I remembered climbing on the stone horse, being hoisted up
to sit between the humps of the camel's back, and running between the
legs of the elephant. Then they had stood on a barren dusty road, massive figures of men and beasts, lonely-looking despite their grandeur.
Now the road was paved, rows of trees planted, and grass and shrubs
filled the empty spaces. The once lonely figures stood before a curtained
backdrop of graceful willows. They looked serene and comfortable,
framed in shades of green, the soft tones of the willows behind and the
darker tone of manicured grass beneath their feet.

Having been to both the Forbidden City and Coal Hill before, I
was not overly disappointed when John and I had to pass them up be-

cause of an emergency dental problem. I had no emotional ties to the Forbidden City, remembering only its many vast empty courtyards and its impressive collection of clocks. However, I was sorry that John missed the southward view of the city from Coal Hill where one can see the full sweep of golden tiles of the Forbidden City, beyond that to the main gate of what had once been the Tartar City, and beyond that to the triple blue-tiled roofs of the Temple of Heaven. But that was a minor disappointment. At the municipal hospital, in the special wing for foreign emergency treatment--the Chinese take good care of their foreign tourists--a young female dentist took care of John's tooth quickly and efficiently. At our request, she then directed us to the old Peking Union Medical College, the hospital once headed by my friend Edie's father. The beautiful old Chinese-style buildings with their green-tiled roofs were still there, now more beautiful when compared to some of the unattractive new buildings that surrounded them. We peered into the auditorium where I had once starred in our high school play. A group of young children were on stage rehearsing a choral number. All the performances in which my friends and I had participated through the years flashed through my mind: the grade school plays my mother had directed, the dance performances, the piano recitals where I had performed so miserably. I could see them all. It was there my nostalgia trip really began.

While the children were sightseeing, John and I went in search of old homes. We looked first for the main guesthouse at 29 Hsi Tsung Pu Hut'ung. It was gone. The street's name had not changed but the numbers had. An obvious old timer assured us that a large four-story building built by some investor from Singapore was on the former site of number 29. Farther down the street we searched for Number 10 where I had spent the war years. Through an open gate in the approximate vicinity of Number 10 we could see people, some elderly enough to have been long-time occupants. As was the case everywhere we went, we were immediately identified as visitors from abroad, and several occupants of the property gathered around us to talk. I asked if we could go in, that I wanted to show my foreign husband the inside of a courtyard house. They snorted. "Courtyard? We have no courtyards left. They have been filled up with rooms." But nonetheless the occupants led the way into the first of what had once been a courtyard. We could still see the tiled roof-lines of the rooms that had once framed the original courtyard, but as we had been told, families in overly cramped quarters had built into the courtyard area. Now unsightly additions of brick and board left only a small passageway of open ground. We did not go farther. It was enough. The house was now Number 45, but the occupants said it used to be Number 11. Next-door must have been Number 10, where we had lived during the war years. *Had these people once been our neighbors?* I had never known our neighbors at any of the houses where we lived. John was surprised at that, but in those days each family lived within its own walls. The rest of the world was outside. Number 10, our former house, was now a primary school. It was Sunday and the gate, brand new, was closed. We walked back the way we had come.

However, the search was not a total loss. On our way back up the street, no longer preoccupied with locating the houses, we came across clouds of steam rising from a stack of bamboo steamers. The stove looked like an old oil drum; perhaps that's what it was. We asked the woman tending the steamers if we could see what she was cooking, and quite obligingly she lifted the lid to reveal the small steamed *pao tze* (round filled dumplings) inside. Who could resist? It was part of *my* Peking that I wanted to show my foreign husband, just as my mother, in starting the guesthouse, had wanted to show *her* Peking to foreign visitors. John and I, standing in the street, each had one; then two; then three. The next day we took the children. The woman could hardly keep up with us. She had no sooner handed each of us one *pao tze*, than the first person was ready for a second. She had a hard time counting how many we had eaten and figuring out how much we owed. The *pao tze* cost less than U.S. four cents apiece. As with our street breakfasts, we stood there in the *hut'ung*, six adults and a child, gorging ourselves on Chinese dumplings.

In our search for the North City house, the home of my earliest years, I was more hopeful. Perhaps it was still there. With the help of our driver we had no trouble finding the street. It seemed like the *hut'ungs* of old. No tall buildings had changed the street's façade. I felt sure I could locate the house. Our gate had been the only large one on the north side of the very short street. We drove up and down its length several times and found only one large gate. I was sure it was the one. The recessed entryway was in immaculate condition, the wide double gate bright red and obviously newly painted. Our house had been Number 15. I expected the numbers to have been changed, but this house had no number on it at all even though the neighboring houses were all numbered. The driver and I left John in the van. I had been advised that a foreigner in tow would arouse unnecessary suspicion if indeed the house was occupied by a high official. Hoping to get a glimpse of the entry court, I tried to peek through the crack between the double gates, but I had barely put my eye up to the crack when a guard in military uniform came out of the small door set into one side of the gate. He had appeared so quickly. There must have been an electronic eye outside the door that had alerted him. He was hostile and very belligerent and demanded to know what I was doing there. I tried to explain that I was from America, that I used to live on this street and was looking for my old home, but he cut me off short. He demanded again, "What is your business here? Show me your identification! Where is your passport?"

My passport was in one of those hidden wallets that tuck inside and under the waistband. It seemed to take forever to get it out, during which time the guard kept yelling at me to hurry up. When I finally produced my passport, he scrutinized the picture and apparently accepted my explanation. He became slightly more civil, but it was obvious that he did not intend to be helpful. I explained again that I was looking for my old home and asked what number this house was. He didn't answer the question and waved us away brusquely, saying, "This is not your house. Go look farther down the street." John reported later that as we walked away, another guard had come out and the two had stood watching us and talking for several minutes before disappearing into the gate. I was sure the house had been ours and could have identified it positively if I had been allowed to look into the frontcourt. I asked one of the passersby if he knew who lived there. He said, "Oh, some big shot. I don't know who." So that was that.

The only house left to find was our summer home in the Western Hills. Luther had tried to find it when he visited Peking in the eighties, but at that time the road had been blocked off and that area declared off limits, presumably the exclusive preserve of high-level government officials. Our house was located between two of the eight temples that comprised the *Pa Ta Ch'u* area (literally, the "Eight Important Sites") Both temples were still mentioned in one of the current guide books on Peking. If I could find *Ch'ang An Ssu*, the lower of the two, where my friend Edie had spent her summers and my brother Richard had spent one summer brushing up his Chinese, I could surely find the house.

It took over an hour to reach the Western Hills in our rented van, but once past the congested traffic of the city, I couldn't help being impressed by the trees that lined the roads. Fifty years before there had only been poorly maintained dirt roads and I remembered the swirls of dust that arose with even the slightest gust of wind. Now they were paved, and the tree trunks, the lower four feet painted white, created a tidy avenue. Throughout our brief stay in China, again and again I had to give credit to the Communist government for its tree-planting efforts. When I was a child, though there were beautiful trees in the courtyards of private homes, in the public gardens, and certain parts of the city, many streets had been bare of greenery. I could not remember there being any trees at all on the street where our hotel was located, formerly a business center for western shops. But now it was bordered by feathery locust trees whose branches arched over the street.

When we reached the Western Hills we found that much of the *Pa Ta Ch'u* area had been made into a public park. *Ch'ang An Ssu*, the temple we were searching for, was not a part of it. Always pressed for time, we decided to forgo the park and search for our house instead. None of the old landmarks were there. Gone was the dry riverbed where Luther and I had drawn our multicolored pictures with the soft river stones. Gone was the gully where we had splashed in the small pool under the bridge. But the temple was there. Or parts of it. The temple gate as I remembered it was gone. None of what remained resembled Edie's courtyard or Richard's.

Two courtyards remained with a few small, new buildings at the rear. It was being used as a hospital. The facilities looked very primitive, and through the open windows we could see several patients in hospital beds. I looked up the hill but could not see our house. Then my son Bean spotted a part of a wall that went up the hill. I recognized it instantly, the large stones, the configuration. I shouted, "That's it! That's it! That's our wall!" Nick and ten-year-old Jae were on their way up the hill before I had the words out of my mouth. "No, no, it's on the other side of the wall. The house is on the other side," I shouted. They came sliding back down to start up again on the far side. Looking up we could see only trees and brush. No house was visible. But then we saw the broken remains of two stone pillars and beyond that a path overgrown with weeds but the center still clear. The stone pillars had once framed the double red gates and had held up the tiled roof above. The path, once about four feet wide, now shrunk by encroaching growth, was two feet wide in some spots, only a foot wide at others. Steps, fallen away at the sides, led to the next terrace where the wisteria arbor and grape arbors had once been. The walls between the terraces were gone; only sloping piles of stone and rubble, half hidden by weeds and wild creeping vines, remained. The same for the next terrace and the next. But at the end, instantly recognizable, the house. The porch that had surrounded the house on three sides was gone. As was the case with those living in the courtyard houses in Peking, the occupants had enlarged their living space, but instead of building inward into the courtyards, here they had built outward into what had been the porch. Except for the center, the porch had been filled in with brick or with boards. The original columns that supported the porch roof were gone; in their place some rough round poles propping up the now-sagging roof. We did not ask to go in. We were told that five families now lived there. We tried to go around the

Western Hills house 1995. Compare to earlier picture, Page 172.

house to the back where the vegetable garden, and above that the tennis court, had been, but that side of the grounds was blocked by barbed wire. Remnants of the days when the house had been used as a VIP hostel?

Perhaps. We were able to get around on the other side. But at the back I was shocked to find a high retaining wall rising immediately behind the house itself. The wall was no less than forty feet across and must have been at least ten feet high, which brought the land behind it up to the level of our former tennis court. Above that, an ornate red brick wall about eight feet high. Obviously someone had commandeered that part of the property, but when we asked who or what was up there, we were given the usual reply, "oh, some big shot." They didn't know who. The term most commonly used was "*kao chi kan pu*" (high-level government official).

We walked back through the overgrown grounds. The gardener's cottage and our schoolroom were gone, as was the *t'ing tze* where we had so often sat enjoying the evening breeze and watching the children playing in the village below. In their place, just piles of rubble. But on each terrace we found the oblong excavations in the ground that had held the pumps for the "artesian well" that was to have pumped water up the hill for our swimming pool. The excavations were lined with brick and had once had fitted wooden covers. Now they were only partially covered with loose boards that in turn were obscured by wild growth. The interiors were littered with trash. I couldn't help thinking how easily a child, or an adult for that matter, could fall into one. But luckily they were located on the side of the property. Going back through the two stone pillars at the entrance, we came to the landing where the garage had been. Again there was only a pile of rubble. I thought of Mother struggling to turn around her heavy Auburn on that small landing. Strangely, as we left I did not feel depressed, only exhilarated that we had found the house. Depression came later.

Going up the hill we had been so eager to find the house that we had not even noticed what was below. Builders were working on six or seven large pretentious-looking houses, some almost completed. We were amazed. This was a socialist society. Who had the money to buy these mansions? Two young men in business suits, looking officious with their cellular phones and clipboards, seemed to be involved in the development. They answered our questions. Some were already sold to wealthy investors from Singapore and Hong Kong, others to businesses. Some were not yet sold, but they were confident that buyers were there. The houses cost about $400,000 in U.S. dollars. Land alone was worth about U.S. $3000 a square meter. Thoughts flashed through my mind about the possibilities of reclaiming our property. Our house and the area we owned around it must have occupied two or three acres. The land had been ours; had never been sold. I had photographs of the step-by-step construction of the house, but I had no deeds to prove ownership. I wondered who had laid claim to the property, who owned it now, and who was reaping its financial benefits. The state? Some high official? It did not matter now. I had no wish to spend summers here again.

That same day we also visited the Sleeping Buddha Temple and the Summer Palace. The large reclining Buddha seemed to have shrunk. I realized I was no longer the small child who had once been unable to peer over its huge bulk. On leaving the temple and climbing back into our van, the memory of the child I had once been, sitting on Uncle Walter's lap, squirming as his hands probed beneath my skirt, flashed through my mind. It was only a fleeting moment. I pushed it aside.

The Summer Palace was as I remembered it, but now there were throngs of tourists, mostly from other Asian countries. The beautiful long covered gallery with its fretted balustrades was so crowded that we chose to walk beside it rather than under its hand-painted ceiling. A large motorized barge was ferrying groups of tourists across the lake. From a distance we saw the famous marble boat but did not take the time to board. I thought of the many times my friends and I had sat on it drinking jasmine tea.

Another day we visited the Temple of Heaven. The triple blue-tiled roofs of the temple were even more beautiful than in my memory. The Altar of Heaven, like the Sleeping Buddha, seemed smaller than I remembered it, but nothing could dim the beauty of those triple tiers of gleaming white marble. The surrounding balustrades under the morning sun were so bright they dazzled the eye. On the disk at its center, where once only the emperor had been allowed, daughter-in-law Nora, ever the tourist, sat cross-legged in her shorts and walking shoes to have her picture taken. I wondered why we had never held the high school dance there that we had spoken of so often.

The Winter Palace, of which I had more happy memories than anywhere, left me feeling strangely flat. Perhaps I was looking for too much. The lotus flowers were no longer in bloom. Parts of the North Lake were still covered with the large plattered lotus leaves, but many were withered and brown. Why had I thought we might rent a barge and that a coolie might pole us out to sit among the lotus blossoms once again? We saw no barges at the boat dock. Perhaps it was too late in the season. And if the barges had been there, I knew they would no longer have been the small ones for private rental; they would be like the motorized one we had seen at the Summer Palace, overly large and overly bright, to appeal to the tourists they ferried from shore to shore. I was told that there was still skating on the lakes in the winter but wondered if the rinks too had been commercialized beyond recognition. Did they still provide chairs on runners for beginning skaters and the non-skating elderly? I did not see the *t'ing tze* where we had danced in the moonlight. It had only been a small isolated structure at the far end of the lake, a resting spot for tired strollers, not even deserving of a name or title.

Any disappointment I had felt at not being able to bring back experiences of the past was totally dispelled by our evening meal. Once again we passed up any thoughts of eating in the hotel or in a fancy restaurant. Instead we headed for the evening market near our hotel where we had been told the street was filled nightly with food vendors. We wanted to see for ourselves. The street was closed to automotive traffic. One side was completely filled with a row of adjoining stalls. Our taxi let us off at one end, and we slowly ate our way to the other. Even in the old Peking I had never seen such a profusion and variety of foods in one place. Now there were not only the foods I remembered from my childhood, but additional specialties from other parts of North China. All the items that have become popular in America were there: spring rolls, *wonton*, steamed *chiao-tze*, and fried pot-stickers. But in addition there were paper-thin pancakes to be wrapped around a variety of stuffings, fried breads filled with either meat or vegetables, and steamed dumplings of various styles with different fillings. There were also all kinds of meats on skewers: lamb, beef, pork, and chicken of course, but also chicken or duck gizzards, hearts, or livers; various kinds of tripe; fish, either whole or in chunks; frogs' legs; boiled quail eggs; whole baby sparrows. The variety seemed infinite. At some stands the skewers were deep-fried in enormous woks of sizzling oil, at others, grilled on flaming coals. There were stalls selling fried noodles, some of wheat flour, others of rice flour. Other stalls sold soup noodles. There were salty fried crullers, and baignet-like crullers sprinkled with moist Chinese sugar; plates of sweet gelatins; puddings of "purple rice," fried glutinous rice balls filled with red bean paste or jujube jam; and *t'ang hu lus*, the candied fruits on sticks that I remembered so well from my childhood. These were only a few of the sweet dishes that filled the stalls. It was too much.

We started at one end of the street, ordering only one plate of each tempting item for seven of us. We each had a taste. If we liked it, we ordered more. If not, we moved on. Everything looked so good; we were carried away. One of us would be trying something several stalls away, crying for the others to come try. Others would still be munching from the last trial plate. Our enthusiasm must have rubbed off on others. They could tell that this was new to us. This street was not for tourists, but for the local population. Some perfect strangers offered us tastes of their selections. One thrust a skewer of frogs' legs into Nora's hands, insisting that she try them. Another offered Kathy a skewer of baby sparrows, heads and all. They were delicious. We were all standing on the street. Other than a few stools at the noodle stands, there were no chairs anywhere. In the middle of the road, on the ground for the unwary to stumble over, sat large plastic tubs in which to put the used bowls, plates, spoons, and chopsticks. Throughout the evening, elderly women moved from tub to tub collecting the dishes and discarding the disposable chopsticks. How or where the dishes were washed, with hot water or cold, we did not know or care. All pre-trip advice about carrying our own bowls and warnings about the lack of sanitation were forgotten. We were submerged in glorious, delicious, delectable, irresistible food. We would never forget this evening. Sated, we taxied back to the hotel for a cup of hot tea in our rooms to end the day. Nick made the mistake of using a ginseng tea bag instead of a regular tea bag and was dismayed to find at checkout time that he was charged U.S. $5 for this much-touted aphrodisiac.

Not everything in Peking gave us as much pleasure as the food. My mother used to say there was no place in the world where the skies were as blue as in Peking. She could not have said that today. We had been told of the pollution, of course, but had hardly expected the skies to be as uniformly gray as they were. We had also been told of the congested traffic, but it was not until viewed firsthand that I realized that the leisurely pace at which the scattered bicycles and rickshaws had moved along the roads fifty years before was a thing of the past, never to be seen again. Now, on the major streets the traffic was hard to believe. Cars, buses, and trucks competed with bicycles and pedestrians for their share of space on the streets. Pedestrian crossings and traffic lights were generally ignored even with traffic police on duty. Just crossing the street was a precarious undertaking. Yet time and again we would see a young woman with a bicycle, often with an infant on the back, pushing directly into the path of oncoming traffic. Miraculously, woman, bicycle, and child would reach the other side safely.

On about our fourth day in Peking, Kathy announced that she had figured out the system. "The trick is to walk very, very slowly," she said. "and never never under any circumstances jerk to a stop when you see a car or bicycle coming toward you. Just keep on moving steadily forward." John and I were skeptical, perhaps not having the courage of the young. We stood by and watched as Kathy then put her theory into practice. With ten-year-old Jae in tow, she stepped out confidently into oncoming traffic. Buses, trucks, taxis, and bicycles hurtled toward her, but she moved slowly but surely to the opposite side. The traffic, like water, simply flowed around her as it did around others who had long ago learned the technique of street-crossing in Beijing. As Kathy had said, stopping suddenly would have broken the rhythm of the flow. Though she had proved her point, John and I still looked for the safety of an overpass when crossing busy streets.

What all of us noticed was the total absence of anger or frustration at the horrendous traffic conditions. No taxi drivers cursing at others who failed to yield the right of way; no one leaning out the window to give someone else the finger; no yelling at pedestrians or bicyclists to get out of the way; and very little beeping of horns. Communism had taught patience. Or was it the inborn nature of the Chinese people?

Pollution, traffic congestion, and the enormous amount of construction, much of it quite ugly, none of this was as disturbing to us as visiting the home of a friend, my old schoolmate Clemy's brother. Before the children arrived, Eddie had spent the day with us and together we had gone to his home for dinner. It was after dark when we arrived, but the darkness did not soften the harsh lines of the gray concrete building. A small elevator, resembling a freight elevator in all but size, took us to the tenth floor. The gray concrete hallway led to the door of his apartment. Inside, a small living room, but big enough for a couch, coffee table, and two easy chairs; a dining area with room enough to seat four; a bedroom, kitchen, and bathroom. The apartment building had no hot running water. In the kitchen, water still had to be boiled on the gas stove for dishwashing, but Eddie had recently had a small electric water heater installed in the bathroom. Though the apartment was small, it seemed quite comfortable and was what I had expected. But I could not help comparing it with their old home that I remembered so well. The family had been affluent. Their home, like our guesthouse, had also once been the palace of a Manchu prince. In their east garden there had been a lovely fishpond in which Clemy had first learned to swim. Besides the garden and the family courtyards, there had been a courtyard for her father's concubine and her children, and another courtyard at the rear of the property for the use of their poorer relatives, a far cry from the modest apartment Eddie and his wife now occupied.

Eddie was U.S.-educated, a structural engineer from Cornell, and before retirement had been the second man in the Beijing Building Institute. His wife had been head nurse at a large hospital. Now the two together had pension incomes that were generous by Chinese standards, but a pittance by American standards. They had stereo equipment, a TV of course, a microwave, a VCR, and a brand new computer. They also had a maid two hours a day. They had no thoughts of trying to move to another country. They had made the adjustment and were willing to live out their lives in place. They seemed content.

In 1988 Eddie visited us at our home in McLean, Virginia. It was his first trip out of China since he had returned there in the early fifties, and all his old schoolmates from pre-Communist days were warmly welcoming him to America. It was on his third day with us that he said to me, "You know, of all my friends' homes that I have visited in the past month, yours is one of the nicest. But I can't help noticing that you don't have a microwave, or a VCR. And I'm surprised that you have only one TV, and that your stereo system is not as good as mine." We were amused at that, and had a hard time convincing him that the reason we didn't have the things he found so essential was that we didn't want them or need them. He found it hard to understand why we, who lived in an American world of material luxury, could think so little of the things that in China were so highly prized.

After leaving Peking, the rest of our tour covered the other "musts" for first-time China visitors. I had never been to Xian or Guilin. The terra-cotta armies had not been discovered when I left China in 1945. Magnificent as the spectacle was, I was more eager to see the city walls, among the few that still existed in China. I hoped they would give my family some idea of what the Peking city walls had been. The part we visited was beautifully restored, but again its very newness was disconcerting. It was sterile. I mourned the loss of our Peking wall, stones crumbling in parts, grass sprouting among the stones. I thought of the parting of four good friends on that wall so many years ago, when we had dramatically smashed at our feet the single glass from which we had drunk the grape juice pledging our eternal friendship.

In Guilin there were no disappointments. As we cruised down the Li River, a light rain was falling. A fellow passenger, Chinese, told us that foreigners always hoped for good weather and the Chinese for rain. We felt more Chinese than foreign. Neither sunshine nor clear weather could possibly have improved the scene around us. The gray mists that accompanied the rain floated among the limestone mountain peaks, creating scenes that seemed to have been drawn from a dream sequence. For the first time in my life I saw that these subjects of centuries of Chinese paintings were real and not the exaggerated creations of a fertile imagination.

All our hotel accommodations thus far had been quite grand, especially the lobbies. This one in Guilin, however, had not a single place to sit. Not a sofa, a chair, or even a bench. When we asked for a reason, we were amused when the management told us that if chairs were provided, all the prostitutes would come in and occupy them. On looking outside the main entrance, we did see a large number of young women milling about the street, but we saw no vinyl miniskirts or Suzie Wang-style *ch'i pao* slit up to beyond the thigh; no heavy mascara, and no sleazy come-on behavior. They all looked to us like young housewives or schoolgirls, but our guide assured us that most of these were prostitutes.

Finally we reached Shanghai. In planning our trip I had not even wanted to include it. I had never liked the city and had no desire to return. But my remaining relatives were there. Was it important to see them again? With the exception of one of my biological brothers, Ling

Ling, whom I had seen once in 1984 on a trip to Hong Kong (when he had shed tears at our meeting) I had not seen for over fifty years my few remaining cousins: Helen, Second Uncle's daughter; Amy, Fifth Aunt's daughter; Gracie, daughter of my oldest cousin Chao Yuen (the one suspected of fathering Mabel); and Ch'iang Ch'iang, the fourth of my biological brothers. For fifty years they had not been a part of my life, nor I of theirs. We had been worlds apart, physically, culturally, and emotionally. I wondered if when we met, memories we shared so long ago would tie us together once again, if my visit would mean anything to them at all.

My questions were answered when we reached Shanghai. I had written Helen to tell her the date of our arrival but could not give her an exact time. I called her when we arrived. It was 5:30; late. I didn't know how many of the family she could round up on such short notice. But barely an hour later, at the restaurant where we had arranged to meet, all were there at the entrance, waiting to greet us when we arrived. Our gathering blocked the restaurant doors. Other diners pushed impatiently past us. All doubts about feelings, theirs or mine, were gone. We hugged; we embraced. I wrapped my arms around Gracie, always small but now shrunken further by crippling osteoporosis. The tears welled up in my eyes. With help, she and her near-blind husband struggled up the restaurant stairs. We were too many for one round table. We sat at two. John and I with my cousins; my children at another. Midway in the meal my daughter Kathy replaced John at the relatives' table. Then my son Bean. Some spoke no Chinese; others spoke no English. We struggled with conversations, half in one language, half in the other, laughing through it all. It was a happy occasion, but sad. The restaurant crowd was noisy. We yelled across the table, the deaf ones cocking their heads to one side to put their better ears closer. When we had last seen each other we had been young, but no more. My two brothers, their once-curly hair now straight and sparse, not quite covering their balding heads, were the personality kids, talkative, animated. Ling Ling, eighty-one, and Ch'iang Ch'iang, seventy-six, now looked like twins.

Though Helen had told me in correspondence that the family wanted to take us to dinner, this was my treat. I did not want them to spend the money. However, I had to defer to Ch'iang Ch'iang on selecting the menu. The meal was good, and sumptuous by U.S. standards, but modest by Chinese. His effort to save me money. My intentions of sparing them any expenditure was pointless. They insisted on hosting us to lunch the next day. By this time my children had left for home, all returning to their jobs in America. John and I were staying an extra day. This time the food was sumptuous. The cost? More than they should have been spending, I know.

After lunch Ling Ling asked us to his place for coffee. Helen joined us. She volunteered to take us first to see the apartment where for a year and a half I had lived with her family, but we had already been there on our own while the children were still with us. The building had a brass plate at the entrance designating it a "Municipal Preserved Building." It had once been one of the nicer apartments in the then-French Concession. We had climbed the dark unlighted stairs. Despite the building's supposed "preservation," its once-polished terrazzo stairs were grimy and chipped. The doors to the apartments looked as if they had not been painted in fifty years. One was open a crack and we could see the worn floorboards and the dingy peeling plaster of the walls inside. We went to the back of the building where I could point out the window of the room that had once been mine. The whole thing was dismal and depressing. "Preservation" seemed only to mean that the building was not to be destroyed, to remain standing.

When we arrived at Ling Ling's I was surprised to find he lived in the same house where I had first met him and the rest of my natural/biological family in 1943, fifty-two years earlier. I thought, "Surely he had not been allowed to keep the house." Back then I had thought it ugly, but it had been comfortable for their family. Now the wooden stairs were grimy, the stair boards sagging in some places. The hand railing was black and worn. On the second floor Ling Ling ushered us into his room. It had once been the living room. It was there that the family had first greeted me when I was a girl of eighteen. I remembered the apathy I had felt. I felt closer to Ling Ling now than I had then. Now the room was filled with all his worldly belongings, including a refrigerator in one corner and just inside the door a two-burner gas plate that served as his kitchen. An array of cooking equipment was on the shelf beneath the gas burners. Five families now occupied the house. He was fortunate in having been allowed to keep the largest room for himself but had to share one of the two bathrooms with two of the other families. I needed to use the bathroom and was dismayed to find the toilet bowl stained with rings of brown, a blackened well at its base. The wooden seat was cracked. The washbasin was streaked with the rust of dripping faucets, and the fixtures pitted with corrosion. The tub was obviously not in use. It was covered with boards, on top of which were numerous enamel basins and all manner of other utensils. I don't know what I had expected, but not this, not this.

But Ling Ling appeared happy. Like Eddie in Peking, he had adjusted to his changed circumstances. I learned later from Helen that he went every morning to a public dance hall to ballroom dance. I'm sure he was quite good. At eighty-one, he walked more brusquely and faster than either John or I. We had barely been able to keep up with him as we walked along the street. Now he heated some water and made us powdered coffee, American, from a jar he kept in the refrigerator. His three sons all lived abroad. They sent him money to supplement his pension. He could afford luxuries like Maxwell House coffee.

Ling Ling brought out old photo albums and we talked of the past. He spoke of my father. He remembered going to the hospital with him almost fifty years ago, when Yi Tai Tai was dying of cancer. He had seen the tears in my father's eyes and was deeply moved. "I knew of the love between them," he said. Listening to his words, my thoughts went back to those early days when I had first learned of my father's relationship with Yi Tai Tai. For years I had known of their affair and the products of it: first Mabel, and four years later, Luther. For years I had judged my father harshly for his infidelity. But now, for the first time, while not condoning, I thought of him not as an unfaithful husband, but as a young man in love with a woman he could not hope to claim, his father's concubine. Had he loved her even before he married my mother? Did he marry Mother knowing that his love for Yi Tai Tai was hopeless? I will never know. His story died with him. Even if he were alive today, I could not, would not, have asked him.

After leaving Ling Ling's place we went on to Helen's. She too had only a single room. When her husband was alive they had had two rooms, but the second was taken away when he died. She was lucky that the second room had been given to another widow, so there were only two to share the bathroom and small kitchen space. Her bed, a double, occupied the whole center of her room with only three feet of space between it and the furniture lining the walls. She received a pension of less than U.S. $40 a month. Helen was not complaining; she was merely stating the facts of her life. But I had eyes to see and ears to hear. And I could also foresee what her remaining years would be as rising inflation further reduced her already meager pension.

As we boarded the plane, I was glad to be going home, to America. I had seen the home of my childhood. It was no longer home to me. I was glad I had made the trip. In many ways it had been wonderful, but it had ended on a depressing note. All the wonders of China remained. Seeing again the Great Wall and the parks and temples of Peking, and seeing for the first time the spectacular archeological discoveries in Xian, the beauty of Guilin's mystic hills, and Suzhou's lovely gardens brought home the wonders of my origins. I had reveled in rediscovering some of the places of my childhood and in showing these small bits of their heritage to my children. Our eating forays on the streets of Peking too would be with me, and them, forever. But I could not forget the dilapidated condition of houses that had once been beautiful, the courtyards that had shrunk to narrow passageways, and the shoddy brick and board structures that had filled them. Most of all I could not forget Ling Ling's and Helen's rooms.

Today as I sit looking out at the pond behind our house, a blue heron stands motionless under the willow tree. He starts his awkward gait along the water's edge, then spreads his wings and soars upward in a graceful arc. Five mallard ducks, four males and one female, glide peacefully across the water. They look slightly hunched, their heads pulled down among their feathers. The weather is turning cold. Across the pond the trees, now red and gold, are mirrored in the water below. The leaves are starting to fall; they drift softly in the autumn air, finally coming to rest gently on the water. I think about the daffodil bulbs yet to be planted and the fence post that must be replaced before the winter freeze.

My thoughts return to Peking. My fears that old memories of my childhood would be tarnished by our visit to the new Beijing were unfounded. Old memories remain, clearer and more cherished than before. New memories, shared with my family, have been added. I have them both, old memories and new, each separate from the other. The old Peking walls are gone, but in memory I see them and walk along them still. The small barges of the Winter Palace may be no more, but they too remain with me. I can hear the voices of family and friends singing my mother's songs among the lotus blossoms of the North Lake. Our North City home may have been closed to me, but in the recesses of my mind I can see beyond its now-guarded red gates to the inner courts, to the terrazzo porch where we sat under the clustered wisteria, and to Yi Tai Tai's house with its fragrance of cassia and August lilies. Mrs. Ch'ien's Guesthouse too is gone. My mother is not here to welcome guests to her Chinese home, nor my father to host a banquet in his silken robes.